Globalizing Cricket

Globalizing Sport Studies

ISSN 2045-225X

SERIES EDITOR: **John Horne, Professor of Sport and Sociology,
University of Central Lancashire, UK**

Public interest in sport studies continues to grow throughout the world. This series brings together the latest work in the field and acts as a global knowledge hub for interdisciplinary work in sport studies. Whilst promoting work across disciplines, the series focuses on social scientific and cultural studies of sport. It brings together the most innovative scholarly empirical and theoretical work, from within the UK and internationally.

Books already published in the series:

Global Media Sport: Flows, Forms and Futures
David Rowe
ISBN 9781849660709 (Hardback)
ISBN 9781849666756 (Ebook)

Japanese Women and Sport: Beyond Baseball and Sumo
Robin Kietlinski
ISBN 9781849663403 (Hardback)
ISBN 9781849666688 (Ebook)

Sport for Development and Peace: A Critical Sociology
Simon Darnell
ISBN 9781849663441 (Hardback)
ISBN 9781849665919 (Ebook)

Globalizing Cricket: Englishness, Empire and Identity
Dominic Malcolm
ISBN 9781849665278 (Hardback)
ISBN 9781849665612 (Ebook)

Forthcoming:

Global Boxing
Kath Woodward
ISBN 9781849668101 (Hardback)
ISBN 9781849667999 (Ebook)

Localizing Global Sport for Development
Davies Banda, Ruth Jeanes, Tess Kay & Iain Lindsey
Publication date: September 2013

Sport and Global Social Movements
Jean Harvey, John Horne, Parissa Safai, Simon Darnell & Sébastien Courchesne-O'Neill
Publication date: September 2013

Sport and Technology: An Actor-Network Theory Perspective
Roslyn Kerr
Publication date: April 2014

Globalizing Cricket

Englishness, Empire and Identity

Dominic Malcolm

B L O O M S B U R Y
LONDON · NEW DELHI · NEW YORK · SYDNEY

Bloomsbury Academic
An imprint of Bloomsbury Publishing Plc

50 Bedford Square   1385 Broadway
London   New York
WC1B 3DP   NY 10018
UK   USA

www.bloomsbury.com

Bloomsbury is a registered trade mark of Bloomsbury Publishing Plc

First published 2013
Paperback edition first published 2014

© Dominic Malcolm, 2013

ⓒ ⓘ ⓢ

British Library Cataloguing-in-Publication Data
A catalogue record for this book is available from the British Library.

ISBN: HB: 978-1-8496-6527-8
       PB: 978-1-4725-7657-6

Library of Congress Cataloging-in-Publication Data
A catalog record for this book is available from the Library of Congress.

Printed and bound by CPI Group (UK) Ltd, Croydon, CR0 4YY

Contents

Globalizing Sport Studies
Series Editor's Preface

There is now a considerable amount of expertise nationally and internationally in the social scientific and cultural analysis of sport in relation to the economy and society more generally. Contemporary research topics, such as sport and social justice, science and technology and sport, global social movements and sport, sports mega-events, sports participation and engagement and the role of sport in social development, suggest that sport and social relations need to be understood in non-Western developing economies, as well as European, North American and other advanced capitalist societies. The current high global visibility of sport makes this an excellent time to launch a major new book series that takes sport seriously, and makes this research accessible to a wide readership.

The series *Globalizing Sport Studies* is thus in line with a massive growth of academic expertise, research output and public interest in sport worldwide. At the same time, it seeks to use the latest developments in technology and the economics of publishing to reflect the most innovative research into sport in society currently underway in the world. The series is multi-disciplinary, although primarily based on the social sciences and cultural studies approaches to sport.

The broad aims of the series are to: *act* as a knowledge hub for social scientific and cultural studies research in sport, including, but not exclusively, anthropological, economic, geographic, historical, political science and sociological studies; *contribute* to the expanding field of research on sport in society in the United Kingdom and internationally by focussing on sport at regional, national and international levels; *create* a series for both senior and more junior researchers that will become synonymous with cutting edge research, scholarly opportunities and academic development; *promote* innovative discipline-based, multi-, inter- and trans-disciplinary theoretical and methodological approaches to researching sport in society; *provide* an English language outlet for high quality non-English writing on sport in society; *publish* broad overviews, original empirical research studies and classic studies from non-English sources; and thus attempt to *realise* the potential for *globalizing* sport studies through open content licensing with 'Creative Commons'.

Professional cricket has undergone a transformation into an emergent force in the global spread of consumer culture in recent years, especially on the Indian sub-continent. The development of the Twenty20 (T20) format of cricket, including the Indian Premier League (IPL) in India in the 2000s, promised to shake up the format of the game in ways that had not been seen since the late 1970s when a 'rebel' league (World Series Cricket) was established by Australian media tycoon Sir Kerry Packer. The IPL established by the Board of Control for Cricket in India (BCCI) in 2008 composed of players from across the cricket world 'bought' for short-term, but highly lucrative, hire in an auction to perform largely outside of their normal playing season.

Dominic Malcolm's *Globalizing Cricket* is an excellent guide to understanding the trajectory that the sport has taken from its earliest beginnings to the recent past. It is much more than that in so far as it is a very well written and readable *historical sociology* of cricket that covers the emergence of the game in England to its globalization in the twenty-first century. Underpinned by the figurational sociology of Norbert Elias he demonstrates that early nineteenth century accounts of the game contained an account of cricket that was closely aligned to the sense of English national character that was more widely emerging at this time. He also shows that, like the emergence of Englishness more generally, 'it entailed a portrayal which obscured an elitist and violent past'. He expertly brings together discussions of the influence of social class, commercialisation, violence, formal innovation, national consciousness, and the projection of empire on cricket in its formative years. The book also explores the 'failure' of 'diffusion' of the game in North America.

At its core the book is interested in *explaining*, not simply asserting, the relationship between cricket and Englishness. The book explores how and why this relationship began, and what the enduring but changing consequences of this relationship have been. For Malcolm cricket is more than a reflection of Englishness but is also an active agent in the production of the identity of English people. *Globalizing Cricket* thus provides an analysis of the development and global diffusion of cricket that also contextualizes the changing ways in which the game influences and intersects with contemporary English/British society.

John Horne, Preston and Edinburgh 2012

Acknowledgements

This book is the product of around sixteen years of work so there are many people to thank who have helped along the way. In particular, I am grateful to the small number of people with whom I have collaborated on cricket-related research over the years: Alan Bairner, Graham Curry, Jon Gemmell, Nalin Mehta, Matt Parry and Phillipa Velija.

I would also like to thank John Wiley and Sons for kind permission to reprint aspects of Dominic Malcolm, 'The Diffusion of Cricket to America: A Figurational Sociological Examination', *Journal of Historical Sociology*, June 2006, pp. 151–173; Dominic Malcolm, 'It's Just Not Cricket: Colonial Legacies and Contemporary Inequalities', *Journal of Historical Sociology*, September 2001, pp. 253–275, and Taylor & Francis for kind permission to reprint excerpts from Dominic Malcolm, Jon Gemmell and Nalin Mehta, 'Cricket and Modernity: International and Interdisciplinary Perspectives on the Study of the Imperial Game', *Sport in Society*, May 2009, vol. 12, Issue 4–5.

Thanks also go to colleagues both at Leicester and Loughborough universities who have been happy to chat about cricket and who I have mined for ideas over the years, especially Eric Dunning. Most of all, though, I would particularly like to thank my family who firstly fostered my fascination with cricket and who subsequently have had to learn to tolerate it.

Disclaimer

Introduction

Globalizing cricket

*I have often thought of how much better a life I would have had,
what a better man I would have been, how much healthier
an existence I would have led, had I been a cricketer.*
Sir Laurence Olivier

*Cricket civilizes people and creates good gentlemen. I want
everyone to play cricket in Zimbabwe; I want ours
to be a nation of gentlemen.*
Robert Mugabe

*It is not true that the English invented cricket as a way of making
all other human endeavours look interesting and lively; that was
merely an unintended side effect. I don't wish to denigrate
a sport that is enjoyed by millions, some of them awake
and facing the right way, but it is an odd game.*
Bill Bryson

*If everything else in this nation of ours was lost but cricket ... it
would be possible to reconstruct from the theory and practice
of cricket all the eternal Englishness which has gone to the
establishment of that constitution and the laws aforesaid.*
Neville Cardus

Cricket polarizes opinion. To some it holds quasi-religious status; to others it is a point of fun. Despite their obvious devotion, some (particularly English) cricket spectators are remarkably impassive. Inextricably linked to what defines Englishness, cricket is also venerated by those who have publicly and vigorously fought against imperial oppression. It has the aura of a genteel game which builds character, yet it is amongst the most injurious sports played in the United Kingdom (Sports Council 1991). Suicide rates among England's test cricketers are almost double that of the UK male population as a whole (Frith 2001). The mythology of cricket enables some to make rather far-fetched statements about the consequences of playing cricket and its effect on cultural life, while for others the game is simply unfathomable. Cricket is seen as the quintessential English game but also the sport, *par excellence*, of the *British* Empire. Such a paradoxical beast is ripe for sociological investigation.

On one level it is difficult to see why cricket divides opinion so deeply. At its most basic cricket is a bat and ball game. It was 'invented' in England, though others have claimed that it has Celtic origins (Bowen 1970), and that it was played by the Dalraid Scots from northern Ireland around 500 AD (Lang 1912, cited in Bateman 2009: 5). An alternative account is that it was invented in France and that its name derives from the French word 'criquet', meaning wooden gate (Altham and Swanton 1948: 19). Ashis Nandy famously describes cricket as 'an Indian game, invented accidentally by the English' (1989: 1). But it could also be argued that bat and ball pastimes of this type are culturally universal, as evidenced by the many similarly structured games around the world, such as Brännboll (Sweden), Danish Longball, Gilli-danda (India), Kilikiti (Samoa), Lapta (Russia), La Lippa (Italy), Oină (Romania), Pesäpallo (Finland), Syatong (Philippines) and, of course, baseball.

One reason why cricket divides opinion so sharply is that it contains some peculiar rules and esoteric customs. A game of cricket can take an incredibly long time to complete. A 'timeless test' played between South Africa and England in 1939 lasted twelve days (including three rest days) and was concluded without a result because England's players needed to catch a boat home. In traditional forms of the game the two sides wear near identical white clothes which make it difficult for the casual viewer to tell the teams apart. The umpire can only give a batter out if the fielding side 'appeals', and specifically asks whether, in the umpire's opinion, the player was legally dismissed. To be given out 'leg before wicket' (LBW) the ball must not simply be blocked from hitting the wicket by the batter's leg, but the umpire must also consider where the ball pitched (bounced) and whether the batter was playing a shot. Leg byes (where a batter runs when the ball hits his/her legs but not the bat) can only be awarded if the batter attempted but failed to hit the ball (or avoid being hit by the ball). Four runs are awarded if the ball crosses the boundary, but also in cases where in stopping the ball the fielder touches the boundary his/herself. A batter may be out if caught over the boundary as long as the fielder returns to the playing area before his/her feet touch the ground. The fielding side can 'improve' but not deliberately deteriorate the condition of the ball. Cricket is a team game but only sixty per cent of players compete at any one time and for long periods players essentially perform as individuals. In no other sport is the captain so important in making decisions which are material to the outcome of the game. While many claim that cricket builds moral character, the game has an increasingly active anti-corruption unit. It is the only game (although golf comes close) for which the 'spirit' in which it should be played is explicitly laid down in the laws.

These characteristics could be dismissed as a series of ad-hoc quirks but there is a more systematic rationale underpinning the peculiarity of cricket. This can perhaps best be illustrated through a comparison of the game with the characteristics that have been identified as distinguishing *modern* sports from their pre-modern counterparts. In a classic statement on this, Guttmann (1978) identified seven interdependent characteristics which distinguish the sports developed in Europe (and latterly North America) from c. 1750. These are:

1) secularism – modern sports are rarely related to formal aspects of religious worship;

2) equality – in modern sports considerable stress is placed on the importance of equal opportunity for participation (in the sense that nobody is formally excluded) and on literally and metaphorically providing participants with a 'level playing field';

3) specialization – in modern sports we clearly distinguish between game forms and increasingly expect elite participants to specialize in a particular role within one sport;

4) bureaucratization – modern sports are not *ad hoc* or spontaneously organized, but are administered centrally, often by people who are not themselves participants;

5) rationalization – modern sports are structured according to an instrumental rationality which leads events to be staged in purpose-built venues with increasing human control over environmental conditions, equipment which is standardized and regulated, and participants who are prepared using the latest scientific techniques and knowledge;

6) quantification – in modern sport actions are translated into numerical data and participants' performances are measured, recorded and compared; and

7) the quest for records – participants in modern sports are expected to produce increasingly advanced performances by which the progression of humanity can be seen.

Cricket, of course, exhibits many of the characteristics of a modern sport. While religious terminology is often used to exalt the game – for instance, the annual publication *Wisden Cricketers' Almanack* (hereafter Wisden) is often described as the 'bible' of cricket, Lord's cricket ground as the game's 'spiritual home' – cricket is a secular game in the sense that it is not formally played in honour, or with the blessing, of Gods. Few sports are as widely accredited as being infused with an ethos of equality and no sport has provided as many phrases to the English language which encapsulate honour and fairness (for example, 'it's not cricket', 'playing with a straight bat'). Cricket has a long history of bureaucratic control starting with the formation of the Marylebone Cricket Club (MCC) in 1787 and the Imperial Cricket Conference in 1909. The latter's successor, the International Cricket Council (ICC), currently has 105 members, divided between Full (10), Associate (36) and Affiliated (59) status.[1]

The game's rules are notoriously elaborate and complex. Its 42 Laws (and five appendices) currently encompass 116 pages (MCC 2010), and are periodically reviewed by a panel of non-playing experts. Cricket also exhibits extreme forms of quantification, with perhaps only baseball fostering a similar veneration of statistics and records. The average edition of Wisden contains approximately 1,000 pages of numerical data and fifty pages of text. Records are kept not only of highest scores or seasonal averages, but of the minutiae of the game (for example the highest partnership for a particular wicket against a particular team at a particular venue). The act of 'scoring' in cricket is thought of as an art and those who do it, like the late Bill Frindall, become celebrities. Cricket websites are packed with statistics, showing the contemporary relevance and cross-cultural appeal of this aspect of the game.

Yet in other respects cricket is peculiarly *un*modern. Cricket defies the modernist rationalization of team sports. For instance, whereas football teams represent towns, cities or nation-states, cricket teams often represent rural entities and sub- or supra-nation-states. In Britain domestic cricket is based upon 'counties'. One of these, Glamorgan, is seen by many as the representative of a nation (namely Wales), although an entity called 'Wales' competes in the 'minor counties' competition. While most international sports federations only recognize and grant membership to nation-states, two of the ICC's ten full members would fail to meet such criteria. The West Indies, for instance, is a multi-state confederation, parts of which (the ten English-speaking territories) have only briefly been politically united (as the Federation of the West Indies between 1958 and 1962). The other – which the ICC lists as 'England' – is a nation submerged within a nation-state (the United Kingdom). While always referred to as 'England', the side actually represents the England and *Wales* Cricket Board (ECB), and has historically drawn players from Scotland and Ireland which are ICC associate members in their own right.

Furthermore, cricket has multiple and co-existing game forms; that is to say, 'test' or 'first class' matches, the so-called one-day game consisting of one innings per side of approximately fifty overs,[2] and most recently Twenty20 cricket. Whilst other sports have alternative game forms ('five-a-side' football, rugby 'sevens', Pee wee [American] football), their respective relationships to the 'main' game are qualitatively different. First, the hierarchy of game forms in other sports is much clearer. Whereas the Fédération Internationale de Football Association (FIFA) produce (for each sex) a single table ranking the football playing nations of the world, the ICC produce three, one each for test matches, one-day internationals (ODIs) and Twenty20. It is an anomaly that the premier cricketing competition – the ICC Cricket World Cup – is based on the one-day format and thus formally defined in cricket nomenclature as the secondary form of the game (i.e. not first class). Second, equipment is not standardized between the different forms of cricket. One-day cricket may be played at night under artificial lights, by teams wearing coloured outfits, and using a white ball which many believe behaves differently to the red ball used in the longer version of the game; all anathema to devotees of test cricket.

Cricket is also peculiarly *un*modern in terms of the rationalization of the duration of play. As noted, the prolonged nature of cricket is a source of bemusement for the uninitiated, but compounding this *un*modern-ness is the *flexibility* of time which cricket may fill. Association and American football matches are scheduled for 90 and 60 minutes respectively, but test matches are scheduled for *up to* five days, and they may end at any point before that. Other sports require that certain components be completed (3/5 sets in tennis, 18/72 holes in golf) but the 'declaration' and 'forfeit' in cricket enables matches to end after any number of innings of any duration or number of wickets. Given this flexibility, it is ironic that no other game so completely embraces the possibility of contests having no clear outcome. A dead heat is possible in many sports but only in cricket are two words – tie and draw – used to differentiate between the ways in which a match can finish without a clear winner. A draw has traditionally been the most likely outcome in test match cricket (Steen 2010), but a tie is incredibly rare, with only two in almost 150 years of this form of the game. Paradoxically, in shorter versions of the game (which are temporally fixed to last between 20 and 50 overs per side) the cricketing authorities employ a complex set of equations to enable a result to be calculated based on the performance of the respective sides prior to the curtailment of play (known as the Duckworth-Lewis system). No such mechanism exists for longer versions of the game in which undecided contests are obviously more frequent.

Cricket, moreover, has not been subject to the same degree of spatial rationalization as other sports. Though the dimensions of the wicket are specified within the laws of the game, the maximum and minimum sizes of the playing area are not regulated. Not only does cricket embrace a greater variation of playing conditions than any other modern sport, but such diversity is positively celebrated. That the pitch at the WACA in Perth, Australia will provide pace and bounce, the Headingley pitch in Leeds will help seam bowlers, and spin bowlers will dominate at Galle, Sri Lanka merely adds to the interest for cricket officianados. The valuation of such diversity can be seen in relation to recent ground developments in England. When a 200-year-old lime tree within the playing area of the St Lawrence ground, Canterbury was damaged by high winds in 2005, rather than embrace the spatial standardization forced upon them, the ground's owners planted a new tree (albeit adjacent to the playing area) to replace it. When the playing surface at Lord's was excavated to enable the installation of a new drainage system in 2002 the traditional slope was restored to its original form when the ground was re-laid (the south-east side of the playing surface had been 2.5 metres lower than the north-west). Ironically therefore, the owners of the most revered cricket ground and the guardians of the spirit of the sport most directly linked to the notion of fair play, literally chose to *not* have a level playing field.

Thus despite the rhetoric linking cricket with fair play, a prominent feature of the game is a relative indifference towards equality. For instance, no sport is quite as subject to the vagaries of the weather as cricket. Other sports may stop due to rain (baseball, golf), or even because the light is poor (tennis), but the competitors in other sports normally expect that, when they return to play, conditions will either be approximate to what they were before and/or that their opponents will be similarly (dis)advantaged by the new environmental conditions. But in cricket rainfall can affect the speed with which the ball runs over of the outfield, humidity can affect the extent to which the ball 'swings' (moves laterally in the air), and dampness can increase 'seam' movement (deviation when the ball bounces on the pitch), all of which may disadvantage the batting side. Conversely, when the sun shines players will feel that it is a good time to bat. As the light is rarely artificially enhanced, players must accept that, within limits, they will be advantaged/disadvantaged by having to bat in light of differing quality. While artificial lighting is gradually being introduced, cricket administrators have not sought to regulate for the provision of equal playing conditions with the same vigour as their counterparts in other sports. Wembley and Wimbledon have retractable roofs but Lord's does not.

Almost regardless of weather conditions, however, longer games of cricket have the in-built inequality of a pitch which (generally) deteriorates over time and thus presents different challenges to each team at different stages of the match. Invariably the fewest runs are scored in the fourth and final innings of a first class match. Conventionally the pitch initially favours fast bowlers and comes to favour spin bowling as the game progresses. As in other sports a coin is tossed at the beginning of a game and the winning captain gains an advantage (through choice of ends, first possession of the ball, etc.), but in cricket there are no subsequent mechanisms for the equalization of playing chances, such as swapping ends or giving the other team possession at the start of the second half. Rather, in cricket the advantages of this initial success may exert a significant influence over the entire match. Only cricketers talk of a 'good toss to win' because only in cricket is this chance element potentially so central to the outcome of the game. Only cricketers talk of a 'good toss to lose' because only in cricket are the environmental conditions so difficult to predict. The relative reluctance to use non-grass pitches illustrates the lack of enthusiasm to investigate equality-enhancing measures in cricket compared to many other sports.

Cricket's laws are again unusual in paying scant regard to equalizing individuals' and teams' playing chances. In one-day cricket there is no limit to the contribution of each batter but bowlers contribute no more than twenty per cent of the overs bowled. While most modern team sports allow injured and unfit players to be substituted, substitutes for injured cricketers are uniquely barred from the central aspects of the game; namely batting, bowling, and the specialist fielding position of wicketkeeper. An injured batter may, however, have a substitute to run for him/her, meaning that some injured players (bowlers and wicketkeepers) are treated differently to others (batters). Unlike most other team games, tactical substitutions are not allowed in cricket. Teams must be selected prior to the toss and personnel cannot be altered to adjust for the conditions that teams subsequently face.

A final *unmodern* characteristic of cricket regards what Guttmann calls specialization. While the advent of the IPL has marked the emergence of specialist 'portfolio players' (Rumford 2011) who travel the world only playing Twenty20 cricket, most cricketers play all of the game's multiple forms. Moreover, fielding positions in cricket are remarkably fluid, with players expected to fill a variety of roles during the game, potentially changing after each ball bowled. Conversely, North American sports in particular have rules facilitating the participation of those with specialist skills – the NFL kicker, the 'designated hitter' in baseball's American League, the 'enforcer' in ice hockey – but the restriction of substitutes in cricket ensures that players must contribute to all aspects of the game. The cricketing all-rounder is often the linchpin of the side, whereas 'utility players' in other sports are often valued for the backup they provide.

Thus cricket contains a number of features which stand in contrast to the developmental trends of modern sport. Cricket followers revel in these peculiarities. Conversely, neophytes find them a barrier to gaining an understanding of the game. But the specific structure of cricket cannot entirely account for the deification and disinterest the game seems to evoke in equal measure. Indeed, these peculiarities should be seen as the *outcome* of who plays the game, not the cause of its differential popularity. These peculiarities provide part of the stimulus for writing this book, but they are not the central problem which the book seeks to address.

The aims of *Globalizing Cricket*

To understand why cricket has these peculiarities, and therefore why it is both revered and ridiculed in equal measure, it needs to be understood in its historical and social context. As noted, the game stems from, or at least was first codified in, *England*. A glance at the list of countries which currently play cricket shows the degree to which colonization as part of the British *Empire* was responsible for its diffusion around the globe. The game's contemporary social significance rests on the meaning which people attach to cricketing contests. For many people in cricket playing nations, no other sport delivers such meaningful contests which resonate so closely with their historically generated sense of *identity*. Conversely, in many non-cricket playing countries the game has little bearing on the way people conceive of their 'self'.

Consequently this is a book about the development of cricket. The story starts around the time when a particular group of human beings decided that it would be useful to write down a set of rules for the game and examines who these people were, and why they behaved as they did. The book charts how cricket became defined as the 'national game', how a particular set of rules became adopted by a broader range of groups within England, and how it simultaneously diffused to various places around the globe. It examines how cricket was adopted, adapted and rejected in different countries. The journey concludes by looking at the role of cricket in contemporary society; in particular, the way in which the game influences the lives of post-colonial migrants to the United Kingdom, the effect of the game on the way in which the English perceive themselves, and the way in which the English use cricket to frame their understanding of 'Others'.

While this book inevitably offers a history of cricket, it is a specific type of history. This book does *not* primarily attempt to *describe* the development of cricket. A number of these more 'conventional' or 're-constructionist' histories (Booth 2005) of cricket exist which fulfil this task. For instance, Altham and Swanton's *A History of Cricket* (1948) and Wynne Thomas's *From Weald to World* (1997) represent histories of cricket which mainly focus on key matches and personalities in an attempt to re-present the past as it 'actually was'. Nor is this book quite like those written by what Booth calls academic or 'constructionist' historians. Examples of this genre include Birley's *A History of English Cricket* (1999) and Stoddart and Sandiford's *The Imperial Game* (1998) which seek to interpret such events by developing a narrative which locates and gives meaning to them within the broader context. Birley, for instance, looks to examine how 'the English took this game and made it into one of their most cherished institutions' (1999: ix), while Sandiford argues that the playing of cricket within the former British Empire 'is really ... [a story] about the colonial quest for identity in the face of the colonisers' search for authority' (Sandiford 1998a: 1).

Rather, this book is a *historical sociological* analysis of cricket. This approach is based on the belief that the most adequate way to analyse human societies is as an amalgam of processes rather than a series of separate events, and that the commonsense distinction made between past and present fatally severs our ability to understand the contemporary manifestation of those processes. The particular type of historical sociological approach which guides this book relies on some particular theoretical assumptions which are spelt out later, but for now it is sufficient to note that in terms of their 'fundamental pre-occupations, history and sociology are and always have been the same thing' (Abrams 1982: x). Their divorce, moreover, 'makes historians needlessly allergic to the very idea of structures, and sociologists afraid of dealing with single events' (Goudsblom 1977: 136). 'We need the variety provided by history in order even to ask sociological questions, much less to answer them' (Wright Mills 1970: 146). Thus, while this book describes various key phases and processes in the development of cricket, it is more centrally guided by an attempt to *explain* how and why the role and social significance of cricket has changed over time.

The focus of this book is also geographically and temporally distinct. Like most accounts of the development of cricket, this book is focused on a particular territory. 'Constructionist' histories of cricket tend to relate to particular places such as India (Majumdar 2008), New Zealand (Ryan 2004), the Caribbean (Beckles 1998a; 1998b; Beckles and Stoddart 1995) and South Africa (Gemmell 2004). There are even some very good academic histories of cricket in the United States (Kirsch 1989; Melville 1998). This book has a similar geographic bias, but whether that is towards England, Britain or the United Kingdom is a more debatable point. Such precision is easier when the temporal focus of a book was more limited. Underdowns' *Start of Play: Cricket and Culture in Eighteenth-Century England* (2000), Sandiford's *Cricket and the Victorians* (1994) and Williams' *Cricket and England: A Cultural and Social History of the Inter-War Years* (1999) illustrate how a shorter time period lends itself to a more clearly defined geography.

In attempting a broader developmental sweep this book must necessarily be sensitive towards, and go beyond the narrow confines of, socially constructed national borders. In so doing this book addresses the way in which the game has globally expanded, and the effects of that global expansion on the identities of those who now inhabit the place in which the game was originally developed. But this book is *not* about the globalization of cricket *per se*. It does not, for instance, seek to comment on debates about the homogenizing, creolizing or glocalizing consequences of these developments. It does not explore the transnational movement of finance, mediatized images or personnel. Rather, this text is a sociological analysis of the historical and contemporary social significance of what is widely described as the quintessential English game, and how this has changed as the game has globally diffused.

A framework for understanding the development of cricket

While no other text has attempted to examine cricket in this way, a number of (historical) sociological texts have scrutinized the development of other sports. A comparison with four similar texts provides some indication of the approach taken here. The first such text was Dunning and Sheard's *Barbarians, Gentlemen and Players: a sociological study of the development of rugby football* (1979/2005). The title conveys what are seen as the key developmental phases of the game; namely the social control of violence and conflicts over amateurism and professionalism. In addition to this, *Barbarians* was concerned to examine the worldwide trend towards the growing seriousness or commercialization of sport, and the relationship between this process and 'the alleged trend towards greater violence in modern sport' (2005: 15). Gruneau and Whitson's *Hockey Night in Canada* (1993) is an attempt to 'examine the changing character of hockey in Canada as one small part of the making of modern sports, of commercial entertainment, and indeed of modern experience itself' (1993: 4). They chart how (ice) hockey developed out of a tradition of Victorian moral entrepreneurship, embraced consumer culture and national branding through the emergence of the NHL, and has more recently engaged with post-national capitalism. At each stage, there is a degree of contestation and negotiation over the ideological meanings and the social practices associated with the game. Significantly, however, Gruneau and Whitson's interest in hockey stems from the sport's 'powerful grip on the imaginations and collective memories of Canadians' (1993: 3). The cultural politics of the conceptualization of national identity is infused with debates about 'locality, consumerism, ethnicity, class, race and gender' (1993: 7). Third is Giulianotti's *Football: A Sociology of the Global Game* (1999). Arguing that the game's global appeal owes something to its simplicity and plasticity, Giulianotti seeks to examine cross-cultural differences in the way the game is interpreted and practiced. Following analyses of the development of the game in the nineteenth and twentieth centuries, chapters focus on themes such as supporter cultures, stadia, business, aesthetics and cultural politics. Giulianotti argues that the development of football can be seen through a continuum of 'traditional', 'modern' and 'post-modern stages', and that a cross-cultural comparison shows that 'the game's valued characteristics tells (sic) us something fundamental about the cultures in which it is performed' (1999: xii). Finally, Sugden's *Boxing and Society: An International Analysis* (1996) locates the 'noble art' in its broader social, economic and political context. Sugden combines chapters on the history and political economy of boxing with ethnographic case studies of its practice in three cultural settings (the United States, Northern Ireland and Cuba) which together 'provide a balanced view of the submerged world that exists beneath the ring' (1996: 7).

Globalizing Cricket has parallels with each of the above. A key similarity with both *Barbarians* and *Hockey Night* is that this book is structured in a broadly chronological way. *Globalizing Cricket* shares *Barbarians*' underlying theoretical framework (the figurational sociology of Norbert Elias), but the empirical themes addressed here are more similar to those discussed in *Hockey Night*. Gruneau and Whitson see the link between hockey and Canadian identity as historical, ubiquitous, natural, unique, quintessential, oft-stated, and commonsensical. Here, therefore, are obvious similarities with the way the relationship between cricket and the English is typically viewed. While aspects of *Hockey Night* locate the development of Canadian ice hockey in the context of globalization, as noted above, the analysis undertaken here is not an exploration of globalization *per se*, but similar to Giulianotti's and Sugden's emphasis on discussing cultural comparisons in the meaning and practice of a particular sport. Like Giulianotti, I consider why a particular sport appeals to diverse communities. Like *Boxing and Society*, this book provides case study chapters focussed on the sport's cultural meaning in specific settings.

Like *Barbarians* and *Football* this text is underpinned by the view that sport can be seen to have passed through distinct phases and that these phases relate the broader social structure of societies in which the game is played. Like all of the above, *Globalizing Cricket* is centrally about a sport which is a 'male preserve' (Sheard and Dunning 1973) and thus says relatively little about female sporting experiences. Uniquely, however, *Globalizing Cricket* focuses not only on the cultural diffusion of a sport, but the ramifications of this diffusion on the 'diffusers'.

While a more detailed discussion of sociological theory will be deferred to the Conclusion, some core ideas need to be introduced here. At its heart, this work is informed by Elias's conception of human beings as both inherently social and interdependent animals (Elias 1978). Consequently, people's thoughts and actions are determined by the relations that they form with other humans. As the organization of societies becomes more complex – in line with technological developments in travel and communication, for instance – so the context in which humans think and act becomes more complex, with individuals both influencing, and being influenced by, a greater range of people. Human action may have an initial purpose but the consequences of human actions may not be wholly intended; like ripples in a small pool, they re-bound, and directly or tangentially intermingle with other intended actions and unintended outcomes. Human actions have consequences that extend beyond the life of the individual such that the context in which today's cricketers play the game is shaped by the actions of all kinds of historical figures: the eighteenth century Duke of Richmond; William Lillywhite; Harry Wright; Frank Worrell and Charles Lawrence.

As Liston (2011: 161) rightly observes, Elias's most well known and arguably most significant book, *The Civilizing Process*, 'has become synonymous with Elias's figurational sociology'. According to Elias human groups typically seek to define their behaviour as distinct and distanced from animals and those humans they see as inferior to themselves; in other words, as 'civilized'. While *The Civilizing Process*, and indeed much of the figurational research on sport and leisure, has been viewed through a substantive focus on violence and its social control, an arguably more nuanced view is that Elias undertook an 'analysis of the historical development of emotions and psychological life … in relation to the connections … with larger scale processes such as state formation, urbanisation and economic development' (van Krieken 1998: 353). Within the context of sport, emotions and psychological life are most evident in relation to two interconnected factors – social identities and the rules and customs by which sports are played. The former is an expression of the relationships which people consider to be significant, the latter an expression of the norms by which people expect, and expect others to expect, their social lives to be lived. As the content of *Globalizing Cricket* amply demonstrates, these two things are radically interdependent. Yet because people rarely reflect on either – who they are, why they play/watch certain sports – because they are so deeply ingrained in humans due to socialization processes, they become part of *habitus*, or second nature. Within the context of twenty-first century western sport, the larger scale processes which affect habitus go beyond state formation, urbanization and post-Fordist economic development, and include colonialism, postcolonialism and the formation and movement of diasporas; processes which are fundamentally more global in scope.

While this book is not about imperialism, the role of cricket in the British Empire is inescapable. While this book is not about race, it speaks to and of British race relations. While this book is not about English national identity, inevitably it discusses how such self-perceptions change as a consequence of cricket's global spread: *Englishness, Empire, Identity.*

Conclusion: Cricket and Englishness as a pleonasm

The empirical focus of this book is the way cricket both structures and is structured by local (English, sometimes British) and global relations. Yet drawing a link between cricket and the English is hardly a novel idea amongst social scientists who write about sport. Jack Williams (1999: 4) has argued that between the wars writers frequently 'praised cricket as the epitome of moral worth'. Leading sports geographer John Bale similarly argues that 'the landscapes of cricket are projected as not only being bucolic and rural but as being overwhelmingly English and Southern in location' (1994: 159). Literary historian Tony Bateman suggests that 'cricket and literature ... have played particularly privileged and significant roles in the historical construction of Englishness' (2003: 27), and Joseph Maguire (1993: 297), a sociologist of sport, has argued that 'Cricket is seen to represent what "England" is and gives meaning to the identity of being "English". The sport fixes "England" as a focus of identification in English emotions'.

A range of publications more directly focussed on Englishness and English national identity replicate such claims. Colls (2002), Easthope (1999), Fox (2005), Haselar (1996), Kumar (2003a) and Langford (2000) draw on cricket for ready-made examples of manifestations of English national identity. For instance, in *Englishness and National Culture,* Anthony Easthope argues that 'English national culture, profoundly secular as it is, seems to treat only two things as genuinely transcental – cricket and its own sense of humour' (1999: 162). Similarly Stephen Haseler, in *The English Tribe,* argues that cricket is 'the most exalted icon' of what he calls 'theme park heritage Englishness', in which the game has become 'a metaphor for the celebration of the English and rural nostalgia' (1996: 59). More populist readers, like Jeremy Paxman's *The English* (1999), Clifford and King's *England in Particular* (2006), and Bill Bryson's *Icons of England* (2010) would also be incomplete without references to cricket. Paxman refers to the 'curiously passionless devotion' that the English have to cricket (1999: 204), whilst Clifford and King cite cricket's timeless character which evokes fair play and selflessness. For many, Clifford and King (2006) argue, cricket is the epitome of Englishness.

Cricket and Englishness therefore frequently appear as a couplet, but these two words are so frequently put together that their relationship has become a largely commonsense, and therefore unexamined, assumption. But while there is no shortage of people who recognize a relationship between cricket and Englishness, it is my contention that no one has yet fully explored how and why this relationship began, and what the enduring but changing consequences of this relationship have been (to date only one relatively brief publication has explicitly addressed 'The "Englishness" of English cricket' (Simons 1996)). For those examining changing conceptions of English national culture and identity, cricket is merely used to provide occasional illustration. Nothing approaching a sustained analysis exists. Indeed the ubiquity of cricket in these analyses is matched only by the superficiality with which these authors tend to engage with the sport. Kumar (2003a), for instance, whose work I draw on extensively, refers briefly to the 'Tebbit cricket test', and John Major's citation of cricket in response to the (perceived) threat to British sovereignty posed by the expanding powers of the European Union, but does not see cricket as sufficiently important to include, for example, in his index. For most, perhaps all, of those who write about English national identity, cricket is a reflection of Englishness rather than an active agent in the production of the identity of English people. Their engagement with cricket is akin to what Carrington has called 'the repetitive and perfunctory "Jamesian" nod' (2010: 48), via which mention of *Beyond a Boundary* (James 1963) is deemed sufficient recognition of sport amongst postcolonial theorists. Indeed so interchangeable, so synonymous, are these words that 'Englishness and cricket' amounts to a pleonasm (the use of more words than is necessary to express an idea).

Globalizing Cricket is an attempt to correct that omission. Just as Gruneau and Whitson (1993: 25) argue in relation to the cultural analysis of hockey in Canada, an element of intellectual snobbery may account for the absence of analytic insight. It is probably also because the connection between cricket and the English is so widely made that no one has thought it necessary to subject it to sociological scrutiny. The task of this book is to put flesh on these bones, to provide an analysis of the development and global diffusion of cricket in order to contextualize the changing ways in which the game influences and intersects with contemporary English/British society. What characteristics of the development and structure of this society account for the development of a sport with the peculiar characteristics described at the beginning of this introduction?

1

The Emergence of Cricket

In Jamaica, on 29 January 1998, a test match between England and the West Indies was abandoned after just fifty-six minutes of play.[1] During that time the England team's physiotherapist had treated injured batsmen on six separate occasions. Ultimately the umpires, in consultation with the team captains and the match referee, decided that the unevenness of the wicket made the ball's bounce too unpredictable and thus that play posed an unacceptable risk to batters' safety. An editorial in *The Times* stated that 'Somebody could have been killed. Test cricket is not a game for the faint hearts. But neither should it be turned into an intimidatory dice of death' (30 January 1998). Remarkably this was the first time that this had occurred in 122 years of test cricket.

The perception of cricket as a genteel game is inextricably linked to the cricket-Englishness couplet. To examine this relationship more fully we need to appreciate how the modern sport we now call cricket emerged. Who was responsible for drawing up cricket's laws and what specific choices did they make? How did this process relate to the broader social context of which it was a part?

From folk game to modern sport

As Major notes, 'the search for the birth of cricket has been as fruitless as the hunt for the holy grail' (2007: 17). This is because it is a fundamentally misconceived search, for while the Oxford English Dictionary (Simpson and Weiner 1989) may cite the first recorded use of the phrase 'cricket ball' as Edward Phillipps' 1658 poem, 'Treatment of Ladies as Balls and Sports' (and the sentence, 'Would my eyes have been beat out my head with a cricket ball'), we have little way of comprehending the similarities between the game played with that 'cricket' ball and the modern form of cricket we know today. Such was the structure of medieval societies that identical games could have a variety of different, locally specific names, or that one name could be used to describe a variety of locally specific rules. The kind of uniformity people expect today was neither possible nor considered particularly important for it is only when social interdependencies are relatively broad and varied that a lack of standardization is thrown into sharper relief. Indeed Strutt (1801: 107) in the landmark *The Sports and Pastimes of the Peoples of England* specifically notes this as a characteristic of early cricket, stating that its rules were 'subject to frequent variation' and evidence presented in Chapter 6 further suggests that variations were apparent throughout the British Isles at this early point in the game's development. More adequately therefore we should conceive of sports as having multiple origins and antecedents. This enables us to focus on two sociologically more useful questions: what were the structural characteristics of nascent sport forms such as cricket, and why did they change at a particular time and in a particular place?

As discussed in the Introduction, modern sports like cricket are structured in distinct ways. This structure, moreover, distinguishes them from the antecedent sports-like activities out of which they emerged. Brookes (1978) argues that it is possible to identify three general types of 'folk games' which existed in the European middle ages:

1) team games in which moving players (on foot or on horseback) propelled a 'ball' (or similar object) towards a 'goal' or fixed point in order to score points;

2) individual games in which a stationary player hit a ball at a target (into a hole, through hoops); and

3) team games in which a stationary person propelled an object away from him/her self and scored by running between two or more fixed points.

Cricket emerged from this latter group which, in the sixteenth and seventeenth century, included bat and ball folk games such as 'club ball', 'stoolball', 'trap-ball', 'tip cat' and 'cat and dog'. Variations of these could have been as similar to each other and as distinct from modern cricket as the international variants listed in the Introduction (for example Lapta, Oină). In each, however, rules were relatively few, relatively simple and transmitted orally rather than in written form.

The process by which folk games transformed into modern sport forms can be described as 'sportization' (Elias 1986a). Evidence suggests that this process first occurred in eighteenth-century England and involved sports such as boxing, cricket, horse-racing and fox-hunting (golf was also codified at this time, but in Scotland. See Stirk 1987). For each of these sports more precise and explicit rules were written down and enforced in stricter and more efficient ways than in the past. The contemporary global significance of cricket is partly a consequence of the fact that it emerged in a coherent form which could relatively easily be communicated before any other similarly structured game did. The question is, therefore, who was responsible for this sportization process and why?

Sportization occurred in conjunction with a parallel process called parliamentarization. Britain was characterized by an end to a 'cycle of violence' in the late seventeenth, early eighteenth centuries as, post-English Civil War (1642–1649), the state became more effective in curbing the violence characteristic of the previously ruling 'warrior nobility' (Elias 1986a). Relatively peaceful means for deciding political issues began to emerge with, for example, the development of parliamentary rules, relatively high levels of mutual trust, and mechanisms for the peaceful transference of power between political parties. In contrast, Britain's European neighbours remained relatively disunited (such as Germany and Italy) or highly centralized and subject to a form of absolute rule (for example France). Parliamentarization did not cause sportization and sportization did not lead to parliamentarization. Rather, these were corresponding processes which not only occurred at roughly the same time but also involved largely overlapping groups of people. Moreover, both processes exhibit a peculiar set of social norms which were emerging in conjunction with these broader structural changes. In Elias's words:

> Military skills gave way to the verbal skills of debate ... rhetoric and persuasion ... which required greater restraint all round. It was this change, the greater sensitivity with regard to the use of violence which, reflected in the social habitus of individuals, also found expression in the development of their pastimes. The 'parliamentarization' of the landed classes of England had its counterpart in the 'sportization' of their pastimes. (Elias 1986b: 34)

Two aspects of the relationship between these political changes and the development of sport should be stressed. First, the relative freedom of association combined with the relative unity of the British aristocracy as a national social class, led their activities to become increasingly centred around the twin foci of government and social life; around Parliament and gentlemen's clubs (and to a lesser extent aristocrats' country estates). Although incipient levels of organized cricket existed in rural areas (and historians such as Wynne-Thomas (1997) and Birley (1999) stress the prominence of the game in the South East of England in particular), it was when the aristocracy met in London and began to play the sport against each other that the need for some kind of agreed statement which drew together the similar forms of the game customarily played in different parts of the country emerged. It was in this context that cricket began to resemble a modern sports form and for this reason that the governing bodies for the sports that emerged at this time took the form of *clubs* (i.e. the MCC, horse racing's the Jockey Club and the Royal and Ancient Golf Club) rather than sports associations or unions (i.e. the Football Association and the Rugby Football Union). The close link to parliament is also seen in the use of 'laws' rather than 'rules' to regulate the game.

Second, the shift towards the relatively peaceful settlement of disputes in political conflict facilitated the competition for social status to take place via non-violent means. Behaviour characterized by stricter personal self-control and self-discipline became socially valued, and ultimately ingrained as part of this social class's habitus. It is, therefore, entirely logical that sports rules invariably restrict the means by which individuals can achieve sporting success and therefore reward similar behavioural characteristics.

Thus, in providing a sociological explanation of the emergence of cricket, a number of features need to be examined. Emphasis should be placed on the construction of formal sets of written rules, on the social classes of which the people who developed those rules were a part, and the degree to which those rules illustrated a decline in the prevalence of violence and injury in the game. As will be seen, cricket provides a very clear illustration of the convergence of these developments; the interplay of identity and behavioural norms.

Early cricket matches

Much of what we know about early cricket matches comes from London's 'new crop of single sheet papers' (Harris 1998: 18) launched following the relaxation of state control over information post-Charles II's enforced acceptance of Habeas Corpus in 1679. Government censorship on printing was 'lifted entirely from 1696' (Birley 1999: 14). The content of these publications was initially structured around business, law and politics, but sport, and cricket in particular, grew in prominence in the first half of the eighteenth century. Notices advertising the staging of cricket matches at this time indicate that the game was played by aristocrats for whom gambling was both frequent and significant. Notices also indicate that the participation of women in cricket was not uncommon. As we will see, these matches served as the stimulus for the development of the first sets of written rules for the game and thus the standardization of variously termed folk games into a coherent and subsequently communicable game form. First, however, it is important to say something about the violent tenor in which these sports appear to have been played.

Injury seemed to be an ever-present danger of playing early forms of cricket. On the one hand it may be argued that this was because it was only the occurrence of such incidents that made games newsworthy (Harris 1998: 22). McLean (1987: 18) states that 'almost all accidental references to cricket' stemmed from Puritan hostility and thus associate the game with violence and drinking. Yet newspaper reports of severe injuries and deaths largely passed with little comment, and where the reporting of a game was restricted to the production of its scorecard 'a host of gory titbits about collisions, charges and crashes' would have been omitted (McLean 1987: 33). That some players, notably Hambledon's David Harris, were notorious partly for the injuries their bowling inflicted (Altham and Swanton 1948: 49), suggests that these were sufficiently frequent occurrences to be considered a normal part of the game.

Not only was injury a danger inherent in playing; many writers have referred to the frequency of spectator disorder at games. Ford (1972: 131) argues that largely because of the problems associated with gambling and heavy drinking, 'when there was not some sort of commotion it seemed to be thought unusual'.

Major (2007: 56) similarly states that a 1731 match between the Duke of Richmond and a Mr Chambers ended in 'the near-obligatory affray'. Other notable incidents include the reading of the Riot Act at a match in Writtle, Essex in 1726 and the abandonment of a women's match between Charlton and Westdean & Chilgrove, Sussex in 1747 due to a pitch invasion (Brooke and Matthews 1988: 133). A cricketer called John Smith died in 1737 due to a cut from a stone thrown by a spectator (McLean 1987: 33). Leicester's victory over Coventry in 1788 led to 'a scene of bloodshed ... scarcely to be credited in a country so entirely distinguished for acts of humanity' (*Coventry Mercury*, cited in Brookes 1978: 69), and the *Birmingham Gazette* commented on the same incident: 'At present we have not heard of any lives being lost, though the weapons used in the contest were the most dangerous and alarming' (cited in Lambert 1992). Ford cites a report from the 1776 *London Chronicle* when, at a Kent vs Essex match at Tilbury Fort, a dispute over a player's eligibility led to 'a battle'. One of the Kentish men,

> ran into the guard-house, and getting a gun ... fired and killed one of the opposite party. On seeing this, they all began running to the guard-house, and there being but 4 soldiers there, they took away the guns and fell to it, doing a great deal of mischief. An old invalid was run through the body with a bayonet, and a sergeant ... was shot dead. (Ford 1972: 45)

As Harris notes, fighting between teams could lead to 'wholesale mayhem' (1998: 24).

Admission prices were used to keep undesirables out, and individuals or groups were employed to keep the peace. For instance, Brookes (1978: 50) notes how entrance fees to London's Artillery Ground were altered, first to attract a more reputable crowd, and latterly to keep events economically viable. Similarly, at Walworth Common London in 1744, a joint cricket match and smock race was staged and, according to the *Penny London Morning Advertiser*, 'Captain Vinegar, with a great many of his bruisers and bull-dogs, will attend to make a ring, that no civil spectators may be incommoded by the rabble' (cited in Underdown 2000: 85).[2] 'Recent violence' is cited as the reason why the Corporation of London prohibited cricket matches at the Artillery Ground (London's premier cricket venue prior to the establishment of Lord's) from 1780 onwards (Underdown 2000: 114).

Although Brookes (1978: 53) claims that members of the aristocracy exerted a calming influence at matches, disorder was evident at fixtures involving society's elite. In the eighteenth century, teachers at Westminster and Eton frequently attempted to prohibit boys from playing cricket (Brookes 1978: 72). A game in 1731 between '11 of London' and '11 of Brompton' ended when 'several engaged on both sides for nearly half an hour, and most of the Brompton Gents were forced to fly for quarter, and some retired home with broken heads and black eyes, much to the satisfaction of the other side'

(Wagham 1906, cited in Brookes 1978: 53). A dispute over a catch during a match between Kent and Surrey in 1762 led to the players coming 'to blows, several heads were broken and a challenge issued between "two persons of distinction"' (Altham and Swanton 1948: 39; see also Scott 1989: 6–7 on cricket-related duels).

There is evidence that the legal authorities considered a broader prohibition on the game (Ford 1972: 39) though cricket escaped the sort of restrictions imposed on football and its folk antecedents which were prohibited by state and local authorities more than thirty times between 1314 and 1667 (Dunning and Sheard 2005: 20). Some disputes were, however, referred to the emerging legal system. Wynne Thomas (1997: 27) records a legal case concerning Thomas Hatter who died in 1648 having been struck by a cricket bat. A similar case involving Henry Brand was heard at Arundel the same year (Major 2007: 24). In 1693 Thomas Reynolds, Henry Gunter and Elenor Lansford sent a petition to the Queen seeking remission from their fines which had been imposed for riot and battery, 'they being only spectators at a game of crickett' (cited in Scott 1989: 177). Underdown (2000: 14) is probably correct to interpret this plea as 'implying that violence at matches was common enough to be excusable'.

Gauging the violent tenor of life from documentary evidence is a relatively subjective task. For each piece of supporting evidence there will be match reports which say nothing of this theme. It is the case however, that the majority of those who have written about eighteenth century cricket, producing both populist (Ford 1972, Major 2007, McLean 1987) and academic (Guttmann 1986, Underdown 2000) histories concur with the view expressed here (Bowen 1970, Birley 1999, and to some extent Brookes 1978, do not share this emphasis). Underdown's conclusion that eighteenth-century cricket was 'part of [a] vibrant, if violent, rural culture' (2000: 122) seems equally applicable to the aristocratic, urban forms of the game.

The sportization of cricket

The 1727 Articles of Agreement between the Duke of Richmond and Mr Brodrick (an Irish statesman and the heir to Viscount Midleton (Birley 1999: 18)) is the oldest document relating to cricket laws. However, the earliest version of what could be called a 'full' and systematic set of laws was published in *The New Universal Magazine* in 1752 and described as 'The Game of Cricket, as settled by the CRICKET CLUB, in 1744 and play'd at the ARTILLERY-GROUND LONDON' (Rait Kerr 1950: 13). Subsequently a set of rules, 'As Settled by the several CRICKET CLUBS, particularly that of the Star and Garter in Pall Mall' (cited in Rait Kerr 1950: 91) was published in 1755 which, in all respects agreed with the 1744 rules except for what essentially amounted to some modernization of the wording.[3]

The early rules defined the standard size of the wicket and some of its markings, though made no reference to boundaries or the care and maintenance of the wicket.[4] The maximum and minimum sizes of the ball were included in these rules but no restrictions were made relating to the width or length of the bat. The number of balls per over and what constituted legal and illegal bowling was outlined, as was the scoring of fair and unfair 'notches' (a term only superseded by 'runs' around 1811). In addition to this the methods of dismissal were described and individual sections were devoted to specific laws for the wicketkeeper and umpire, indicating that umpires not only *upheld* the laws at this time, but were *subject to* the laws due to their status relative to the aristocratic team leaders or captains.

Gambling was deeply implicated in much of the game's early violence and thus was addressed in the early rules. For instance, a 1731 match on Chelsea Common terminated in a free fight among the spectators due to a disputed wager. In delivering judgment on the case, a London magistrate observed: 'It (cricket) is a manly game, and not bad in itself, but it is the ill-use that is made of it by betting above £10 that is bad and against the law, which ought to be constructed largely to prevent the great mischief of excessive gambling' (Harris 1907, cited in Brookes 1978: 76). Ford also records how the Duke of Richmond and his team were assaulted by a mob in 1731 because they turned up late for the resumption of a match so depriving their opponents of the opportunity to win the game and how, in 1777, the crowd 'prevented the Stowmarket gentlemen from going in' in order to save their side from losing and hence their stake money (1972: 131–32).

Such was the prevalence of and consequences that followed gambling that, in one sense, the 1727 Articles of Agreement drawn up between the Duke of Richmond and Mr Brodrick were an attempt to avoid physical conflicts over deciding the outcome of the game (Brookes 1978: 42). The regulation of gambling reached its height with *The London Club*'s 1774 code of laws which contained an additional section with three clauses relating specifically to the resolution of such issues. These were:

> If the notches of one Player are laid against another, the Bet depends on both Innings, unless otherwise specified.
>   If one party beats the other in one Innings, the Notches in the first Innings shall determine the Bet.
>   But if the other Party goes in a Second Time, then the Bet must be determined by the numbers on the score. (Rait Kerr 1950: 19)

As Major (2007: 42) concludes, 'a rough and tumble, or an illegal affray, was a frequent accompaniment to a competitive game or an unsettled bet, and in a violent age that may have been an added attraction'.

That these early rules were the products of aristocrats and gentlemen meeting at their London clubs provides a 'measure of the central position of the club in London cricket and of London cricket in English cricket' (McLean 1987: 42). The 1755 set of rules is particularly significant, however, in that it marks the beginning of the MCC's influence over the game. The Star and Garter Club (with a French affectation common amongst the English aristocracy at this time (Langford 2000), it was sometimes known as the *Je Ne Sais Quoi* Club) whose members were significant among the framers of the 1755 rules, had an overlapping membership with the White Conduit Club (to the extent that they were often mistaken for each other). In 1787 members of the White Conduit Club were central in forming the MCC. The crossover between this emerging administrative structure for the game and the gentry and aristocratic political elite, substantiate Elias's linkage of parliamentarization and sportization processes. Frederick Louis, Prince of Wales, was the perpetual Chairman of the Star and Garter Club (coincidentally he died in 1751 from a cricket inflicted injury). Interestingly Birley argues that the Prince's 'desire to be English was such that he had cricket bats shipped out to Hanover, where he was educated' (1999: 22). Lord Frederick Beauclerk, the Earl of Winchilsea and the Duke of Dorset (Ambassador to France, later Steward of the Royal Household) were among the other prominent founding members of the MCC.

Why did these aristocrats become involved in establishing laws for the game of cricket? The resolution of gambling disputes and the avoidance of crowd disorder provides only a partial answer. Rules to clarify the outcome of bets are a necessary but not sufficient reason for the emergence of a standardized game. Rather, rules were required because these bets were a symptom, rather than a cause of, status rivalry. Aristocrats advertised their matches because cricketing success enhanced their social status. Cricket was a venue for conducting the kind of 'reasonably friendly rivalry' (Harris 1998: 23) that predominated after the cycle of violence ended in the seventeenth century and the process of parliamentarization began. By having sets of rules that were consistently applied, status competition became more transparent. In letters to friends nobles expressed their shame at having lost matches and return matches were a common courtesy. Almost without exception all the early patrons who exerted a significant influence over the early game – Sir William Gage; Lionel, Charles and John Sackville; John Russell, Duke of Bedford; the Duke of Newcastle; the Duke of Richmond – were politically active noblemen. By-election candidates would 'attend games as part of their campaign' (Major 2007: 58). A recurrent notice in the 1747 *Daily Advertiser* stated that matches between Kent and England would be postponed due to players' commitments in that year's General Election (Harris 1998: 25). The Duke of Richmond in particular used cricket matches to entertain allies, attract new followers, and publicly confront political opponents such as William Gage (McLean 1987: 25). Richmond sent his steward to cricket games as part of his political campaigning and attended a match between

Slindon and Portslade in 1741 because he anticipated that the Tory candidate, Thomas Sergison, would be there. Sometimes such meetings resulted in violence. When Sergison's supporters chanted insults '"a bloody battle" ensued in which a lot of heads were broken' (cited in Underdown 2000: 61).

At this time, therefore, politics and cricket were closely linked. Both were forms of status competition. Both were undergoing a process of pacification, with more violent elements of each undergoing relatively rapid change. Both became standardized through the introduction of increasingly precise, complex and written laws. Other forms of cricket were certainly played at this time but due to the relative status and power of participants they would not come to have an enduring and global impact on social life. Rather, these particular codes endured because 'the assumption of authority in relation to the organization of cricket was a modest side effect of the more generalized dominance of a ruling elite' (Harris 1998: 24).

Law changes and the control of violence

Aspects of the particular laws that emerged illustrate the way in which personality structures and emotional norms were changing in conjunction with the identity of this particular class. Nine ways of dismissing a batter were outlined in the 1755 code: caught; bowled; stumped; run out; hit wicket; handled ball; hit ball twice; obstruction of a fielder; and 'retirements' (such as timed out, etc.).[5] The other major alteration to the game in this respect, LBW laws, was introduced in 1774. The implementation and modification of four of the original nine – obstruction, hit ball twice, run out and stumped – have occurred, not necessarily because of, but certainly with reference to, issues of violence and injury. That is to say, in what is perhaps the most fundamental part of the game, we can see a consistent trend which links the emergence of cricket to the significant decline in violence in the broader social context.

One of the most obvious consequences of restrictions relating to obstruction was the reduction in contact between the players on each side. This worked in two ways. One of the laws in the 1755 code refers specifically to batters obstructing the fielding side:

> When the Ball is hit up, either of the Strikers may hinder the Catch in his running Ground; or if it is hit directly across the Wickets, the other Player may place his Body any where within the Swing of the Bat, so as to hinder the Bowler from catching it; but he must neither strike at it, nor touch it with his Hands. (Cited in Rait Kerr 1950: 95)

Thus the batter would only be dismissed if, in attempting to obstruct a fielder, he/she left his/her 'running ground' (defined, presumably, as the area between the two wickets). *Within* the running ground, however, either batter could prevent the catch so long as they did not use his/her bat or hand; a practice called 'charging down' in the 1727 Articles of Agreement. McLean records the case of a man called John Boots who in 1737 was killed 'by running against another man in crossing the wicket' (1987: 33). In 1787 the wording of this law was changed such that any contact with a fielder attempting a catch would result in dismissal. This was further revised in 1884 with the batter given out if the umpires judged the fielder to have been *intentionally* obstructed at *any time* during the game. Restrictions were, however, also imposed on the fielding side. A second law in the 1755 code made provision for the umpire to penalize the fielding side for obstructing a batter: 'They (the umpires) are the sole Judges of all Hindrances; crossing the Players in running, and standing unfair to strike, and in case of Hindrance may order a Notch to be Scor'd' (Rait Kerr 1950: 98). A version of this law remains today.

Similarly, hitting the ball twice appears to have been prohibited partly in order to prevent injury. Under 'The Laws for the Strikers' in the 1755 code, 'If a Ball is nipp'd up, and he strikes it again wilfully, before it came to the Wicket, it's out' (Rait Kerr 1950: 94). One of the consequences of this law was to contribute towards the spatial separation of the fielding and batting sides, for in matches where the batter *was* allowed to hit the ball twice, at which point fielders might legitimately try to gain control of the ball, the potential danger to other participants would have been considerable. This is illustrated by an inquest held at West Hoathly in Sussex in 1624 which heard how Edward Tye hit the ball into the air and attempted to hit it a second time before it landed. Meanwhile Jasper Vinall attempted to catch the ball. Tye either did not see Vinall or did not care and hit him on the front of the head with his bat. Vinall died two weeks later as a consequence of this injury. The inquest passed the verdict that Vinall had not died feloniously but by misadventure and through his own carelessness (Scott 1989; Wynne Thomas 1997). Green (1988: 29) has interpreted this practice in the following way: 'This terrifying weapon in the batter's armoury ... sheds a lurid light on the original spirit in which the game was played ... the clear implication being that up to now the conventional tactic had been to wallop the fielders with the bat.' Nowadays the batter is prohibited from hitting the ball twice, except to protect his/her wicket.

Rule changes concerning attempted run outs and stumpings were introduced with more explicit reference to the reduction of injury. Contained within the specifications for the layout of the pitch in the 1744 code is a particular reference to the popping crease which, Rait Kerr states, was a relatively new development at this time. To complete a run, a batter had to get from his/her batting position in front of the wicket to the bowler's end before the fielding side could return the ball to the bowler or wicketkeeper whilst his/her batting partner ran to the opposite end. By 1744, to be 'in' (i.e. to have successfully completed the run), the batter had to cross the popping crease before the fielding side could 'break' the wicket with the ball. Prior to this it appears that a run out was awarded if the fielding side put the ball into a 'popping hole' before the batter could fill that hole with his/her bat (Rait Kerr 1950: 67). Subsequently the rule was changed so that a run was deemed to have been completed if the batter touched a stick held by the umpire before the fielding side could touch the stick with the ball. Altham and Swanton (1948: 29) record a further variation, noting that William Goldwin's poem *In Certamen Pilae* (c. 1700) implies that the batter completed his/her run by touching the umpire's body. These various rules/customs clearly had differing consequences for the safety of the fielders, batters and umpires, and Rait Kerr argues that the 1744 development – whereby the stick or popping hole was replaced by the bat crossing the popping crease and the ball breaking the wicket – was linked to the desire to reduce injury through the spatial separation of the batter and fielder. Nyren (1833a/1948: 44) stated that, when the popping hole was used, 'Many severe injuries of the hands was the consequence of this regulation; the present mode of touching the popping crease was therefore substituted for it.'

Whilst the law relating to hitting the ball twice appears to have been influenced by a concern to limit the movement of the batter which could lead to the injury of opponents, laws relating to stumpings appear to have been influenced by attempts to protect the wicketkeeper from his/herself. The batter was deemed stumped out if, as in the case of a run out, the wicket was 'put down' (broken) when both feet were outside the popping crease. However, the wicketkeeper was restricted to standing a 'reasonable Distance behind the Wicket, and shall not, by any Noise, incommode the Striker; and if his Hands, Knees, Foot, or Head, be over, or before the Wicket, though the Ball hit it, it shall not be out' (Rait Kerr 1950: 96–97). When preparing to strike, the batter would normally stand within the popping crease which, in 1744, was specified at 46 inches from the wicket (increased to 48 inches in 1821). There was no restriction on the length of the bat which could be used until 1835 when a limit of 38 inches was introduced, and bats tended to be longer and more curved than they are today (similar to the sticks used in hockey or hurling). The prohibition on wicketkeepers being 'over or before' the wicket suggests that such a tactic was known and, given the above dimensions, it would appear that this would have been somewhat hazardous. Altham and Swanton's (1948: 53) interpretation of this is that, 'there must, it seems, have been some lusty "obstruction" between batsmen, wicket-keeper and the bowler in the old days'. Indeed the stumping law has since been refined further such that the batter will be deemed 'in' with *either* part of the bat *or* the foot behind the popping crease. Such a change serves to further separate, and therefore reduce the potential for injurious contact between, batter and wicketkeeper. This law may, of course, relate back to the previous practice in relation to run outs whereby the batter was dismissed if the ball was placed in the 'popping hole' before the batter could fill it with his/her bat.

In addition to the structure of the game, the physical environment in which cricket was played was highly significant in terms of the potential for injury to players. Consequently, this issue was also addressed by a number of the early law changes. Initially there was little preparation of the playing area and no formal drawing of boundaries. Nyren, for instance, provides detailed advice on pitching wickets to favour particular bowlers (1833/1948: 49). John Bowyer recalling playing for All-England at Lords in 1810, noted that, 'it was no joke to play without pads and gloves on a bumpy down ... The rough ground made the long hops so difficult. First you had to mind the shooter and if the ball pitched short and rose she would be on your knuckles' (cited in Wymer 1949: 162–63). By 1788, however, with the mutual consent of the captains, the laws allowed for the rolling, covering, watering, mowing and beating of the pitch *during* the match. The 1823 edition of the laws saw the first moves towards standardization of pitch selection with this responsibility transferring from the respective captains to the umpires. Also introduced in 1823 was the provision for moving the pitch or introducing a fresh wicket at any time during the match if the old one became unsuitable (Rosenwater 1970: 131). By 1849 the rolling or sweeping of the wicket between innings would be granted by the umpires if requested by *either* side within a minute of the end of an innings. To improve the quality of the pitch surface further, covers protecting the wicket from the weather were introduced. Although from 1788 the laws allowed for coverings to be used (again with the mutual consent of the captains), it was not until 1872 that pitch covers were used on a regular basis at Lord's (Rosenwater 1970). Even as late as 1820, batters at Lord's were thought to have deliberately got themselves dismissed due to a fear of injury (Altham and Swanton 1948: 59–60).

The clarity of the definition of playing and spectating areas also impacted upon the potential for injury. One of the differences between folk games and modern sports is the move towards a clear distinction between playing and spectating roles. Central to this distinction is the introduction of a physical barrier – in cricket the boundary, in boxing the ring – which designates the spatial area from which non-participants are excluded. In early games, spectators watched from wherever they could and early artwork shows scorers and gentlemen wearing top-hats seated amidst the fielders (see for example the plates in Major 2007). The hazards of this, as well as the social acceptability of injury, are illustrated by a 1778 incident involving the Duke of Dorset. *The Morning Post* records that, while he was batting, the 'Hampshire people' crowded the Duke such that he felt inhibited from playing a stroke:

> His Grace gently expostulated with them on this unfair mode and pointed out their dangers, which having no effect, he, *with proper spirit*, made full play at a ball and in so doing brought one of the Gentlemen to the Ground. (Brookes 1978: 40; Birley 1999: 38. Emphasis added)

The problems associated with the informal nature of such an arrangement are highlighted in the first ever reference to cricket to appear in *The Times* on

22 June 1785. The report featured the forerunner of the MCC, The White Conduit Club:

> It is recommended to the Lordling Cricketters who amuse themselves in White Conduit Fields, to procure an Act of Parliament for inclosing their play ground, which will not only prevent their being incommoded, but protect themselves from a repetition of the severe rebuke which they justly merit, and received on Saturday evening from some spirited citizens whom they insulted and attempted *vi et armis* to drive from the foot path, pretending it was within their bounds. (Cited in Williams 1985: 2)

Vi et armis is a legal term for trespass accompanied by violence – literally meaning by force and arms – and it seems likely that this sort of incident provided part of the motivation which led Thomas Lord, acting on the advice of the Earl of Winchilsea, to establish Lord's cricket ground in Dorset Fields, London in 1787.

The first recorded use of boundaries occurred in 1731 and the first provision of a 'stand' for spectators in 1772 (Brooke and Matthews 1988: 128–129). Although the standardization of the separation of players and spectators took place in a slow and uneven manner, where relatively large numbers of spectators were regularly attracted to matches some sort of provision became (perhaps financially) necessary. On 22 June 1787 *The Times* reported on a match at The New Cricket Ground, London: 'Upwards of 2000 persons were within the ground, who conducted themselves with the utmost decorum; the utility of the batten fence was evident, as it kept out all improper spectators' (cited in Williams 1985: 4). But where players and spectators were not clearly separated, spectators were liable to incur the same sort of injuries as participants. Often, however, these were not viewed as particularly serious. When the *Hampshire Chronicle* (September 1786) reported on a spectator whose eye was injured by the ball, it concluded, 'but he was only a spectator and therefore [the incident] did not mar the sport' (cited in Ford 1972: 130). Thus, the introduction of boundaries was both 'in the interest of spectator safety ... (and) the maximization of space' (Sandiford 1994: 135). It was not, however, until the publication of the 1884 code of rules that the first official mention of boundaries appeared in the laws of the game (Rait Kerr 1950: 81).

Finally, mention should be made of the development of the game's mechanism for conflict resolution. As has already been shown, central to the early law codes of cricket was the standardization of dispute settlement by investing authority in a third party, namely the umpires. In the 1755 laws, provision was made to allow an injured batter to retire and to resume his/her innings at a later time (a further indication that such injuries were relatively common), but not to be replaced or substituted.[6] Presumably due to the suspicion that such a regulation would be flouted (and the ramifications this would have for bets placed on matches), an additional law decreed that the umpires were to be judges 'of all frivolous Delays; of all Hurt, whether real or pretended' (Rait Kerr 1950: 97–98). Further to this, the 1727 Articles included provision for, and sanction against, the questioning of the umpires' decisions: 'If any of the gamesters shall speak or give their opinion on any point of the game, they are to be turned out and voided in the Match; this not to extend to the Duke of Richmond and Mr Brodrick.'

Given the relatively violent character of cricket in its earliest developmental stages and the imprecise authority of the umpires in this context, it is likely that the people filling the role of arbiter had a particularly difficult task. Ford notes that it was not unusual for newspaper reports to note the umpires' good standing as credentials (1972: 105). Furthermore, it seems that in the early game it was customary for the umpires to carry a stick or bat. The 1727 Articles indicate that the stick was used for recording the number of 'notches' scored. As already noted, a common practice *circa* 1700 was for a batter to complete his/her run by touching a stick held by the umpire (for example, eighteenth-century artwork shows one of the umpires standing in a 'position of imminent personal peril' very close to the batter (Altham and Swanton 1948: 29)). However, McLean further argues that these 'staves' were probably also used by umpires for self defence (1987: 33).

Conclusion

Through the development of a range of cricket laws and practices we can see how the prominence of physical violence in the game has changed over time. Because of the overlap of personnel involved, this suggests an interconnection between broader social structural change (i.e. parliamentarization) and changes at the level of personality (i.e. increasing emotional control). While subsequent sports (notably rugby and football) would develop amidst an explicit debate about tolerable levels of violence (Dunning and Sheard 1979/2005), for cricket there was little such discussion and no evidence that any particular individual or group had the specific intention to develop the sport in this way (Malcolm 2005). Consequently, the distinct pattern of violence reduction as part of the clarification and standardization of cricket's rules has to be understood as indicative of a broad and deep-rooted social change towards increased intolerance of witnessing and experiencing violence in everyday life. There is no evidence that these developments were thought out in a particularly coherent way, simply that they seemed to 'make sense' to the individuals involved because they aligned with this group's changing social habitus.

Also unintentional at this time was what this game would subsequently become; a nationally standardized and latterly globally diffused game. Although the MCC issued a number of early statements on the laws of cricket, it did so in an 'advisory' rather than 'regulatory' capacity for the first 100 years of its existence. MCC members were more concerned with organizing their own leisure than they were with enabling the game's national standardization as a precursor to global diffusion. Indeed the standardization which enabled cricket's emergence as a modern sports form took place largely for parochial purposes. This was consistent with the mindset of parliamentarians who developed English law more generally. A disdain for general ideas was a unifying feature of eighteenth century Englishness (Haselar 1996: 20) and this was evident in the creation of laws which, Colls notes, largely rested on the defence of 'certain persons who at certain times and in certain places did this and that' (2002: 28). This stands in contrast to the notions of universal rights that more commonly developed in mainland Europe and England's closest geographical and social rival France in particular. Cricket could only emerge because a national class with specific interdependencies and specific freedoms of association came into existence. But the British Isles was a fragmented and pluralistic place at this time and while the landed aristocracy was one of the few nationally unified sectors of society, the members were not, at this time, embarking on a nationalistic project. Evidence of this would start to emerge in the nineteenth century and, as we will see in the next chapter, this time debates about the role of violence in the game would become explicit.

Brief mention should, however, be made of the role of Hambledon in the emergence of cricket. Many believe that cricket was first played on Broadhalfpenny Down in this small village fifteen miles north of Portsmouth in Hampshire (Major 2007). This, however, is a misguided belief for while cricket may well have been played at Hambledon at an early time: a) it would be fallacious to argue that it was not concurrently being played anywhere else; b) there is little evidence to link the game played at Hambledon with the specific Law codes which would ultimately develop into the game as we know it today; and c) as well connected as the cricketers from this village were, it is difficult to believe that they held sufficient social power to have such a telling impact on the wider society. Moreover, as I will show in the next chapter, the veneration of Hambledon derives from both the re-invention of the game in the nineteenth century based on a nostalgic desire to identify specific types of origins for cricket, and the creation of the cricket-Englishness couplet.

The way a sport is structured is neither essential nor eternal, and while the laws of cricket have continued to change, they change more rapidly and more significantly at particular points of time. The periods of relatively marked change are linked to periods in which more fundamental shifts in social structure occur. The emergence of cricket occurred in conjunction with one of the most fundamental shifts in English social structure, the development of parliamentary democracy. Given that cricket was the only team game to emerge alongside parliamentarization, it is easy to see how these two institutions should come to be seen in the same exalted light (poet E.V. Lucas, for instance, called the Lord's pavilion 'the Houses of Parliament of cricket'). The English would subsequently come to view their specific and relatively peaceful process of parliamentarization in contrast to the relatively violent democratic revolutions in America and France. As Langford (2000: 3) notes, 'Foreigners came to England, it was said, in search of government, as they went to Italy in search of arts.' But visitors also observed a game, peculiar in its specific form, which captured the imagination of the people integral to the process of parliamentarization. Thus cricket, like parliament, came to be seen to embody the character traits which the English regarded as the source of their distinctive and distinguished status. It is to this that we now turn.

2

The 'National Game'

Cricket in nineteenth-century England

As significant as the codification of cricket was, the game as it was played at the end of the eighteenth century was distinctly different from that played today. The crucial difference relates to the style of bowling, for the nineteenth century saw under arm bowling replaced by round arm and subsequently over arm bowling. The cultural significance of cricket also changed fundamentally during the nineteenth century as cricket became the 'national game'. These two developments were symbiotic. Like the emergence of cricket, both also relate to broader social structural developments and changing interdependency ties in English society.

What do we mean when we refer to cricket as England's national game?[1] As Bairner notes, the concept of a national sport 'is a slippery one' (2001: 167). National sports range from those activities 'invented' in a particular place (for example baseball) and/or which remain exclusive to a particular nation (such as Gaelic games in Ireland), to those in which a nation has been particularly successful and/or developed a specific style of play (for example football and Brazil, rugby union and New Zealand). Paradoxically therefore both international isolation and international competition can enable a game to become a national sport. A game may also attain this status by being the nation's most popular sport, but again this is not a necessary qualification (for instance, football is as widely played in Wales as the national sport of rugby union). National sports do, however, generally entail the greatest 'depth of celebration' or the 'most widespread attention' (Bairner 2001: 18–19).

Cricket's status as the national game of England is in part based on it being seen to have been 'invented' in England. Cricket also exhibits a peculiar balance between international isolation and competition, being limited to a particular group of nations (discussed further in Chapter 3). The English can certainly be associated with a distinct style of playing (and watching) the game, though this only became apparent when other nations diverted from established patterns and developed their own contrasting styles (see Chapter 5). Moreover, cricket is not, and probably never has been, the most widely played sport in England. At times the English have been particularly successful at cricket, but cricket's place in the nation's culture does not depend on playing achievements.

Rather, cricket's distinction as the English national game stems from the correlation between the supposed national character of the English people and the behaviour of those who play the sport; that is to say, why cricket and Englishness is a pleonasm. Importantly, however, national character should not be viewed as some kind of essential or unchanging set of traits, but as 'a construct, an artifice. Whoever defines or identifies it is at best selecting, sifting, suppressing, in the search for what is taken to be representative' (Langford 2000: 14). For Elias, however, the personalities and behavioural forms which constitute national character are not entirely subjective or free-floating but change according to the broader social structure of which people are a part. While this chapter delineates the correspondence between notions of Englishness and the character of cricketers, a fuller discussion is deferred to the Conclusion. The aim here is to explain how and why this connection first occurred at this particular time. This necessarily entails a discussion of the interweaving of an amalgam of social processes which influenced both English society and the game of cricket during the nineteenth century.

National identity and Englishness

The sociological study of nations and nationalism 'can appear esoteric, requiring specialized knowledge and using a language and conceptual apparatus entirely its own' (Day and Thompson 2004: 2) and while McCrone (2000: 3) argues that a lack of consensus over key terms stems from the historical diversity of experience, some definitional work is necessary to structure this discussion. The existence of a national game presupposes a *nation*. Nations are geographical units but rarely are their boundaries fixed and uncontested. Often, but not always, nations exist as political units – as *nation states* – but nations are also inherently social entities which rest upon some shared conception of identity – a *national identity*. Attempts to forward the status of a nation(-state), or indeed to establish its political structure or identity politics, is perhaps better defined as *nationalism*. The similitudes which are believed to form the basis of this shared sense of national identity may be biological (leading to ethnic nationalism) or cultural (civic nationalism) but they are always somewhat arbitrary, identifying certain commonalities as significant (such as not being French or German) while obscuring manifest differences (for example being Cornish or Geordie). National identity is ultimately a conceptual tool for organizing the world into 'we' and 'they' groups (Elias 1991) and thus the notion of 'Englishness' can be defined as, 'those distinctive aspects of national life' that both insiders and outsiders have described as characteristic of the English (Langford 2000: 2). The way a group would like themselves to be seen, and their ability to persuade/coerce others to agree, are deeply implicated in this process.

English national identity is often portrayed as peculiar. Kumar (2003a: ix) describes it as an 'enigma', more elusive and difficult to pin down than for other nations. Writers note the strong tendency to deny the very existence of an English national identity. In part this relates to the use of 'British' and 'English' as synonyms which, it is argued, stems from the creation of Great Britain (Colley 1996) and led the English nation and the British nation-state to become conflated entities. Allied to the British imperial experience, this led the English self-conception to be defined by inclusion and expansion rather than exclusion and inwardness (Kumar 2003a). As a consequence of this peculiarity, and in contrast to the 'virtually universal consent' that nationalism was a nineteenth century invention (Kumar 2003a: 23), a number of authors have argued that the English case pre-dates these developments. The eighth (Hastings 1997), sixteenth (Greenfeld 1992), seventeenth (Kohn 1940) and eighteenth (Newman 1987) centuries have all been claimed as the earliest manifestations of English national identity or nationalism (Kumar 2003a cites the late nineteenth century as the 'first moment of Englishness').

Different interpretations of the emergence of English national identity/ nationalism essentially follow the debates between 'modernists' and 'ethnicists'. Briefly stated this entails the idea that nationalism is a cultural and political ideology produced by modernity, versus the view that modern nationalisms require a sense of common history, unifying myths and symbols, and cultural practices characteristic of ethno-cultural communities. However, the difference between these two positions, 'seems to come down to how much invention; to matters of degree rather than of kind' (McCrone 2000: 16). Is a self-conscious sense of Englishness sufficient, or is the political expression of that identity necessary? How widely must that identity be shared? Does it matter if that identity exists among political elites, the masses or both? We do not need to resolve these questions here. Rather, for present purposes it is enough to note that there is considerable agreement that there were significant social changes during the late eighteenth and early nineteenth centuries which impacted upon the way in which (some of) the English viewed themselves and attempted to disseminate and propagate such views. Two largely complimentary accounts of the making of Englishness are particularly relevant to the development of cricket.

Langford (2000) argues that 'national character' became a fashionable idea in late eighteenth-century England and that over the next fifty years a remarkably stable and consistent model emerged. The English national character became perceived to be practical yet lacking in subtle appreciation. The English were independent, upright and honest to the point of tactless. They possessed unflagging energy. They were self-disciplined and dedicated. They persevered and did not know when they were beaten. The 'radical reassessment of the importance of England and things English' (Langford 2000: 3) between 1650 and 1850 occurred in conjunction with England's/Britain's rise as a European power. Following the political reform noted in the previous chapter, England's history of 'violence, turbulence and instability' (Langford 2000: 5) was forgotten. Commercial and industrial developments driven by an ethos of improvement and innovation came to be admired by Britain's European neighbours, but within England a cult of 'Old Englishness' developed as a reaction to the speed of change. Where the British aristocracy had affected French mannerisms as part of their cosmopolitan outlook at the beginning of the 1700s (remember the *Je Ne Sais Quoi* Club), by the nineteenth century the ability to speak English became valued on the continent. The process of identifying English national character enabled the people rather than the social elite to be accredited for this rapid development and enhanced international status. It also enabled the continental influence on sport, which had the potential to undermine claims for its distinctively English character, to be obscured.[2]

Haselar similarly argues that 'in the space of a few short decades in the latter part of the eighteenth century the idea of England began to form' (1996: 17). He defines the emerging sense of Englishness as pre-modern in that rather than being dominated by urban commerce and democracy (as, for example, in France), it was built upon the pre-industrial trinity of 'land', 'class', and 'race'. Englishness was defined by a small group of non-entrepreneurial land-owners (i.e. the social equivalents of those who codified cricket in the mid-1700s) but the emphasis on land meant that wealthy Celts (for example Matthew Brodrick, see also Chapter 6) could be easily assimilated. This essentially feudal perspective on social class hierarchy exalted the rural over the urban. The ideology of Englishness was fortified by an aristocracy reacting to revolutions abroad and in France in particular. Faced with the choice of remaining distinct from or embracing the lower classes and emerging bourgeoisie, the aristocracy took the latter course. They were aided in this by the new literary classes which 'helped define and describe the new national identity' (1996: 26). The newly invented Englishman was honourable, upright, and noble. Key attributes included 'innocence, honesty, originality, frankness, above all truthfulness and moral independence' (1996: 27). The English were anti-intellectual and particularist, valuing the traditional, familiar and practical, and showing 'disdain for general ideas and theories' (1996: 21) such as the rather abstract notions of rights and democracy which drove the French revolution.

Cricket and Englishness

The ideological connection between cricket and Englishness emerged concurrently with these late eighteenth- and early nineteenth-century developments. In the same way that sportization and parliamentarization were concomitant processes, so the identification of English national character and cricket as the national game corresponded. Like English national character, cricket's social significance was championed by a literary elite. Both sets of writers venerated the rural over the urban, both embraced an ambiguity over Britishness and Englishness, and both were formed in opposition to the peoples of the European mainland. It did not matter that, 'until the early nineteenth century the British were famous for their *disorganized* games: rowdy, bloodthirsty, cruel sports' (Perkin 1989: 146). It did not matter that emerging interpretations of the game stood in direct contradiction to some of the evidence of the way the game had been played in the eighteenth century. It did not matter that the world's first industrialized nation, and ultimately most urbanized was 'exalted for its countryside' (Haselar 1996: 106). This was a time of wholesale re-imaging. The invention of cricketing tradition (Hobsbawm 1983) was concurrent with the invention of Englishness.

Cricket was first portrayed as a symbol of British/English national identity in James Love's *Cricket: an heroic poem* (1740). Love refers to the 'glorious, manly, *British* game' and contrasts the qualities of manliness and athleticism with the emasculating influences of European culture. But it was nineteenth-century literaturization of cricket which truly established it as England's national game (Bateman 2009). Mary Mitford's *Our Village*, serialised in *The Lady's Magazine* between 1824 and 1832, is typical. For Mitford,

> I doubt if there be any scene in the world more animating or delightful than a cricket match. I do not mean a set match at Lord's Ground for money, hard money ... No! the cricket I mean is a real solid old-fashioned match between neighbouring parishes ... (the spectators are) retired cricketers, the veterans of the green, the careful mothers, the girls, and all the boys of two parishes ... There was not a ten-years-old urchin, or a septuagenary woman in the parish, who did not feel an additional importance, a reflected consequence, in speaking of "our side". (Cited in Guttmann 1986: 78)

Our Village was fundamentally nostalgic. It combined pastoral imagery with notions of inclusive, passive and cohesive community. Cricket became a vehicle through which various strands of the broader concept of national identity could be drawn together.

Probably the most significant literary works in the elevation of cricket to a national sport, however, are Nyren's *Cricketers of my Time* (1833a/1948) and Pycroft's *The Cricket Field* (1851/1948). Nyren's *Cricketers of my Time* was originally printed in conjunction with *The Young Cricketer's Tutor* (1833b). The former is essentially a description of the men who played for the Hambledon village team around the 1770s, while the latter is an instructional manual for playing the game. Pycroft's text is a more self-conscious and explicit attempt to chart the history of the game. The messages these texts convey closely resonate with ideas of English national identity. This in turn explains their fame and subsequent significance relative to similar texts (for example Lamberts' *Instructions and Rules for the Playing of the Noble Game of Cricket* (1816); Lillywhites's *Illustrated Handbook of Cricket* (1844); Denison's

Cricket: Sketches of the Players (1845)). Nyren and Pycroft did not simply reflect a particular ideology of the game they were instrumental to its construction.

Cricketers of my Time opens with an introduction by Charles Cowden Clarke (1833/1948: 14), the first line of which reads, 'Of all the English athletic games, none, perhaps, presents so fine a scope for bringing into full and constant play the qualities both of the mind and the body as that of Cricket.' Clarke goes on to list the characteristics of a good cricketer. The good cricketer will, of course, be a man. He will also be manly. Consistent with the anti-intellectualism identified by Haselar, rather than celebrating intelligence as a virtue, Clarke merely says that a good cricketer will not be stupid. He will, however, be active and a physically competent all-rounder. The notion of self-discipline is relayed via the term 'cool tempered'. Perseverance and unflagging energy are conveyed in the claim that the good cricketer will be able to endure fatigue. Clarke urges younger readers to adhere to 'the sterling qualities of integrity, plain dealing, and good old English independence – the independence of native worth and moral rectitude, not of insolence and effrontery' (1933/1948: 15). There are, therefore, direct crossovers between the projected character of Nyren's cricketers and the broader narrative of English national character that was developing at this time. The physicality of sport made it an ideal vehicle for the advancement of practicality over subtle appreciation.

Nyren is less explicit but nonetheless consistent in his evocation of national character. The contrast between his opening line – 'The game of cricket is thoroughly British' (1933/1948: 16) – and Clarke's description of cricket as 'English' shows the easy elision of these national identities after the formation of the Union. Nyren describes the beer drank at Hambledon as strong, 'unsophisticated John Bull stuff', and thus Bateman (2009: 24) notes that, 'the rambunctious energies and virility of late-eighteenth century rural cricket provide [Nyren with] a point of contrast to the relatively temperate, effete and Europeanised present'. Consistent with the inclusionary motif of English national identity, Nyren portrays cross-class harmony. In describing yeoman cricketers as possessing integrity, independence and honesty he identifies the lower classes as the embodiment of English virtues and, by extension therefore, responsible for the dramatic improvements in Britain's international status.

But in order to make this connection between cricket and English character Nyren had to 're-invent' cricket through a portrayal which strategically belied eighteenth-century evidence. Nyren 'consistently euphemised the sport's violence through a process of aestheticisation' (Bateman 2009: 26). His claim that 'like true Englishmen' the Hambledon spectators 'would give the enemy fair play' (2009: 27) when a cricket ball was knocked amongst them, seems rather romanticized given that games at Lord's continued to be disrupted in this way well into the latter half of the nineteenth century (Malcolm 2002a. See also the conclusion to this chapter). Through the emphasis the text gives to Hambledon, the game is located as essentially rural and therefore linked to the land. While

Nyren notes that Strutt's *The Sports and Pastimes of the Peoples of England* (1801) suggests that cricket had no popular ancient roots, he omits to mention Strutt's assertion that the game was particularly popular among 'nobility and gentlemen of fortune' (1801: 106), or indeed that it was codified in London as a consequence of a commingling of political classes and therefore had an essentially urban genesis. While he describes each of the Hambledon players in considerable detail, he deems it sufficient to merely list the predominantly aristocratic and upper-class members of the MCC. The essentially nostalgic tone is enhanced by the fact that these are described as childhood recollections. It is a moot point whether these are cricketers of Nyren's time (as the book title claims), or in fact cricketers of his father's era.

Published twenty years after Nyren, Pycroft's *The Cricket Field* is more self-congratulatory. A chapter on 'The General Character of Cricket' begins thus: 'The game of cricket, philosophically considered, is a standing panegyric on the English character'. Pycroft continues, 'none but an orderly and sensible race of people would so amuse themselves', thus perpetuating notions of a peaceful and rational English people. The description of the game and its players contains a number of notable similarities with other portrayals of English national character. A player, we are told, must 'be sober and temperate. Patience, fortitude, and self-denial, the various bumps of order, obedience, and good humour, with an unruffled temper, are indispensable' (Pycroft 1851/1948: 62). Another chapter title proclaims that cricket was 'Generally Established as a National Game by the End of the Last Century' and thus attempts to give cricket's new found status a sense of longevity.

Pycroft is also more explicit than Nyren in contrasting Englishness (and cricket) with the characteristics of other nationalities. Though unusual in its explicit highlighting of differences between British nationalities, Pycroft conforms to an anglo-centric view of power relations where the English are portrayed as both partners in, and leaders of, a Union that was as much 'Greater England' as Great Britain (Haselar 1996: 30). Of England's closest neighbours he writes:

> As to physical qualifications [of a good cricketer], we require not only the volatile spirits of the Irishman *Rampant*, nor the phlegmatic caution of the Scotchman *Couchant*, but we want the English combination of the two; though with good generalship cricket is a game for Britons generally. (1851/1948: 62)

However, Pycroft's reference to England's continental neighbours draws a sharper distinction:

> The game is essentially Anglo-Saxon. Foreigners have rarely, very rarely, imitated us. The English settlers and residents everywhere play; but of no single cricket club have we ever heard dieted either with frogs, sour crout, or macaroni. But how remarkable that cricket is not naturalised in Ireland! The fact is very striking that it follows the course rather of ale than whiskey. (1851/1948: 63)

Both in relation to cricket and more broadly (Langford 2000), national differences were identified as culturally rather than biologically based. If the French, Germans and Italians changed what they ate, and best of all if they drank beer, there was no reason to think that they could not also become proficient at cricket just as the German-born Frederick Louis had. Similar ideas are expressed in John Mitford's review of Nyren's *Cricketers of my Time* which appeared in the *Gentleman's Magazine* just months after the latter's publication. Mitford contrasts cricket, 'the pride and the privilege of the Englishman alone', with pastimes specific to the French (Tennis), Swiss (Shooting), Italians ('ballone') and Dutch (skating). 'A Frenchman or a German would not know which end of the bat to hold' (Mitford 1833/1948: 122). As we will see in Chapter 6, the concern to link cricket to Englishness may have led to the obscuration of the popularity of cricket in the Celtic nations of Britain at this time. As we will see in Chapter 9, the role of cricket in the process of 'Othering' continues today.

Pycroft's assessment of the relationship between cricket and intelligence further resonates with the broader discourse of Englishness. Pycroft makes three descriptions in this regard. Initially he says, 'For intellectual virtues we want judgment, decision, and the organ of concentrativeness ... the cricketer wants wits down to his fingers' ends' (1851/1948: 62). He subsequently writes that the cricketer should 'have *nous* in perfection, and be instinct with sense all over' (1851/1948: 64). Finally he states that,

> there is something highly intellectual in our noble and national pastime. But the cricketer must possess certain qualifications, not only physical and intellectual, but moral qualifications also; for of what avail is the mind to design and the hand to execute, if a sulky temper paralyses his exertions ... or if impatience dethrones judgement. (1851/1948: 66)

Thus while cricket is portrayed as a cerebral pursuit and thus not a childish or foolish game, the intellect required is instinctual rather than learned, practical and applied rather than theoretical and abstract. There is no indication that a man should apply himself to, or would benefit from, study of the game. Pycroft implicitly suggests that abstract intellectualism can be detrimental to character and thus is more broadly problematic. English cricketers, he tells us, are pragmatic.

Pycroft replicates Nyren's 're-invention' of cricket as non-violent. In a section titled 'Chapter of accidents – Miscellaneous', he claims that 'Fatal accidents in any legitimate game of cricket there have been none' (1851/1948: 107). He further describes various incidents of injury and mishap in the game only to systematically deny the *real* harm or significance of risk in each case: 'all this proves little as to the danger of the game' (Pycroft 1851/1948: 108). At one point he states, 'these are hardly the dangers of cricket: men may run their heads together in the street' (1851/1948: 110). He notes, for instance, the physical proximity of multiple matches on common ground like Oxford's Cowley Marsh but concludes, 'The wonder is, that twelve balls should be flying in a small space for nearly a day, yet I never heard of any man being hit in the face – a fact the more remarkable because there was usually free hitting and loose bowling' (1851/1948: 111). Thus Pycroft tells the reader that while cricket might look dangerous, one would be foolish to make this assumption:

> Let any man of common judgement see the velocity with which the ball flies from the bats of first-rate players, and how near the fieldsmen stand to the hitter; and then let him feel and weigh a ball in his hand, and he would naturally expect to hear that every public cricket ground was in near connection with some casualty hospital, so *deceptive is a priori reasoning*. (1851/1948: 107. Emphasis added)

Characteristic of the ideology of Englishness more generally, cognitive reasoning is contradicted by practical experience, universalism by particularism. Ultimately however the length to which Pycroft goes to stress the peaceful nature of the game is matched only by the empirical weakness of his position.

There were, therefore, two key characteristics of early nineteenth-century cricket literature. First, it contained an account of cricket which was closely aligned to the sense of English national character that was more widely emerging at this time. Second, like the emergence of Englishness more generally, it entailed a portrayal which obscured an elitist and violent past. But *why* did these texts so closely match the broader discourse of English national character? It is to these that we now turn.

Cricket and social change in nineteenth-century England

The identification of cricket as the game which both reflects and defines the English national character occurs in conjunction with a number of broader social processes which influence the emergence of a sense of Englishness in the late eighteenth and early nineteenth centuries. The social composition of the ruling aristocratic elite was changing as it became untenable for this group to govern simply on the basis of social status as they had in the eighteenth century. Commercial opportunities were increasingly open to a wider range of people. Industrialization created new wealth and these emergent classes were subsequently incorporated into an aristocracy more open and more nationalistically minded post-French revolution. This was a period of rapid innovation and marked change in which the romanticism of Old Englishness emerged as a reactionary force (Langford 2000).

Similar social processes influenced and were evident in cricket. The game became increasingly subject to commercial considerations. The aristocracy's governance of the game changed. As we have seen, cricket's history was re-invented. This was a reaction to both societal changes and also something more parochial and specific to the game; the development of round arm and over arm bowling. Nyren and Pycroft's texts can be understood as the outcome of both broader structural social changes and the 'local' conflicts in cricket which these changes fuelled.

In response to the development of lob bowling (under arm, with the ball spinning on pitching) batsmen started 'running down' to meet the high tossed lob before it bounced (also termed 'giving her the rush' (Altham and Swanton 1948: 65)). This led to the domination of batting over bowling and thus longer matches. Bowlers responded by bowling faster and, in doing so, raising their arm from vertically down, to horizontally round. While Nyren claims that Tom Walker first introduced the 'system of throwing instead of bowling' (1833a/1948: 34) and was immediately censored by his Hambledon teammates, the actions of John Willes were ultimately rather more significant. Willes' first recorded game was for the Gentlemen in the inaugural Gentlemen vs Players match of 1806. By the following year a match report in the *Morning Herald* claimed that 'the straight-armed bowling, introduced by J. Willes Esq. was generally practiced in the game' (cited in Read, 1898: 86–87). Willes' style of bowling caused much controversy. In 1821 the *Morning Herald* reported that, 'Mr Willes and his bowling were frequently barred in making a match and he played sometimes amid much uproar and confusion. Still he would persevere until the ring closed in on the players, the stumps were pulled up and all came to a standstill' (cited in Rae 2001: 99). The issue came to a head in 1822 when Willes played for Kent against the MCC and was no-balled by the umpire. 'Willes threw down the ball in disgust, jumped on his horse and rode away out of Lord's and out of cricket history' (Altham and Swanton 1948: 66). Birley (1999: 64) speculates that the umpire was acting on the orders of Lord Frederick Beauclerk, the most influential aristocrat cricketer of his day and subsequently President of the MCC.

The momentum of bowling innovation changed with the emergence of two Sussex professionals, William Lillywhite and Jem Broadbridge. Lillywhite so perfected this technique that he became known as 'Nonpariel' and defeated opponents, many of whom were also professionals and whose livelihoods also depended on playing success, objected to 'Lilly and Jem's' methods. However, Lillywhite and Broadbridge had an influential ally in G.T. Knight, a leading MCC member who was himself a round arm bowler. Through a series of letters to *The Sporting Magazine* in 1827–28, Knight set out the case for legalizing round arm bowling. He argued that the dominance of batting was detrimental to the game, that attempts to regulate round arm bowling had continually failed because of the difficulties in precisely defining a 'throw', and that other proposals to correct the imbalance between bat and ball (such as increasing the size of the wicket) would be retrograde steps. Furthermore, Knight claimed that this style of bowling was not at all new, that historical precedent existed (citing Tom Walker of Hambledon as one example) and, finally, that there was nothing to fear about the new style, because it 'makes it quite impossible to bowl fast and dangerously'. Mr Denison, replying for the MCC, stated that the change would lead to scientific play being replaced by chance hits, that the new style was throwing 'pure and simple', and finally that 'It must lead to a dangerous pace, such as cannot be faced on hard grounds, save at the most imminent peril.'[3]

Knight also persuaded the MCC president, H. Kingscote, to sanction three 'experimental matches' between Sussex and All England in 1827. After Sussex won the first two, the nine All England professionals (indicating that this was no straight batsmen-bowler, amateur-professional, class conflict) refused to play the final match, unless the Sussex bowlers 'abstain from throwing' (Altham and Swanton 1948: 67). The side's batting was strengthened by the inclusion of two further amateurs and, with Knight's own round arm bowling particularly successful, the All England team secured victory in the final match. For now, however, the MCC resisted calls for change and Law X was modified only to clarify and re-assert the existing position (Rait Kerr 1950: 76). Despite this, round arm bowling persisted and the law was finally altered in 1835, 'legitimising any ball not thrown or jerked in which the hand or arm did not go above the shoulder' (Birley 1999: 67). Birley notes that 'the march of intellect' was 'the term used by the opponents of the innovative style of bowling that was disturbing cricket's equilibrium' (1999: 63). The phrase, widely used at this time by those optimistic about social progress, was sarcastically mocked by their reactionary critics. As with the innovation and social change of early nineteenth-century England more broadly, these new bowling techniques were met with nostalgia-based resistance.

The protracted nature of the dispute over bowling was a consequence of a particular set of power relations evident in the game at this time. By the early years of the nineteenth century, with the increasing commercialism of English society, there were 'unprecedented openings' for skilled cricketers to make money (Birley 1999: 67). The MCC increased the number of professionals contracted at Lord's to perform various cricketing duties for members. Harrow became the first public school to hire a professional coach. 'Lilly and Jem' were not only the most popular and successful bowlers of their day, they were commercially proactive. Lillywhite, having severed links with his local employers, had come 'up to London to seek his fortune' (Denison 1845/1948: 60). Together they helped Sussex attain 'a celebrity it never before acquired' (Denison 1845/1948: 65). They attracted numerous imitators. It is therefore not surprising that the matter of legal and illegal bowling was ultimately 'to be decided not by debate or by committee edict but by a demonstration of the growing power of market forces' (Birley 1999: 66).

The dispute was also influenced by the aristocracy's relatively weak governance of the game. As the game nationally diffused (or at least its folk games antecedents became nationally standardized) cricketers in different parts of the country became increasingly interdependent. For instance, Knight argued that round arm bowling had been 'commonly practiced in various parts of England for many years' (Denison 1845/1948: 80). 'One or two' local men were included in the England team for the first of the three experimental matches between England and Sussex played in Sheffield. Tellingly the proficiency of such players 'convinced the cricket world that the *South* must not, as heretofore, presume to wear the wreath forever' (Denison 1845/1948: 82). While Denison noted that the authority of the MCC had 'never hitherto been disputed' (1845/1948: 65) club members were ill-disposed and ill-equipped to govern the game for a more demographically diverse population. For the first half century of the club's existence members were largely happy just to turn up and play cricket. Few showed any inclination towards administrative matters and what influence over the game they held was simply a by-product of their high social status. Most MCC members favoured batting and employed professionals to do the bowling for them. Few, therefore, were inclined towards rule changes which would improve the bowler's prospects. The disparity between what the MCC pronounced and what was practiced undermined the club's position.

The MCC's orientation towards the game was, however, changing. A new outlook stemmed from the club's changing social composition which itself stemmed from changes in the aristocracy more generally. Between 1776 and 1830, 209 new British peerages were created and the number of seats in the House of Lords increased from 199 to 358 (Cannadine 1990). This expansion was driven by industrialization and the emergence of an increasingly affluent capitalist class. The new, wealthy, middle classes 'sought to catch up with the old' by adopting typically aristocratic social practices, acquiring such things as land, art work, titles and honours. To secure their status, the rising middle classes sought to (re-)present themselves just as cricket was being (re-)presented; not as something new, recent or novel, but as something old and organic. While the richest, most well-established, and powerful aristocrats 'looked on with disdain as their inferiors and the parvenus fought it out' (Cannadine 1990: 31), some concessions were made and traditional aristocratic practices relinquished. In cricket the main tradition to be cast aside was the aristocracy-led fashion for gambling. Of course, given the shift in economic power in the nation, the older, more established aristocracy would have had less desire to use wealth as a basis for status competition.

The emergent classes sought to adopt cricket in an attempt to self-aggrandize and thus aid their movement into and assimilation with society's changing elite. Consequently, by 1833, in terms of membership and administration, the MCC could 'scarcely be described as an aristocratic institution since only twenty-five, out of a total membership of 202, possessed titles' (Brookes 1978: 87). This trend continued throughout the remainder of the nineteenth century. For Bradley, from 1860 to 1914, 'the whole feeling of the general committee was more upper-middle class than aristocratic' (1990: 8). However, underlining Cannadine's point that there was a large degree of incorporation of other social classes into the aristocracy at this time, Bradley (1990: 7) notes that even 'those who were not aristocrats certainly moved with ease in that milieu'.

These changes had multiple impacts on the game. Law revisions became more frequent, occurring for instance, in 1811, 1817, 1821, 1823 and 1825. Further revisions in 1828 were the first to be put to an MCC general meeting, and by the 1830s the MCC had a formal and coherent administrative structure. It was also at this point that the distinction between amateurs and professionals became most pronounced. Social distance was maintained by various status-emphasizing practices such as the use of separate gates for entering and exiting the playing field, the listing on scorecards of the professional's initials after, and the amateur's initials before, the surname; the use of separate, usually inferior, travel and changing facilities by professionals. Professionals were expected to help with the preparation of the playing area and to bowl to the amateur batsman in the 'nets' in order to provide him with practice (Dunning and Sheard 1976: 58–9). Furthermore, 'by 1850 the pattern of amateur batsmen and professional bowlers was well established' (Brookes 1978: 92).

These playing, commercial, governance and demographic changes were the stimulus for the Englishness and cricket discourse discussed in the previous section. Mary Mitford's account of cricket in *Our Village* is explicitly contrasted with matches at Lord's played for 'hard money'. The obfuscation of the role of gambling in cricket's codification was, ironically, a response to the increasing monetization of the game. Consequently Pycroft, thirty years later, championed the consignment of cricket-related gambling to 'A Dark Chapter in the History of Cricket.' Pycroft argues that 'the lovers of cricket may congratulate themselves at the present day that matches are made at cricket, as at chess, rather for love and the honour of victory than for money' (1851/1948: 100). He suggests that bookmakers were excluded from Lord's 'many years since' and celebrates the reform of this 'corrupting' practice, even though clauses related to gambling remained integrated within the game's laws up until 1884.

There are however even more compelling grounds to see Nyren's work as an explicit response to the development of round arm bowling. The concluding section of *The Young Cricketer's Tutor* is titled, 'Protest Against the Modern Innovation of Throwing Instead of Bowling the Balls'. Here Nyren predicts that, if the new style of bowling continues, cricket will 'deteriorate in character' (1833b/1948: 40). He claims that no modern player can compare with the old cricketers he describes, that the 'fine style of hitting' will cease, and that 'the elegant and scientific game of Cricket will decline into a mere exhibition of rough, coarse, horse play' (1833b/1948: 41). Furthermore Nyren strategically dedicates *Cricketers of my Time* to William Ward, then owner of the lease for Lord's and a player whose competitive success appeared to wane in the face of the new bowling style (Birley 1999). The dedication explicitly argues that such bowling is 'in direct infringement of a law prohibiting that action' (1833a/1948: 13) and Nyren appeals to the MCC to bring in alternative, stronger, regulation. Of course, if a central objection to round arm bowling was that it would make the game more dangerous, cricket's violent and disorderly past needed to be forgotten. This re-invention of cricket's traditions runs parallel to the collective amnesia over England's violent and unruly past that accompanied the emergence of English national character.

Cricket towards the end of the century

The story of cricket in the second half of the nineteenth century is essentially a continuation of these themes – bowling innovation, commercialization, and governance changes. The legitimation of round arm bowling effectively granted bowlers such as Lillywhite licence to develop their experiment into over arm bowling. Lillywhite's performance in the North vs. South matches in 1836 demonstrated both that he was unplayable under the new regulations and that the severe injuries critics predicted were likely to occur. However Lillywhite's reputation and subsequent economic power meant that few umpires were prepared to declare his style illegal. As leading umpire William Caldecott noted, '(umpires) thought that what Lillywhite did must be right ... it was cruel to see how he would rattle either the knuckles or the stumps' (cited in Brookes 1978: 95). Consequently for 29 years the Laws of Cricket were regularly altered in overt and covert attacks on bowling innovation (see Rait Kerr 1950). In 1845 Law X was reformulated allowing umpires to call no ball whenever the bowler came 'so close' to infringing that it became difficult for the umpire to judge the ball's legality. Penalties for no balls and wides began to be accredited to the bowler in an attempt to make them accountable for any waywardness. Leg byes were introduced and the LBW Law was revised so that, for the batter to be out, the ball had to pitch in a straight line between the wickets (which was thought to restrict round arm bowlers' chances of obtaining such a dismissal).

The most significant commercial development was the formation of domestic touring professional XIs. Starting with William Clarke's All England XI, a series of professional teams was established that were relatively autonomous from the MCC. These toured the country enabling cricket to become 'a national sport as well as big business' (Brookes 1978: 101). Matches involving Clarke's XI tended to be one-sided affairs with the opposition often terrorized by Clarke's two fast bowlers, John 'the Demon' Jackson and George 'Tear 'em' Tarrant. Tarrant's bouncers 'frighten(ed) timid batsmen ... causing them to change colour and funk at the next straight one', whilst Jackson would bowl beamers to batsmen who scored runs off his bowling (Lord Harris, cited in Rae 2001: 89).[4]

But debates over legitimate and illegitimate bowling would not go away and the issue came to a head again in 1862. As Edgar Willsher began his third over for All England against Surrey he was no-balled by the umpire John Lillywhite (coincidentally the son of round arm pioneer, William Lillywhite). His following five attempts were also no-balled at which point Willsher, and the eight other professionals playing for England, walked off the pitch. Play was abandoned for the day but resumed the following morning, with Lillywhite replaced. It is a mystery why Lillywhite acted as he did. Over arm bowling was widespread and widely tolerated by umpires. Lillywhite and Willsher were good friends and subsequently became business partners as secretary and treasurer of the United South of England XI. Willsher was allowed to bowl unimpeded in subsequent matches. Perhaps Lillywhite had been pressured by the MCC, perhaps Lillywhite (with Willsher's knowledge and approval) merely wanted to make a (very) public statement about the current ambiguity in the Laws. Either way, this incident precipitated a debate in the press, a vote by the MCC twelve months later, and finally the revision of the law in June 1864.

The MCC also struggled to grapple with the changing balance of power in the game. In 1835 James Darke purchased the leasehold for Lord's, transformed the ground facilities and upgraded the MCC fixture list. A revitalized MCC made its first general pronouncement on the conduct of the game in 1851. The instruction to umpires to enforce the existing Rule X was largely ignored by bowlers and umpires alike. The MCC launched its first consultation with cricket clubs in 1863, again in relation to (il)legitimate forms of bowling. Despite these moves, Rait Kerr describes 1840–1864 as 'probably … the very worst period of MCC control of the game' (1950: 37). Indeed in 1863 *The Sporting Life* set in motion a move to establish a Cricket Parliament. It was not until the MCC's 1894 'Classification of Counties' that the national game could be said to have had a truly national governing body (Brookes 1978: 137).

Conclusion

By the end of the century cricket had developed into the game that those in the early part of the century had prematurely claimed it to be. It was now nationally played and administered and, in W.G. Grace, had a totemic and popular figurehead who was 'the first national sporting hero' and represented 'a robust kind of old world Englishness of sturdy yeomen and hunting squires' (Holt 1996: 54). From 1890 to 1914 cricket would enter a 'golden age', a time when the game was dominated by amateur batsmen who were lauded as stylish, entertaining, adventurous and chivalrous. With the development of fast bowling cricket assumed a form similar to that which it holds today and while the laws of the game continue to evolve, the codification of cricket was such that the game cannot be said to have assumed its 'modern character' until 1864 (Sandiford 1994: 128).

Further developments counteracted the bowling changes and reduced the element of physical danger in the game. Batsmen increasingly sought to protect their bodies. Robert Robinson 'was laughed out of his invention' when he used wooden boards as leg protection c. 1800 (Wisden 1978: 115). The first 'pads' in the modern sense were invented by H. Daubney of Oxford, c. 1836, and worn by batsmen in the Sussex v England match of 1839 (Brooke and Matthews 1988: 127). Gloves, were first produced by Daniel Day, circa 1827 (Wisden 1978: 115) and refined by Nicholas Wanostrocht who played for Surrey, Kent and the All England XI during the 1830s and 1840s (Sandiford 1994: 132). The first groin protector (now commonly called a box) was shown at the 1851 Great Exhibition. It was described as 'so completely protect[ing] the person from injury, that the most timid can play without fear' (Brooke and Matthews 1988: 128). Head protection would follow in the twentieth century.[5] Playing surfaces also vastly improved. David Jordan in the 1860s and Percy Pearce from 1874 onwards made major contributions to developing the Lord's playing surface into 'the envy of every county club' (Sandiford 1994: 136). Pearce's writings on the subject helped to spread what became known as the new craft of 'groundsmanship'. By 1900, all the major British cricket grounds had been re-laid and levelled. The initial impetus for this, Sandiford (1994: 137) argues, 'was largely the offspring' of the death of George Summers, a batter who was hit by a ball from a fast bowler at Lord's in 1870.

Crowds had also become more orderly, though violent incidents continued to occur. For instance England Captain and MCC President, Pelham Warner, recalled an incident at Lord's in 1866 when a spectator fielded the ball and returned it to the wicket. The batter, presuming that a boundary would be signalled, stopped running and was run out by the fielding side. 'So great was the uproar and confusion', that play was abandoned for the day (Warner 1946: 55).[6] Similarly, following the Eton v Harrow Match of 1873, the MCC called for old boys to ensure order at future matches. For the 1874 game, the MCC warned against 'undue exhibitions of party feeling, hoisting being prohibited' (Warner 1946: 69). Despite such incidents historians largely agree that by the mid-nineteenth century cricket crowds could be described as 'usually quite civilized' (Guttmann 1986: 79). For instance, Sandiford (1994: 123) states that Victorian cricket crowds, 'behaved very well indeed. They were certainly less rowdy than contemporary gatherings at other sports'. Exceptional incidents were attributed to the increase in cups and leagues, over-crowding due to a larger than anticipated turnout and the presence of the so-called 'football element' (Vamplew 1980: 15), or a 'non-cricketing', 'holiday' crowd (Sandiford 1994: 123–5). While cricket does appear to have been more orderly than other sports, there was also a concerted effort to make that *appear* to be the case by displacing the blame for any such disorder away from the game.

Paradoxically the 're-invention' of cricket buried the link between the game and that other particularly significant English institution, Parliament. Such obscurantism was necessary to disguise the foreign influences on the game which came via a social class which, at one stage, had relatively strong interdependency ties with their continental counterparts. Yet subsequently cricket would go from strength to strength as the epitome of Englishness, and as the embodiment and source of national character. Probably the most famous expressions of this interdependence of cricket and national identity is provided by Thomas Hughes in his classic book, *Tom Brown's Schooldays* (1857). Cricket 'is more than a game. It's an institution' states Tom. 'Yes' his friend Arthur agrees, 'the birthright of British boys old and young, as *habeas corpus* and trial by jury are of British men' (cited in Brookes 1978: 86). In further stating that 'there's a place for everyman who will come and take his part', Tom relays the sense of inclusivity consistent with the aristocracy's decision to embrace the emerging bourgeoisie and cite the masses as the source of England's rise in international status. This ideology would subsequently be fundamental to the cultural diffusion of cricket. The continued conflation of England and Britain in descriptions of the game enabled the quintessential English game to become the game *par excellence* of the British Empire. It is to this that we turn in the next section of the book.

Postscript

The developments discussed in this chapter also had radical implications for the participation of women in cricket. Eighteenth-century evidence suggests that female participation in cricket was a fairly frequent occurrence, and McCrone argues that female cricket 'flourished' in the second half of the century only to go into a prolonged slump after c. 1838 when 'two teams of Hampshire hay-makers played the last game of cricket for several decades in which women are known to have taken part' (McCrone 1988: 141. See also Underdown 2000, for a description of the relative prevalence of women's cricket in the eighteenth century). Cricket's evolution into a male preserve therefore coincides with the developments charted in this chapter. Tellingly, Nyren and Pycroft offer no instances of females playing cricket in the eighteenth century. As Bateman concludes, 'as forms of literature positioned cricket within a discourse of moral manliness, women were increasingly positioned beyond the boundary of the cricket field' (Bateman 2009: 27).

On the one hand this concurs with other evidence that suggests that nations and states are gendered institutions. For Nagel (2005: 116), 'Masculinity and nationalism articulate well with one another, and the modern form of Western masculinity emerged at about the same time and place as modern nationalism.' Sport, and specifically cricket and Englishness, provides a particularly clear example of this, for the re-invention of cricket as the national game was fundamentally also the description of it as a manly pursuit. Such an argument would have been rather difficult to sustain had women also been seen to play the game.

Paradoxically, however, women are given a central place in the development of round arm bowling. Pycroft provides what appears to be the first report of the theory that it was Willes' sister who was responsible for this innovation, as she sought to avoid her voluminous skirts when bowling under arm (see also Hargreaves 1994: 98). Subsequently it was claimed that round arm bowling was invented by W.G. Grace's mother. Though widely repeated, the attribution of this technical innovation to a single female seems implausible and probably stems from the attempts to discredit this new style of bowling. Once again we see the interdependence of bowling innovation and cricket's elevation to the status of England's national game. The apparently neutral act of codification therefore reveals a commingling of a range of different class, gender and national relations.

3

The Imperial Game
Cricket and colonization

Concurrent with the various changes to the game in nineteenth-century England was a broader social process of international diffusion which was to have a fundamental effect on the way cricket came to be played, and the meaning that it holds today. The codification which began in the mid-eighteenth century was a notable and necessary pre-condition of the game's subsequent popularity. Its nineteenth century 're-invention' as the national game, as both the epitome and a generator of English national character, was similarly important in giving the game an ideological meaning which mediated the way it was received. It is, however, England's colonial history which is the key to explaining the globalizing of cricket, and thus the relationship between cricket and contemporary identities, for 'Empire continues to play a key part in British consciousness' (Reviron-Piégay 2009: 6).

The description of cricket as *The Imperial Game* (Stoddart and Sandiford 1998) is almost as commonplace as describing cricket as the quintessential English game. For Mangan (1986: 153), cricket was the 'umbilical cord of Empire linking the mother country with her children'. All the leading international sides are former territories of the British Empire. As noted in the Introduction, the first international governing body for the sport was titled the *Imperial* Cricket Council. British sport administrators' contrasting attitudes to the emergence of international governing bodies of sport underscores this point, for whilst the English were reluctant participants in the early bureaucratization of international football and rugby union, they were firmly at the helm of the internationalization of cricket. The (English) Football Association (FA) declined a number of requests to assume leadership of the fledgling international governing body in the 1890s, eventually joining in 1905, a year after FIFA was established. The relationship continued to be acrimonious with the FA resigning its membership twice during the inter-war years. Similarly the RFU was not an original member of the International Rugby Football Board (which initially consisted of Scotland, Ireland and Wales) but joined in 1890, four years after its formation. In contrast to this, in 1907 when Abe Bailey, President of the South African Cricket Association (SACA), suggested that an Imperial Cricket Board be established, Lord Harris and the President of the MCC, Lord Chesterfield, were instrumental in placating initial objections from Australia and hosted the meetings which led to its 1909 formation.

Cricket's literature is replete with quotes linking cricket and Empire. For instance, in 1880 Lord Harris claimed that 'the game of cricket has done more to draw the Mother Country and the Colonies together than years of beneficial legislation could have done' (cited in Holt 1989: 227). He subsequently described the MCC as 'perhaps the most venerated institution in the British Empire' (cited in Bradley 1990: 3). In 1912 Lord Hawke wrote, 'On the cricket grounds of the Empire is fostered the spirit of never knowing when you are beaten, of playing for your side and not for yourself, and of never giving up a game as lost. This is as invaluable in Imperial matters as in cricket' (cited in Bateman 2009: 130). MCC President Pelham Warner would subsequently argue,

> Cricket has become more than a game. It is an institution, a passion, one might say a religion. It has got into the blood of the nation, and wherever British men and women are gathered together there will the stumps be pitched. North, South, East and West, throughout the Empire, from Lord's to Sydney, from Hong Kong to the Spanish Main, cricket flourishes. (Cited in Bradley 1990: 15)

Not only was cricket 'an integral part of Empire' (Birley 2000: 95), it was claimed to be responsible for the development of English national characteristics amongst populations across the globe.

The Imperial game: Some conceptual issues

The ubiquity of the idea that cricket is the game *par excellence* uniting the British Empire serves to obscure a deeper complexity. There are five conceptual points which can fruitfully be addressed. First, the idea of cricket as the imperial game projects a false homogeneity upon the Empire. Perkin identifies the tendency to conceive of the British Empire in terms both too *narrow* in the sense that the British exercised a wider influenced, and too *broad* in the sense that the Empire appears as 'an undifferentiated series of British "possessions"' (1989: 148). Rather, Perkin prefers to see the Empire 'not as a monolith but as part of a continuum in the exercise of British power and influence' (1989: 148). British 'possessions' were ruled in a variety of ways ranging from Crown colonies, through forms of self-government and dominion status. Beyond this, subtle forms of economic and cultural power reached almost all points of the globe. Perkin thus proposes that we consider concentric circles of influence consisting of: 1) an 'informal Empire' of free, self-governing nations which were relatively lawful and offered Britain stable trading relations; 2) a 'formal Empire' of self-governing dominions and dependent states; and 3) an inner circle of British-ruled colonies. 'Looked at from this point of view, the British were everywhere' (Perkin 1989: 149).

Second, although participation is largely mediated through the process of British colonization, labelling cricket the imperial game obscures the unevenness and the heterogeneity of the diffusion process. While accounts of the tremendous popularity of cricket in the West Indies, the subcontinent and Australia are relatively unproblematic, 'the game's unexpected demise [in Canada] is puzzling' (Kaufman and Patterson 2005: 83). Furthermore, the relative strength of the game in Holland and Denmark illustrates how the game took hold outside the formal Empire. The different histories of cricket in these two countries suggest that these exceptions to the rule do not have a singular or simple explanation. The first description of Danish cricket is thought to have appeared in 1802. The game was played in colleges from 1840 and in 1865 English railway engineers formed the Randers club. Dutch cricket is dated to 1856 and the existence of a Utrecht club involving students from the Netherlands and the Cape Colony.[1]

A comparison of cricket in two Greek islands – Corfu and Cyprus – is similarly revealing. Since the eighteenth century Corfu has passed from Venetian, to British, to Greek governance. A British protectorate between 1815 and 1864, the first cricket match in Corfu is thought to have been played on St George's Day in 1823. A cricket pitch remains in the centre of Corfu Town and is claimed to be the only sports field within a UNESCO World heritage site.[2] Cyprus, however, was part of the British Empire for longer than Corfu (from 1878 to 1960) and remains a member of the Commonwealth Games Federation. Cypriots did not take to the game until after the Second World War and its current popularity in Cyprus only dates back to around 2000 and is largely attributed to the remaining British military presence and the Asian diaspora.[3] Thus it would be difficult to produce a model which accounts for all the specificities of cricket's diffusion. While some of those only briefly introduced to cricket in the colonization process continue to exhibit the after-effects, some nations that existed closer to the heart of British imperialism and remain active in the Commonwealth show relatively few signs.

A third issue relates to the commonplace elision between England and Britain noted in Chapter 2. The Empire was, fundamentally, a British venture but cricket was codified by the English and came to be seen as synonymous with Englishness. Williams (1999: 12) provides an example of how easily this slip can be made:

> The nature of cricket as an imperial sport was vital to the assumptions that cricket was a distillation of English moral worth. Cricket was very much a sport of the British Empire … Cricket played between teams from Britain and other parts of the Empire was seen as a highly effective means of strengthening imperial loyalties.

Sen provides another (2001: 240): 'cricket was central to the culture of British Imperialism; playing sport trained middle-class and upper-class Englishmen to play overtly political roles'.

While as Kumar notes (2006b: 5), it was the 'English who were in command of Empire', to fully account for the relationship between cricket and colonization we must therefore also consider the process of 'internal colonialism' (Hechter 1975). Culminating in the 1707 Act of Union which established Great Britain, and was extended to incorporate Ireland in 1801, each Celtic nation experienced a different relationship with England, yet all are widely thought to be areas in which cricket has failed to have gripped the social imagination to any great extent. Thus in addition to the concentric circles of imperial influence identified by Perkin, in discussing cricket and colonization we could add a fourth concentric circle consisting of what Kumar calls 'the first English Empire' (2003a: 60). Complicating the claim for cricket as the game of the British Empire is the inconvenient fact that cricket is seen as the quintessential English rather than British game.

These remarks point to a fourth conceptual point. The distinctions between the imperialists and the colonized, and the colonial and post-colonial eras, are far from straightforward. The first colonial/post-colonial ambiguity relates to the Welsh, Scots and Irish who, once subsumed (to varying degrees as partners) within Great Britain, became a fundamental part of the broader British imperial project. Similarly, while Australia was formed through European expansion, it also had its own colonies such as Papua New Guinea (Hay 2003). Furthermore, at a time when British colonialists were most explicitly promoting cricket as *the* imperial game, inhabitants of Britain's most significant former colony (America) were attempting to diffuse baseball (Roden 1980). We are not, therefore, dealing with a simple process whereby people were exposed to a particular game form and subsequently decided whether or not to adopt it. Rather colonized became colonists and pre-existing cultural forms were abandoned, adapted or advanced by different ethnic groups in different ways in different contexts. Sport and colonization therefore entails a commingling of class, ethnic and national identities rather than a simple binary relationship. Sport and colonization is not a linear process in which the phases of colonialism and post-colonialism form mutually exclusive aspects of a single sequence, but a process with 'no unambiguous division[s]' (Bale and Cronin 2003: 3).

The fifth and final point relates to the sheer diversity of people involved in the imperial process. At its height the (formal) British Empire included at least 660 million people and encompassed more than 12 million square miles (Sandiford 1994), or a quarter of the world's habitable land (Perkin 1989). Emigration from Britain averaged about 250,000 people per year by the 1850s (Gemmell 2011) and by the time of Queen Victoria's death 'there were about 100 million people of British stock occupying territories beyond the United Kingdom' (Sandiford 1994: 144). A significant group amongst these emigrants were the public-school educated gentlemen who had been explicitly trained for imperial service. Sandiford (1994) states that this group accounted for as many as 45,000 who left Britain for the dominions between 1875 and 1900 and Perkin

(1989: 150) largely 'accredits' this group with the diffusion of cricket, arguing that while 'it would be too simple to claim that cricket and rugby were confined to the empire and soccer to the world', it was the case that cricket and rugby were diffused by former public-school boys, and football by those who travelled for more directly commercial reasons. But while it is true that former public-school boys dominated the major institutions of Empire (education, religion and military), and were significant in cricket's spread, the analysis of cricket and Empire requires a broader sweep. There were, for instance, those who provided the manpower for the military or who were active in developing trade links. There were huge numbers drawn from various social classes who, like the Mayflower pilgrims, voluntarily left Britain in search of a more prosperous future. Others were encouraged overseas by the 'systematic colonization' schemes of Edward Gibbon Wakefield who considered the de-population of Britain as a cure for the ills he believed had been created by urbanization and industrialization (Ryan 2004: 12). Finally there were those who were forcibly deported as part of Britain's penal system. Thus in the same way that we must recognize the geo-political heterogeneity of Empire, so we must also address the demographic diversity of the colonizers. Commingling with social class divisions was ethnic diversity. Stimulated by the Scottish Highland clearances and the Irish famine in the mid-nineteenth century, significant numbers came from beyond England. Almost half of the population in New Zealand in 1881 were born overseas and of these, 44.7 per cent originated in England, 19.8 per cent Scotland, 18.5 per cent Ireland and 6.5 per cent Australia. The Irish immigrant population constituted approximately one quarter of the total Australian population at this time (Ryan 2004).

Consequently, detailing the diffusion of cricket could be a book-length task in itself. In defining cricket as the imperial game we must embrace diverse lands, colonized by diverse people, with diverse motives for emigration and performing diverse roles. Thus it is hardly surprising that one of the main outcomes of Stoddart and Sandiford's text comparing the development of the game in each of the major cricket playing nations is to illustrate 'the complexity of cultural imperialism' (Sandiford 1998a: 1). It is not my intention, therefore, simply to recount a series of geographically de-limited histories of cricket in this part of the book. All of cricket's most successful playing countries, and some notably unsuccessful cricket playing nations, have been the focus of texts which provide far greater detail than can be attempted in this chapter. Rather, the aim here is to highlight what have been identified as some of the more common characteristics and some of the ideological underpinnings of this process. Doing so will enable us to understand the historically generated relations of Empire so that we can subsequently gain a deeper appreciation of the role of cricket in constructing contemporary identities. This chapter continues to focus on two core themes discussed so far, social identities and the structure and behavioural norms which govern this particular sport. Through an analysis of cricket and colonization we can highlight the relationships which people consider important at particular times and the way people subsequently orientate their behaviour to develop those relationships.

Cricket and colonization: Dominant trends

A logical conclusion from the previous section is that the relationship between colonialism and cricket belies capture in a single succinct phrase. For instance, Birley's (1999: 81) summary that 'cricket, like the Empire itself, spread somewhat haphazardly and not always for the noblest of motives' is perhaps true as far as it goes, but is of limited analytic use. Sandiford's argument that 'the story of imperial cricket is really about the colonial quest for identity in the face of the colonisers' search for authority' (1998a: 2) also misses the mark, for while *some* consciously and conspicuously sought to implant the game within new cultures, others carried cricket abroad simply because it was part of their 'cultural baggage of emigration' (Bateman 2009: 121). This section seeks to combine the literature on cricket and imperialism with histories of the game in various cricket playing nations in order to identify some of the overarching features of the relationship between cricket and colonization.

One way to make sense of the cricket and colonization process is to focus on the various degrees of adoption, adaptation and resistance which the game inevitably manifested. At its simplest, colonized people either started to play, decided not to play, or played cricket in some modified form. The limitation of this approach can be seen via a comparison of Trobriand Cricket and American baseball. Introduced to the South Sea Islanders in the 1920s and 1930s,[4] Trobrianders played cricket according to a number of rules which departed from the MCC-defined game. These included no restriction on the number of players per team (as long as the sides were even), throwing rather than bowling, a smaller-sized wicket, the incorporation of elaborate dances at the fall of each wicket and feasting at the end of the game (though of course all international cricketers now seem to have their own versions of each of these), and a convention whereby the home side always won. The elements of adoption, adaptation and resistance are clearly evident in this description and have been documented by cricket researchers as evidence of cultural resistance (for example Stoddart 1998a). Yet similar processes were evident in the development of baseball. Like Trobriand Cricket, baseball varied from 'MCC cricket' in terms of, for instance, the number of players on each team, the style of bowling/pitching to the batsman, and the style/shape of bases/wickets. However, scholars rarely depict the development of baseball in such derivative terms but, rather, as something with its own distinct origins. The reason for this disparity, and I expand on this in the next chapter, relates to the relative power of those invoking the adaptations. We therefore need to ask, 'where does the promoting hand of the colonial master stop and where does the adapting and assimilating indigenous tradition start?' (Cashman 1988: 261). When should our accounts give primacy to discontinuity over continuity and vice versa?

A second general tendency is to dichotomize those involved in this process into two competing and mutually exclusive groups: the transmitters or change agents and the adopters of this cultural form (see for example Kaufman and Patterson 2005). Again there are problems with this mode of analysis. First, our knowledge of the respective groups is uneven. The relatively powerful not only had greater resources with which to record their activities, but there was little to stop them (mis)interpreting or exaggerating their results to bolster their self-identity. Similarly some of these accounts may contain post-hoc rationalizations which lead the colonizers' actions to take on an unrealistic aura of coherence and intentionality. For instance, emigrants may have played cricket amongst themselves, the colonized may have played the game (or a variant of it), and the colonizers might have subsequently interpreted this as the intended consequence of their goal to assimilate the 'natives' when in fact the causal connection is far more complex. Furthermore, Cashman argues that accounts which concentrate exclusively on the actions of the proselytizers tend to view 'colonial salesmanship as a monolithic activity' (1988: 261). Given the class and ethnic differences between British emigrants it is reasonable to assume that their respective relationships with cricket, and their desire to share the game with others, were not uniform. Indeed, as we will see, the process of the rationalization and standardization of cricket is such that we cannot always assume that there was only one version of the game being diffused to any particular territory. A third problem relates to the portrayal of the adopters of this cultural product as nationally uniform in accepting (or rejecting) its diffusion. Rather, reception should be viewed as contoured by local differences and conflicts as much as by external influences. The history of cricket shows that the diffusion of a sport may benefit some but not all of the colonists, and its adoption might benefit some but not all of the colonized.

With this in mind it can be argued that, in the beginning of the colonization process, cricket was diffused largely because it was a form of recreation and entertainment with which British emigrants were familiar. Cricket and a range of other leisure pursuits were used in much the same way as they had been at 'home'. However within the relatively fluid communities of Empire, sport also helped to integrate new arrivals and act as 'a means of maintaining morale and a sense of shared roots' (Holt 1989: 208). Cashman argues that playing cricket enabled migrants to establish a perception of normalcy within an otherwise alien and hostile environment. Consequently we can see that some of the first Australian cricket grounds 'attempted to replicate the English rural environment' (Cashman 1998: 35). The parallel between the initials of the Melbourne Cricket Club's and those of its Marylebone counterpart added an air of legitimacy to the former's ascendency in Australian cricket administration. Ryan states that a desire to replicate such essential English institutions as cricket clubs was even stronger amongst those who migrated from Britain after 1840 and suggests that anglophilia continued to strongly influence the structure and administration of New Zealand cricket throughout the twentieth century. Cricket literature ascribed to the game the 'ability to transform aesthetically the colonial landscape, subsuming geographical particularity into a single, generic space of Englishness' (Bateman 2009: 128). A significant aspect of the global diffusion of cricket entailed little conscious or explicit attempt to alter the behaviour of indigenous or colonized populations but simply the continuation of existing cultural practices and traditions.

Subsequently people saw an educative role for cricket within the Empire. It is important to note that the social meaning of the game was not uniform across the process of colonial diffusion. For instance, while the Calcutta Cricket Club was founded in 1792 (Cashman 1998: 116) and cricket was first introduced to South Africa between 1795 and 1802 (Allen 2010: 40), in England in 1796 the Eton headmaster banned the school's pupils from playing against Westminster school (Brookes 1978: 72). At this point in the imperial process cricket had not yet been 're-invented' as a pastoral, peaceful and patriotic game form. Of course, by the end of the nineteenth century there were many, both at home and abroad, who were willing to attribute Britain's success in establishing an Empire to its sporting tradition. Playing sport was seen to build character and the characteristics nurtured were remarkably similar to those previously identified in relation to the ideas of cricket and Englishness which emerged at the beginning of the nineteenth century. As Holt's discussion of the role of sport in the Empire notes, 'The British were perceived as active and resourceful, if academically limited. Foreigners often envied their sheer ability to get things done, especially in relation to the running of an empire, which was ascribed in part to energy and common sense derived from games' (1989: 204). Through Empire, the British came to share the group charisma which the English had devised for themselves, but neither this conflation nor cricket's moral worth were evident at the Empire's outset.

The educational role of cricket fused with a discourse of civilizing mission. The establishment of such an extensive Empire was demonstrably a remarkable achievement and the positive self-image which the British took from this was 'intimately bound up with notions of white supremacy' (Williams 2001: 18). They were the colonizers because they possessed characteristics lacked by the 'inferior races' being colonized. Social Darwinism – an ideology which suggested that the survival of the fittest cultures was a natural and universal process – gave imperialism an aura of inevitable evolutionary development. Apologists for Empire, and especially those whose *apologia* was fuelled by Christian beliefs, framed colonization as a moral obligation to bring their particular form of civilization to those they were conquering; that they would both literally and metaphorically learn how to 'play the game'. As Mangan's (1984) description of Tyndale-Biscoe's activities in Kashmir clearly illustrates, the belief persisted that through sports such as cricket the colonized could come to acquire the characteristics of the English gentleman. What resistance the colonized offered was because they knew no better. They would come to realise the benefits in time. Cricket playing, extensively described in the colonizers' burgeoning literature, became 'living proof of the success of Britain's civilizing mission and of the victorious transference of Anglo-Saxon values on its subjects' (Bateman 2009: 129).

In situations where cultural assimilation could not easily be imposed, cricket offered a vehicle for the colonized to integrate into British cultural norms. In India the Parsees (a group of merchants and liberal professionals of Persian origin based around Bombay) were amongst the first to take up the game. Playing cricket enabled the Parsees to illustrate to the British that they were suitable and reliable collaborators. This facilitated their go-between role for the British and Indian populations. *Pace* Perkin (1989) it also demonstrates the importance of trade links in the development of cricket. Furthermore, the game acted as a 'means of anglicizing the indigenous rulers' of India (Holt 1989: 215) as so vividly demonstrated in the career of Ranjitsinhji. 'Ranji' transferred from Rajkumar College, Rajkot to Cambridge University before going on to captain Sussex County Cricket Club and represent England (Sandiford 1994). Enabled by his unquestioning commitment to both the Empire and the English institutions at its hub, he clearly 'learned the language of muscular Christianity' (Sen 2001: 241). Moreover, he brought 'a peculiarly English genius to batting … the glamorous obverse of the effeminacy, laziness, and lack of stamina that many colonial theorists thought Indians represented' (Appadurai 1995: 30). Playing cricket could be particularly advantageous to some individuals, even if a broader framework of economically and racially exploitative relations remained intact.

We can therefore see that to fully account for the diffusion of cricket we need to consider elements of accident, education, indoctrination and acculturation. In the final section of this chapter, however, I want to place greater emphasis on the ideologies which underpinned the process of cricket and colonization for within these we can see a number of logical inconsistencies. Addressing these ideological paradoxes allows us to explain cricket's relationship to the demise of the British Empire and indeed the social conditions under which the notion of cricket as the imperial game was generated. Through the commingling of intended and unintended consequences we can see how British dominance in colonial relations did not in any simplistic sense equate to absolute control.

Cricket and colonization: Ideological problems

The first of these ideological problems relates to the character building properties claimed for cricket. Similar to the invention of cricket and

Englishness discussed in Chapter 2, proponents of the game assumed seemingly contradictory positions regarding the violence/passivity of the game. While Tyndale-Biscoe used sport to grind 'grit into Kashmir' (Mangan 1984: 193), he and others also saw cricket as able to transform the 'baser instincts' of the colonized and inculcate the degrees of self-reliance, calmness and courage exhibited by English gentlemen (Bateman 2009: 126). Cricket could therefore make one both more manly *and* more genteel. While not strictly speaking oxymoronic, such an ideology barely stood scrutiny, particularly when placed in the broader context of more-or-less violent subjugation through colonization. It is perhaps no coincidence that the ICC should be proposed by a South African in the immediate aftermath of the Boer War. Similarly, the relatively unruly behaviour of cricket crowds in Australia in the 1880s seemed, on the face of it, to contradict the claims for the civilizing virtues of the game, but did little to shake commitment to cricket's character building properties. And if Britain's imperial strength stemmed from a culture of game playing there was something rather paradoxical about introducing such games to those whom they had colonized. As Majumdar (2008; Majumdar and Brown 2007) has argued, part of the appeal of cricket to Bengalis was the game's masculinity validating properties. However, was this not simply training the subaltern for effective resistance? Thus one of the central characteristics of the relationship between cricket and colonalization was that supporting and counter evidence, intended and unintended consequences, were evident in equal measure.

Perhaps the most marked and significant challenge to the character building ideology came during the 1932–33 tour of England to Australia. During this series the England captain, Douglas Jardine, instructed his bowlers to bowl 'fast leg theory' or 'Bodyline' to counter the proficiency of the Australian batsmen, and Donald Bradman in particular. With England set to take a two to one lead in the best of five test match series, and the Australian public becoming particularly enraged when wicketkeeper Bertie Oldfield was hit by a Harold Larwood bouncer,[5] the Australian Board of Control sent a telegram to the MCC. Bodyline, they claimed, '(made) protection of the body by the batsman the main consideration. This is causing intensely bitter feeling between the players as well as injury. In our opinion it is unsportsmanlike' (Wisden 1934: 328). The MCC defended their team but offered the Australians the option of cancelling the tour. Jardine insisted that the accusation 'unsportsmanlike' be retracted, which it was (reluctantly) on the first morning of the next match. While the series continued acrimoniously, perhaps most importantly, the idea that English cricketers possessed some kind of special virtue was undermined forever.

A second ideology underpinning Empire and influencing the imperial role of cricket was the concept of environmental determinism. Environmental determinism is a geographical version of Social Darwinism (Bale 2002) and, according to this highly teleological set of ideas, imperial dominance was partly based on physical and psychological characteristics generated by the environmental conditions particular to Britain. (Indeed this ideology could be further refined to explain differences between the (southern) English and the Scots, Irish and Welsh.) Environmental determinism could be used to explain the perceptions of both British virtues and the weaknesses and failings of the colonized. The converse of the belief that the human body was invigorated by the cold of Northern Europe was that it was equally weakened by the heat of the tropics. However, according to this logic the act of British colonials re-locating to the hot climes of the Empire entailed the risk of physical degeneration. This became a central reason why colonists wanted to play sports such as cricket. Competing (successfully) against teams from the 'Mother Country' was a way of demonstrating that British stock had not declined. This was as true for those who migrated to Australia as it was for those in the Caribbean. Consequently English commentators could congratulate the English 'race' for the victories of Australian cricketers over the English, a rationalization which Bradley (1995: 40) describes as 'an intellectual sleight of hand'. In a similarly ironic twisting of this logic, an ever-increasing number of black players were integrated into the West Indian team to ward off continued defeat at the hands of the 'Mother Country' and thus demonstrate the colonists' continued vigour. This may have been an extension of the English national character of 'getting things done', but what such empirical evidence did *not* seem to do was lead to a revision of the belief system which naturalized and therefore ultimately justified the process of colonization.

A third and perhaps the most enduring paradoxical ideology of imperial cricket related to the game's role in fostering unity. Playing cricket came to be seen as one of the clearest expressions of loyalty to the Crown and commitment to the Empire. At first cricket was used by white emigrants, 'as a celebration of the tight, unbroken bond between themselves and their metropolitan "cousins"' (Beckles 1998a: 2). The white plantocracy in the Caribbean strived to be seen as the most loyal group of colonial subjects and the veneration of cricket was an essential part of, and an ideal vehicle for, this claim. Initially at least, Australian cricket represented 'a highly deferential and pro-imperial nationalism' (Bateman 2009: 125). Ranji, through his playing career and cultural outlook, came to be seen as the embodiment of the legitimacy of the entire imperial process and civilizing mission. But not all parts of the Empire took to the game with equal zeal. While playing cricket was celebrated, those countries which exhibited a relative disinterest in the game were not punished or shunned in any way. Rather such non-conformity was simply overlooked. Moreover, the cricketing histories of populations that did not remain loyal to the crown – America, Ireland – were simply re-written. While these nations sought separation from the Empire, the people continued to play cricket. The English, as we will see in subsequent chapters, were disinclined to give much recognition to this anomaly.

Imperial cricket was also deeply infused with social divisions. Cricket in India was a vehicle for the re-creation of ethnic identities such as Hindu,

Muslim, Sikh and the aforementioned Parsees. A 'separate and culturally pro-British stratum' (Holt 1989: 219), fostered through the racial and social class segregation was reproduced in a variety of Caribbean societies. Here the population was also geographically divided with competition between the different island cultures particularly significant. New Zealand cricket, especially in Canterbury, broadly followed the class infrastructure of English cricket (Ryan 1998; 2004). What seems most remarkable about these cultural formations is that social divisions were identified as the cause of cricket's unpopularity in certain contexts (notably North America), while in others such divisions seemed to actively contribute to the uptake and popularity of the game. For instance the social class differences which characterized English cricket at this time were said to appeal to the Indian princes who adopted the game. Cricket was 'a useful extension of other royal public spectacles that had been an important part of the obligations and mystique of royalty in India', and the employment of white cricketing professionals from England contributed to a 'complex, hierarchical, cross-hatching' of social relations (Appadurai 1995: 29). Perhaps most famously, CLR James (1963) has described the relative acceptance within the Caribbean of cricket clubs stratified according to both race and class.

The credibility of this ideology was further stretched as cricket subsequently came to play a more central role in the generation and expression of national differences and identities. First was Australia, where test matches against England quickly came to be a gauge of the country's readiness for independence (Sandiford 1998a). Next came South Africa, then the West Indies, New Zealand, India and so on (see Table 4.1). Each test playing nation has its own benchmark of progress *vis a vis* the 'Mother Country', but invariably major milestones on this journey include the 'granting' of test match status, and the

Table 4.1 The development of international 'Test Match' cricket

Test Playing Nation	Test Debut	First Victory over England	First Victory at Lords
England	1877		
Australia	1877	1877	1888
South Africa	1889	1905	1935
West Indies	1928	1929–30	1950
New Zealand	1929–30	1977–78	1999
India	1932	1951–52	1986
Pakistan	1954	1954	1982
Sri Lanka	1982	1993	
Zimbabwe	1992		
Bangladesh	2000		

initial victory over England (often first in home conditions and ultimately, if possible, at Lord's). Whether victory over England will in future have the same significance remains to be seen. For Zimbabwe, and Bangladesh in particular, other playing successes may come to be seen as more significant in defining national status.

The key point here is that cricket 'threatened the hierarchical principles of Empire because of its new inclusiveness' (Bateman 2009: 122). The 'level playing field' and the fair play espoused in cricket ideology and nomenclature would eventually struggle to co-exist with the more pronounced structural inequalities of Empire. One response was to produce 'a dichotomous image which emphasized the similarities and differences between the old Country and its colonial offshoots' (Bradley 1995: 38) but the tenuous nature of these images was such that cricket administrators and advocates in the 'Mother Country' increasingly seemed to feel the need to produce statements which bolstered and justified their international influence. Reminiscent of Levi-Strauss's (1967) argument that social phenomena 'become the object of acute analysis precisely when they are ending' (Cole 2000: 440), the most developed narratives of cricket and imperialism were produced at the time when the Empire was beginning to be dismantled. Thus the ubiquity of the notion of cricket as the imperial game depends to a significant degree upon people's increasing awareness of its contradictions and paradoxes. Conversely where cricket was popular in the 1860s and 1870s (as we will see, in American and the Celtic nations) it did not acquire longer term popularity because English cricket administrators at that time were neither in a position (due to domestic weakness) nor particularly interested in the international development of the game. Gemmell (2011) makes the very interesting observation that at the point at which the ICC was formed, it could easily have been claimed that America rather than South Africa was amongst the world's three strongest cricket playing nations. The decision not to include the USA at this time may well have subsequently led to some very significant consequences for the game. But while cricket was England's national game, imperialism meant that it was not explicitly a *nationalistic* game, at least not in the sense that it would become, in England, in the 1990s.

Conclusion

This chapter has sought to examine the widely held notion that cricket and the British Empire are fundamentally linked. On one level this is a truism but like all common sense ideas there is a tendency towards over-simplification. The obvious contemporary manifestations of imperial cricket hide a deep, rich and varied pattern of social relations. This is not, of course, to say that particular trends or themes cannot be identified, merely to suggest that the relationship between cricket and colonization is sufficiently complex to belie summary in a simple umbrella statement.

It is partly for this reason that I will *not* conclude this chapter by developing a model of sports diffusion. Kaufman and Patterson provide what is probably the best of these, but as I have written elsewhere (Malcolm 2006), their model remains far from perfect. Rather, in the following chapters I examine three particular cases which help develop an understanding of the relationship between cricket and colonization. I look first at cricket in America. This study represents one of the most striking cases of rejection and serves as a vehicle for illustrating some of the limitations in existing explanations of cultural diffusion. Within the American case we can see the continuation of the fundamental importance of social class in the development of the game; something which, cf. Haseler (1996), has distinctly English characteristics. Moreover due to the antipathetic relationship that is commonly perceived to exist between cricket and American culture, particularly the highly commercialized sports forms of North America, the fact that Americans do not play cricket in large numbers is fundamental to the continued perception of it as the quintessential English game. The second study relates to cricket in the Caribbean. In many ways this is one of the most remarkable cases of the adoption of cricket and the subsequent use of the game in the process of 'national' self assertion. Within the West Indian case we can see the continuation of the fundamental importance of violence (through fast bowling) in the development of the game. In this regard it reveals a great deal about the concomitant aspects of conflict and cooperation within colonial and post-colonial relations. Finally attention is turned towards the relatively unchartered waters of cricket in the Celtic nations of the British Isles. This chapter is essential for helping us to fit the square peg of cricket's Englishness into the round hole of its status as the British Empire's pre-eminent sport.

Together the three studies develop our understanding of the cricket and colonization process more generally, but they also help form the foundations of the contemporary aspects of identity examined in the book's final chapters. Stoddart (1998b: 163) concludes his overview of the relationship between cricket and Empire by noting that 'while … the sun *has* finally set on the British Empire in the political sense, the persistence and even flourishing of cricket shows that "the imperial game" might well be one of the empire's major lasting influences'. Holt (1989: 222–23) similarly notes that 'cricket has helped both to sharpen a sense of nationalism and to soften its impact on Britain through the maintenance of close sporting contacts between former colonies and the "mother country"'. Dirlik (2002: 444) cites cricket as a particularly apposite example of the durability of colonial relations in contemporary cultural identities. Thus the relationship between cricket and colonization is essential to furthering our understanding of both the globalizing of cricket, and of the role of cricket in structuring and mediating the way in which the English view themselves and others in the twenty-first century.

One final point needs to be made. While this will be illustrated in subsequent chapters, it is important to note at this point that the role of cricket in identity construction was not a process confined to those in the colonies. Rather, cricket also performed a key role in educating the British about what their Empire was and who they, as a colonizing people, were. For instance, the first tour of England by a 'white' Australian team in 1878 (an Aboriginal team had toured England ten years earlier) was marked by the English public's realization that Australians were visually similar to themselves. Moreover, in the same way that the veneration of the English countryside is related to the early and extensive urbanization of Britain (Haseler 1996), the English sense of self was generated via contradistinction with the colonial other. Descriptions of the Australians focussed on their social class; 'good straightforward fellows of the rough and ready sort' (cited in Bradley 1995: 46). Complaints about the money-making activities of Australian cricketers, and the dour as opposed to dashing style of play they favoured reinforced the primacy of the amateur in English cricket. 'By describing what English people were not (Australians), they were attempting to say what English people were' (Bradley 1995: 37). As Loomba (1998: 19) notes, 'postcolonial studies have shown that both the "metropolis" and the "colony" were deeply altered by the colonial process'.

4

Cricket in America

If cricket and Englishness could be said to constitute a pleonasm, within the popular imagination cricket and America are largely viewed in oxymoronic terms. Marqusee's *Anyone but England: Cricket and the National Malaise* begins with an autobiographical statement about his 'discovery' of the game and the way it contrasted with his upbringing in America. He wrote:

> Everything that English people take to be 'American' – brashness, impatience, informality, innovation, vulgarity, rapaciousness and unashamed commercialism – is antithetical to what they take to be 'cricket'. For the English it is a point of pride that Americans cannot understand cricket … As for the Americans, everything they took, until recently, to be 'English' – tradition, politeness, deference, gentle obscurantism – seems to be epitomised in 'cricket'. (Marqusee 1998: 15)

While the American case underscores the idea that cricket is the quintessential English game, it also provides an excellent example of diffusion 'failure'. It enables us to see the unevenness of the role of cricket in the process of colonization and how the development of cricket was influenced by the heterogeneity of British emigrants. It also raises questions about the applicability of describing cricket as the imperial game.

In exploring this argument, it has been necessary to limit the scope of the empirical discussion. It has not been possible to address the role of influential institutions such as schools and universities (see for example Melville 1992) or the popularity of cricket in a wider range of geographical areas (see for example Lockley 2003, or Redmond 1992 in relation to Canada). But this does not detract from the central point; while cricket was essentially taken to America as part of the cultural baggage of English/British emigrants it was in America, perhaps before anywhere else, that ideological beliefs about the game were subject to a degree of scrutiny and, in many cases, that scrutiny led to outright rejection.

Theories of cricket's demise in America

Sports historians largely agree that, outside of the Native American game of lacrosse, cricket was 'the first major team sport and the first organized team sport in America' (Riess 1991: 33). Records of cricket played in America date back to 1709. An advertisement for cricket players was placed in a New York newspaper in 1739 and the first recorded match took place in Manhattan in 1751 (Majumdar and Brown, 2007). However, the period between 1840 and 1860 is generally regarded as a 'golden age'. Centred on New York, and in particular the St George's Cricket Club (established in 1840), the game 'showed considerable strength on the eve of the sectional conflict' (Kirsch 1989: 24). At this time cricket received extensive and largely supportive press coverage and was played in an estimated 125 cities in 22 states. Approximately 500 formally constituted clubs existed and, 'it is possible that there were 10,000 men and boys in the United States in 1860 who had played the game actively for at least one season' (Kirsch 1989: 42–43). After the Civil War, however, the popularity of cricket declined markedly. Baseball, whose first club, the Knickerbocker Base Ball Club, was founded in 1842 and produced its first set of written rules in 1845, was similarly centred on New York and superseded cricket both in terms of participant involvement and spectatorship by the early 1860s (Adelman 1990: 114).

The initial analyses of cricket in America were essentially adjuncts to histories of baseball (for example Seymour 1960; Voigt 1966; Tyrrell 1979). More recently historians such as Adelman (1990), Kirsch (1989) and Melville (1998) have provided analyses which more centrally focus on cricket for, as Melville notes, it is now recognized that an explanation of the demise of cricket is 'critical to the very validity of any theory that purports to explain the urban origin and subsequent development of American team sports' (1998: 2). Most recently Majumdar and Brown have revisited what they describe as the 'old dichotomy "Why Baseball, Why Cricket"' (2007: 139). Two explanations for the demise of cricket in the United States dominate such accounts: the structure of cricket and its incompatibility with American 'national character', and the post-Civil War rise of American nationalism. Both themes, to a greater or lesser extent, are predicated on the belief that baseball essentially replaced cricket. Scrutinizing these two arguments thus allows us to say something more about the (un)successful global diffusion of cricket.

Whilst the chronology of events indicates that the rise of baseball and demise of cricket were co-relative, the evidence for a causal connection is weak. As Waddington and Roderick (1996) have argued with regard to theories of the diffusion of soccer, one of the major problems with arguments that link the demise of one sport with the existence of another is that they are predicated on an implicit and unexamined assumption about 'sports space'. Addressing 'American Exceptionalism' to the global popularity of soccer (see Mason 1986; Markovits 1990; see also Markovits and Hellerman 2001), Waddington and Roderick note that such explanations are based on the 'assumption that in each society there is a limited amount of "space" for sports, and that once this "space" has been "filled" by one sport, there is no room for other sports' (1996: 45). However, when these arguments are cross-referenced, it becomes apparent that 'sports space' is either arbitrarily or teleologically assigned.

For instance, Waddington and Roderick note that just one sport (Australian rules football) is deemed sufficient to fill the 'sports space' of Melbourne in Australia and thus crowd out soccer, whilst in other places many more sports (as many as four in Canada) may be required. Ultimately the 'space' for sports in any given society appears to be determined by the number of sports which ultimately become culturally significant. We cannot, therefore, conclude that just because one sport became popular (i.e. baseball), another (cricket) would necessarily decline in popularity, for in instances where both remained popular, this could/would merely be taken as evidence of a larger 'sports space'. Moreover, if baseball and cricket could not co-exist as summer sports, why was there sufficient room within the 'winter sports space' for both US football and basketball? Given the timing of events it is inconceivable to think that the rise of baseball and the decline of cricket were not in some way related, but a more adequate way of conceptualizing this problem is to see the two sports – or rather, the participants in and advocates of the two sports – as subject to the same general social processes.

The notion of sports space is integral to the argument that the decline of cricket stemmed from the incompatibility of the game's structure and American national character. This theory asserts that various aspects of cricket – its slow pace, long duration, the inequality of opportunity for players to participate in meaningful ways – were at odds with an American national character forged by the experiences of a frontier nation and latterly moulded in the rapidly industrializing and urbanizing America of the late nineteenth century (Tyrell 1979: 207). For instance, Kirsch (1989) develops the idea that baseball's strength was its 'modern' character (relative to cricket), whilst Adelman (1986: 113–14) argues that baseball was structured to generate relatively higher levels of 'action' and 'exciting drama'. Thus many believe, as Melville concludes, that 'cricket failed in America because it never established an American character' (1998: 149).

Such essentialist arguments are problematic in two key ways. First, as we saw in Chapter 2, 'national character' is an artifice, constructed by particular people, with particular interests, situated in a particular social context. As Elias shows us, human personality structures do change over time. Moreover, such changes are more marked in periods of more pronounced social structural change. But even though post-Civil War America was clearly a society undergoing considerable social change, the idea that national characteristics can change so radically and so rapidly as would need to be the case to explain cricket's fall from prominence in the late 1850s, is simply not credible. The popularity of sports changes rather more quickly than can a national psyche (Guttmann 1996) although perhaps just as quickly as an ideological narrative can change. Second, one can invariably find contradictory evidence to such essentialist arguments. For instance, in the late 1850s, a series of conventions of the National Association of Base Ball Players (NABBP) approved the dismissal of batters who continually refused to swing at 'good balls' (thus making games shorter), but also (and more contentiously) agreed that catching the ball on its first bounce (on 'the fly') should not lead to the dismissal of the batter (Kirsch 1989: 63–68). Not only did outlawing catches on the fly make games longer, but moved the rules of baseball closer rather than further away from cricket. Moreover, if we undertake a cross-cultural comparison it is difficult to accept that cricket was sufficiently flexible to fit the 'national' character of the Indian, black-Caribbean, Australian, South African and New Zealand members of empire, but not Americans. The diffusion of baseball to Britain further counters the notion that the game's structure necessarily provided players and spectators with more excitement for the reaction of the English media to the game in the 1880s was to describe baseball as 'rounders made wearisome' (Bloyce 1997: 209). Consequently Kaufman and Patterson (2005: 90) are correct to note that, perceptions of the 'essence' of sports 'are as much an effect of the differential status of sports as a cause thereof'.

The 'nationalism thesis' is both the more popular and more convincing explanation of the decline of cricket in America (Melville 1998: 147), but still one that requires refinement. The first weakness of this thesis is the idea that the rise of American nationalism had a negative effect on the popularity of cricket in the 1850s and 1860s, for at that time cricket rather than baseball was the 'established international sport' (Melville 1998: 43). In other countries, e.g. Australia, playing cricket was a very successful vehicle for uniting the people and generating a sense of national difference. Secondly theses which argue that disassociation from English games was a way of asserting American independence (see e.g. Majumdar and Brown, 2007) are undermined by incompatible timings. It was Harold Seymour, in his 1960 study of baseball who initially proposed the thesis that Americans rejected cricket and chose baseball because the latter was a home-grown game, but Tyrrell (1979: 208) notes that it was not until the 1890s that the American origins of baseball became widely accepted. Indeed, the establishment in 1907 of the Mills Commission, from which the Abner Doubleday creation myth emerged, was in part a response to an audience's assertion that the roots of baseball lay in rounders and rather indicates that a consensus was reached some time after cricket's popularity began to wane. It must therefore be recognized that the early claims made for baseball as the national game were 'essentially propagandistic exercises' (Tyrrell 1979: 208) rather than expressions of popular will. Parallels with the 're-invention' of cricket as the embodiment of Englishness in the nineteenth century are clear to see.

It is, of course, no accident that the rise of American team sports, and baseball in particular, 'coincided with an intense wave of political and cultural nationalism' (Kirsch 1989: 91); these were, after all, key contextual factors in the development of cricket into England's national game. But the American example allows us to refine our conceptualization of the link between nationalism and the differential popularity of sports forms by recognizing the distinction and potential for conflict between different forms of nationalism. The rapid influx of European emigration from the 1850s increased the diversity of *ethnic* nationalisms in America and thus helped to undermine or dilute the 'Englishness' of the United States. Many of these emigrants would neither have had a tradition of playing cricket nor much desire to participate in something so quintessentially English. But, particularly post-Civil War, such ethnic nationalisms were effectively challenged and suppressed as political leaders fostered ideas of *civic* nationalism in order to ensure the state's political continuity. Different ethnic nationalisms proved differentially resistant and, as discussed later, Englishness was one of the more powerful ethnic nationalisms in America at this time. Thus it was not simply the rise of one form of nationalism which explains the demise of cricket, but the interdependence of different forms and types of nationalism which provides a more compelling explanation.

In concluding this section on theories of the demise of cricket in America, it should be noted that previous analyses have fundamentally misunderstood the position of the game in England in the mid-nineteenth century. Melville (1998: 41) and Adelman (1990) argue that a key factor in cricket's demise was that it was too 'mature' a sports form, and too fixed in tradition to be adapted, or 'Americanized'. Kirsch similarly refers to cricket's 'time-honored rules and traditions' (1989: 103). These arguments are fundamentally flawed for, as discussed in Chapter 2, the nineteenth century was a period of considerable flux in English cricket, dominated by debates about the legality of round and over arm bowling techniques. These debates exposed weaknesses in the MCC's authority over the game and the 1884 revision of the laws of the game, which 'fill(ed) gaps previously left to the imagination' (Rait Kerr 1950: 42), was a significant point in the reassertion of the club's dominance. Crucially these rule changes were one manifestation of class tension in the game and wider society at this time. The dynamics of nineteenth century English cricket have largely been overlooked by American historians of the game (for example Adelman 1990; Lewis 1987).

Thus, counter to the situation portrayed by American historians, cricket in the mid-nineteenth century was not fully 'modern' but retained the characteristics of a folk game. What Rait Kerr refers to as 'gaps … left to the imagination' were, in fact, local variations to rules and customs. One example is the practice whereby fielders would scramble to get the ball at the end of the game. Brodribb (1953: 177) claims that this was abolished after an incident in the 1848 England vs Kent match though it appears that a cricketer called George Pinder broke his collar bone thirty years later, during a similar scramble for the ball at the end of the 1878 Yorkshire v Nottinghamshire match at Sheffield. These local variations included physical contact between batters and fielders (laws about obstruction), the spatial separation of players and spectators through the use of boundaries (see Chapter 1), but more centrally the way in which the ball was propelled to the batter (i.e. the debate over round and over arm bowling discussed in Chapter 2). Whilst some clubs in some parts of Britain will have followed the lead of the MCC, it needs to be recognized that there was not simply one cricket form in England at this time. Rather, game forms varied according to social class and geography and if cricket laws varied, then it is highly plausible to think that so too did cricketing customs, traditions and playing cultures.

The arrival of cricket in America

With the greater physical and psychological distance from London, it seems reasonable to suggest that such variations would have been more marked in America. Indeed existing historical analyses of cricket in America provide empirical support for this thesis of co-existing game forms based around class (as well as regional) difference. From the 1840s to the 1870s, the leading cricket club in America was the St Georges Cricket Club (SGCC) in New York. Formed by 'prosperous middle class' Anglo-Americans (Adelman 1990: 117), the naming of the club after the patron saint of England indicates that ethnic group identity was part of the founders' motivations. Indeed, Lewis notes that the English immigrants in ante-bellum New York were 'a group apart', remarkable for their 'clannishness' (Lewis 1987: 321). However, Melville considers that the formation of the SGCC 'may have been as much an attempt to maintain class distinctions common in English cricket at this period as it was to assert national identity' (1998: 11–12) and, in this regard, it is significant that almost from its beginnings the SGCC employed professionals and imitated the status emphasizing mechanisms widely employed in the upper circles of English cricket (and in the Caribbean) at this time.

However, whilst cricket's elite may have been drawn from the prosperous middle class, 'the majority of participants were emigrants from the emerging industrial centres of northern England; as such the sport was "closely bound up with steak and ale", the working class and gambling' (Adelman 1990: 101). Similarly both Kirsch and Riess note that the first Philadelphia cricketers were of 'humble origin' (Kirsch 1989: 23; see also Riess 1991: 21). Indicating that varied cricketing customs and styles of play existed within this working-class group, Kirsch further notes that Northern and Southern English immigrants 'sometimes resorted to "hard blows" to resolve their differences' (1989: 23). The abandonment of the 1846 contest between Americans and Canadians – the first international cricket match – provides a telling example. During the match, 'Samuel Dudson, a "sturdy, strong and rough" Philadelphia artisan was knocked down by a Canadian batsman while attempting to catch an opponent's fly ball' (Kirsch 1989: 35). Dudson reacted aggressively, at which point the

Canadians refused to finish the match. This incident presumably stemmed from the non-standardized character of cricket's laws at this time and the variety of playing customs and traditions of the game which existed both in England and to a more marked extent in America at this time. (Yates (1982: 7) claims that the custom of 'charging down', which was banned in the 1787 Laws, was common in the United States and other colonies until at least 1846. Catching on 'the fly' has only ever been permissible in baseball and does not feature in any of the known codes of rules for cricket.) American cricket historians have largely failed to recognize that the game of cricket being diffused to America was not of a unitary nature. Rather there seems to have been different social groups simultaneously introducing different varieties and styles of cricket to America at this time.

Central to understanding the diffusion of what therefore might be described as a polymorphous game is the specific nature of the interdependent relationships between Anglo-Americans at this time, characterized by a combination of unity (based on their common ethnicity) and division (based on English regionalism and social class). Middle- and working-class English immigrants appear to have been tightly bonded (Lewis 1987: 321) but this relationship can perhaps most accurately be described as one of 'harmonious inequality' (van Stolk and Wouters 1987). The respective status positions were both underpinned by tradition, and reinforced by the context in which the English immigrants were an 'outsider' ethnic group. Where English immigrants were low in number (e.g. New Jersey), cricket clubs were formed which crossed class barriers and forged ethnic identity (Benning 1983: 71). Where numbers permitted (for example New York), middle-class immigrants formed their own clubs and asserted their relative status by employing professionals and vetting club membership. The most common pattern was for clubs to be class based; 'very few clubs had evenly mixed memberships' (Adelman 1989: 152).

How were these ethnic/class interdependencies manifest in the diffusion of the game? Within New York the Anglo-American prosperous middle class which introduced cricket continued to dominate the game (Kirsch 1989: 123). While between the 1840s and 1860s the SGCC became increasingly class exclusive (Adelman 1990: 117), the establishment of the Union Star of Brooklyn cricket club indicates that the English middle classes were probably not united in this approach (Melville 1998: 18–19). At this time relatively few 'American' cricket clubs were formed in the city. The majority of cricketers in the metropolitan area remained English and politically the game was dominated by the social elite of the SGCC. By contrast, cricket in Philadelphia exhibited a rather different pattern. Introduced in the 1830s and 1840s by working-class English immigrants, the game was subsequently adopted by the American upper middle classes such that by the 1860s 80 per cent of Philadelphia's cricketers were white-collar workers and only 10 per cent were English

(Kirsch 1989: 134; see also Melville 1998: 28). Newark exhibited a different pattern again, with a relatively even split between Anglo-American and American players. In marked contrast to Philadelphia nearly 85 per cent of all cricketers in Newark were working class. Thus, the different English groups who were responsible for introducing cricket to different areas of America, experienced different degrees of 'success'. To understand this dynamic it is necessary to examine not simply the actions of the change agents, nor those of the receivers, but their interdependence.

Like the 'colonial' elites in other territories, the Anglo-American elite was held to have a high cultural status, as evidenced through the media's support for the character building properties of sports such as cricket, and 'late nineteenth century upper-class America's tendency to look "to the British Isles for standards of culture and genteel behaviour"' (Jable 1991: 218). Whilst Anglo-Americans were well-integrated into and had good and stable access to the broader American economy, they were by no means dominant. Their position was markedly different to that of the elites in the Caribbean and the Indian subcontinent, which actively promoted the integration of colonized people through cricket to enable imperial expansion and consolidate dominance. Conversely, for this group of Anglo-Americans the cultural assimilation through cricket of those who saw themselves as more unequivocally American was unlikely to increase their influence in economic or political spheres. In short, Anglo-Americans simply did not have much to gain from proselytization. Consequently, members of the SGCC expressed little interest in spreading the game to other groups, or getting involved in the national governance of the sport. However, to retain their cultural status it was important for the Anglo-Americans to be seen to uphold the standards and traditions of cricket from which they derived their social prestige. Rather than adapt the game's customs to be more in line with the local culture, this group actively sought to replicate the status-emphasizing and exclusionary practices used by the elite cricketing groups in England, and thus contemporary critics blamed the exclusionary behaviour of Anglo-American cricketers in New York for stifling the development of the sport in the United States. Contrary to Adelman clubs were not 'formed to promote the sport' (1990: 111), and by resisting (or at least not cooperating with) the establishment of leagues and regular competitions, members of the SGCC were merely replicating the actions and aloofness of their counterparts who ran the MCC. Moreover, it was their association with the MCC which formed the basis of their cultural capital. Whilst others were not formally or explicitly excluded from entering the sport, any attempt by the upper-middle-class Anglo-American elite to incorporate other social classes and groups would have weakened the cultural basis of their social status.

This entrenched position was consolidated by the interdependence of Anglo-Americans and elite groups 'back home'. In part because of the relative independence and economic power of the United States, but more particularly because of the impact of the frontier, Americans were insulated from the kind of questioning of the degeneration of physical stock which stemmed from ideas about environmental determinism. As Mennell notes, there existed a common perception that American civilization was unique, or at least fundamentally different from Europe, with 'optimism and activism towards collective social life and the general good' the dominant theme (2001: 230). Quite simply, the New World did not measure itself solely by the criteria and standards of the Old World. They were able, in a way that would only come to other colonies much later, to reject, revise and refute the ideologies that underpinned cricket's role in the process of colonization. When contrasted with the colonial elites in, say, the Antipodes, we can see how this ethos was empowering for the Anglo-American upper-middle-class cricketers of New York. For Australians, who 'have long had a sense of cultural inferiority to England' (Kaufman and Patterson 2005: 99), '"progress" was measured essentially in British terms against British standards maintained by British institutions' (Stoddart 1979: 126). Cricket in the Caribbean was a similar case in point. But British and Anglo-American interdependence was very different. Consequently there was little external pressure on the Anglo-Americans to drop their exclusionary stance.

In contrast to this, English working-class immigrants did not have such cultural standing and therefore probably neither wished, nor had the capacity (in terms of social power) to act in exclusionary ways. Interestingly, not only did Americans take to the game in greater numbers where it was played by the English working classes, but both the American middle *and* working classes responded positively to the game diffused by the English working class. The diffusion of cricket to the Newark area might be described as homophilous (where change agents and adopters of a cultural form share comparable social positions. See Kaufman and Patterson 2005). There seems to have been a comparatively open reception to the game amongst the working classes, indicative of relatively low levels of ethnic or class competition. In Philadelphia however we see a heterophilous diffusion process (where change agents and adopters are socially unequal). Here upper-middle-class Americans assumed control of the game and came to dominate the Anglo-American working classes who had introduced it. Within the relatively rigidly class stratified community of Philadelphia (Melville 1998: 122) there was cultural capital to be gained from participation in the sport and, in particular, the link between cricket and the public schools of England 'may have impressed the social elite' (Tyrrell 1979: 212). To augment this, they, like the Anglo-American cricketers in New York, adopted much of the refinery and many of the customs of elite cricket in England, including the employment of working-class professionals. Thus whilst the potential existed for cricket to be diffused by working-class English immigrants, such developments were restricted in two ways.

Firstly, the existence of an identifiable Anglo-American elite meant that the working-class imported game came to hold a subordinate status. Secondly, the broader association of the game with high social class status meant that some American upper classes desired involvement in the game, in some cases subsequently marginalizing English working-class immigrants.

The development of cricket in New York, however, appears to have been characterized by more pronounced (class) conflict. New York was central to the development of baseball into firstly a modern sports form and latterly the American national game. Moreover, between 1850 and 1855, 87 per cent of New York's baseball players were white collar workers (Adelman 1990: 126). About half of these Adelman defines as 'professional-high white collar', though baseball in other areas of America appears to have had a broader mix of players, with a greater proportion of artisans and skilled craftsmen (Kirsch 1989). This demonstrates that in New York at this time there co-existed two exclusionary but relatively evenly balanced upper-middle-class groups, Anglo-Americans and Americans. The competition between these two groups was not only important for the eventual demise of cricket in New York, but had ramifications for cricket in America more broadly. The status competition between these two groups requires greater exploration.

Although American cricketers in New York were critical of the more elaborate customs such as the emphasis on after-match dining, two issues appear to have been particularly important – the use of professionals, and multi-club membership. Americans resented the Englishmen's use of professional players for, whilst they criticized the practice on ethical grounds, it also led to continuous and almost inevitable English sporting supremacy. For instance, one contemporary critic noted that, 'it came to be believed that no man who did not drop his H's could possibly win honours at bowling or wicket-keeping' (*Clipper*, 1858 cited in Kirsch 1989: 99). The American cricketers of New York were not so powerful as to see such sporting defeats as meaningless and one option was for Americans to embrace these practices. However, this did not occur. Why? Firstly, the American players did not have the cultural status, augmented by tradition and association with English institutions such as the MCC, to sustain such a 'harmoniously unequal' relationship. The exception to this, but an exception that appears to prove the rule, was in Philadelphia, where the dominance of cricket by the American higher social classes was relatively uncontested. Secondly, the majority of professionals were imported from England. Though the career of the professional tended to be 'peripatetic and insecure' (Melville 1998: 80), given the relatively strong ethnic identity of the English and the retention of links back to the 'Mother Country', Americans were simply not as well placed as Anglo-Americans to recruit cricket professionals. The common ethnic identity and the strength of the social bonding between the Anglo-Americans probably also made them better able to sustain a system of multi-club membership as player mobility was predicated upon close-knit networks of interdependence.

Presented with such structural disadvantage, the American players attempted to alter the rules of the game. In this they failed and they failed because the Anglo-Americans had a relatively high cultural status and, moreover, were able to point to the even higher cultural status and tradition of the game as formalized by the MCC. American cricketers could have sought simply to split from the Anglo-Americans over these issues, but they were not sufficiently powerful to make such a decisive break. Moreover, to lose the backing of the Anglo-Americans may have meant severing links with the ideology of the 'character building' properties which formed the basis of the rationale for their sporting activities. Americans were therefore faced with the prospect of a sport in which their participation was not courted, at which their sporting (and by inference cultural) inferiority was repeatedly demonstrated, and which they were unable to alter to more adequately suit their interests. Though the supposed character building properties of sports participation made cricket an attractive pastime to some, this significant number of negatives detracted from the benefits.

While Americans were not sufficiently powerful to adapt cricket, neither were they so power*less* as to be unable to significantly affect this relationship. This in part helps to explain the rise of baseball. Indeed the debates of the early baseball conventions indicate that status insecurity, and thus players' interdependence with other social groups, was important. Early baseball players were keen to distance themselves from children and younger players through fear of having the respectability and 'manliness' of their activities questioned (Kirsch 1989: 64). This is an apparently consistent trait amongst those involved in the formalization of modern sports forms for, it will be remembered, a similar discourse emphasizing manliness accompanied cricket's establishment as England's national game. Moreover, the staunchly amateur stance of baseball, and the rejection of a form of 'broken time payments' for players indicates that advocates of baseball were also aware of their status relative to their English cricket playing counterparts (Kirsch 1989: 67).[1] Like Gaelic games in Ireland which operated 'within a definition of sport which was essentially English' (Houlihan 1994: 192) baseball combined anti-English foundations with a faithful reproduction of the underpinning English amateur ideology. Consequently while American baseball players, like their English cricket playing counterparts, were socially exclusive, their exclusivity was manifest in different ways and for different reasons. It was not simply the case that the English proponents of cricket acted in exclusionary ways but that different social groups (Americans and Anglo-Americans), between which the balance of power was relatively even, enacted a kind of dual (or multiple) social closure. The different type of closure exhibited stemmed from the specific interdependencies in which these groups were enmeshed.

Cricket's peak and the rise of baseball

The dynamics of American cricket changed in 1859 with the arrival in America of the professional touring XI captained by George Parr. Interestingly, whilst the SGCC took a central role in organizing the tour it was the lower status New York Cricket Club, whose players would have been socially closer to the tourists, which made the initial arrangements (Adelman 1986: 108). Whilst many historians have discussed this team's impact on cricket in America, few have recognized the significance of the broader context of class tensions in which this tour occurred.

The expansive press coverage which the touring team gained meant that the co-existence of different cricketing cultures was given greater exposure than ever before, and thus the potential division between middle and working-class English migrants was thrown into sharper relief. Contemporary American commentators were disgusted by the blatant commercialism of this touring team (Kirsch 1989: 39–40). Clearly this would have appeared at odds with the game as defined by the SGCC, thereby raising questions about the apparently fundamental link between playing cricket and character building. Moreover, given the debate raging in England at this time, it is highly likely that the style of bowling used was somewhat contentious. To date, no empirical evidence of this debate has been uncovered and thus this point remains a matter of conjecture. However, given that this touring team consisted solely of professional players the actions of whom the MCC was continually trying to curb, and given that many of the Anglo-American cricketing elite would have arrived in America at a time when not even round arm bowling had been legalized, it is difficult to think that any such consensus over the laws of the game would have existed.

Moreover, just as the establishment of the William Clarke XI had demonstrated to English professional cricketers twelve years earlier, this tour illustrated the broadening range of commercial opportunities available to American professionals. It is notable that Sam Wright and his son Harry – founder in 1869 of the first all professional baseball team, the Cincinnati Red Stockings – were Anglo-American working-class professionals employed by the SGCC. Both played against the 1859 English touring professional XI (Ickringill 1995), whilst Harry and his brother George subsequently played against the English touring professional XI of 1868. As employees of the SGCC these players would have been expected to perform the kinds of subservient roles required of MCC professionals but, Ickringill notes, the example of the professional side gave Harry Wright 'food for thought' (1995: 148). As harmonious as the unequal relationship was between the elite who ran the SGCC and their professional employees, this tour demonstrated the commercial viability of 'exhibition' cricket matches. If it was possible to become an independent cricket professional in England, why wouldn't Wright, given his status as a player and the greater opportunities for economic and social mobility which America offered, have been even more successful? The significance of this tour, therefore, was that it highlighted the changing nature of the relationship between the Anglo-American elite and working class cricketers and this in turn had significant ramifications for the development of both cricket and baseball.

Ultimately Harry Wright – who later referred to cricket as his first love – would choose baseball rather than cricket as the vehicle for his professional team. The reason why lies in the enabling and constraining effects of the relationships in which he was enmeshed and which constituted the broader American context for cricket. As noted, the social value of cricket in America lay in the perception of its ability to build character (an American version of Pycroft's *The Cricket Field* was published in 1859). As demonstrated by the criticisms levelled at the 1859 touring team, a professional version of the game – as existed in England at this time – was perceived to have a diminished social value. It was also likely that the Anglo-American cricket elite would actively resist professional developments. Consequently there were barriers to the establishment of an American professional touring cricket XI, barriers which Wright and others were not sufficiently powerful to overcome (this was also the case in Ireland in the 1850s). Wright was, however, highly familiar with baseball, and indeed there was considerable overlap of personnel and facilities at this time (Lewis 1989). The fact that baseball was a 'new' sport, and a sport which was not championed by a social elite whose cultural capital was so deeply entwined with the amateur ideology, meant that Wright was less constrained in his pursuit of an independent professional career. We can see, therefore, that the relationships between different class groupings in America, and between different groups in England and America played a highly significant role in creating the conditions both for baseball's rise and cricket's demise. Entrepreneurship and the establishment of leagues stemmed from the networks of interdependency and power balances which existed in this specific time and place. Thus the rise of professional baseball can be explained with reference to the same social processes that led to the demise of cricket, without resorting to an arbitrary or teleological assignment of 'sports space'.

Conclusion

The class and cricketing relations in England in the mid-nineteenth century had a significant impact on the diffusion of cricket to America. This alerts us to the importance of recognizing the polymorphous character of cricket's diffusion process, the variety of groups in 'receiving' countries, and thus the multiple motivations for adopting/adapting/rejecting the game. Examination of the interdependencies between the English and Anglo-Americans, between upper- and lower-class Anglo-Americans, and between

Anglo-Americans immigrants and Americans help reveal why cricket did not become central to the American way of life, and indeed subsequently became antithetical to the way the English understand Americans and Americans understand the English. Thus national identity and nationalism, if not necessarily national character, played a significant role in the diffusion of cricket to America. It played an equally important if rather different role in the development of cricket in the Caribbean. It is to this that we now turn.

5

Cricket in the Caribbean

Of all the histories of imperial cricket, the Caribbean game is probably the best documented. It provides an excellent example of the way in which cricket was taken to a new cultural environment by British colonizers, was embraced by a colonized people, and was subsequently a vehicle for the assertion of a separate and distinct 'national' identity. National is used here in speech marks in recognition of the fact that the Caribbean entity that plays international cricket – the West Indies – is a multinational conglomeration which remains something of a peculiarity in world sport.

The case of cricket in the English-colonized Caribbean has been described as a tale of 'the gradual supplanting of whites by blacks on the field and in society' (Yelvington 1990: 2). However, as the following sections show, this was not a simple, linear process characterized solely by dominance and subordination. Rather, the black population negotiated its way and, at times, was incorporated into the game by the white colonizers. At times various groups of non-whites also sought to discriminate against each other. At times British emigrants were constrained by their relationships with other emigrants, and with groups back in Britain. The history of cricket in the Caribbean is 'a complex mixture of accommodation and resistance … (with) as many struggles over boundaries within and between the lower ranked social groupings as there were within the white elite' (Stoddart 1995a: 81). Indeed, C.L.R. James's (1963) seminal book, *Beyond a Boundary,* is essentially an autobiographical discussion of the seeming contradiction between an appreciation, acceptance and love of cricket (and the values and behavioural mores associated with the game), and a lifetime of resistance against the subordination of non-whites under imperial rule. The West Indian case therefore demonstrates the complexity of the influence of class and race relations on the development of the imperial game, as well as the ideological tensions over environmental determinism and the endurance of the ideology of imperial unity supposedly fostered by playing cricket. In addition to this, fast bowling features as a central aspect in this broader process of negotiation and thus further reveals the problematic linkage of Englishness, cricket, civility and violence.

Cricket in the colonial Caribbean

Beckles (1995a) notes that the first references to cricket in the West Indian press appeared in the *Barbados Mercury and Bridgetown Gazette* in

June 1806. In January 1807 the paper included an announcement of a dinner to be held at the St Ann's Garrison Cricket Club. Two years later the *Gazette* publicized a 'grand cricket match' to be played between the Officers of the Royal West Indies Rangers and Officers of the Third West Indian Regiment for fifty-five guineas a side. These, and subsequent, press reports highlight the central role of the military in the organization of the early game in the region (Stoddart 1995a). Cricket pitches were often a central feature of garrisons throughout the Caribbean. The significance of military cricket was such that the St Ann's Garrison club, for instance, has been referred to as a 'pioneering West Indian social institution' (Beckles 1995a: 37).

Initially members of the military played between and amongst themselves. However, during the period of slavery, blacks had been encouraged to use what leisure time they had 'constructively'. Pursuits perceived as a threat (and this can be taken to mean almost any activity which was unfamiliar to colonists) were prohibited. Consequently, those activities which were familiar (i.e. cricket) formed the few permissible pastimes available to slaves. This is not to say, of course, that the slaves were entirely compliant in this adoption. Many (for example Yelvington 1990) have argued that there may have been elements within the play of blacks which effectively sought to satirize the colonizers' ways. Gradually, however, the slaves were 'incorporated' into the cricket games of the military officers. As Yelvington (1990: 2) notes, blacks 'performed restrictive roles. At first they were "allowed" to prepare pitches ... and a few were "allowed" only to bowl and retrieve batted balls during practice sessions'. Thus from this early stage, the cricketing roles performed by blacks had similarities with the experiences of the working-class professionals in English and American cricket.

While people throughout the British Empire adopted cricket as a signifier of inclusion, in the West Indian case three reasons were particularly apparent. First cricket allowed the white community to demonstrate their loyalty to the Crown. Second, performances on the field of play served to prove that the heat of the tropics had not undermined British vigor as the logic of environmental determinism suggested it might (Stoddart 1995b). Third, once slavery was abolished (in 1838) cricket served to distance the elite from the '"uncivilized" indigenes' (Beckles 1995a: 34). As Beckles (1995a: 36) puts it: 'In exactly the same way that whites defined a political system in which less than 10 per cent of the population was enfranchised as democratic, a place was found for blacks within the cricket culture that enhanced the divisions of labour insisted upon by the plantations.' Cricket's development rested on an uneasy alliance of imperial unity and localized division.

These factors contributed to cricket's dramatic spread in the Caribbean during the second half of the nineteenth century. The major centres of cricket – clubs and schools – were organized on the basis of social ranking with club membership determined on the basis of occupation, wealth and colour, rather than playing ability. In Barbados, for instance, the sons of the white elite (and a few blacks who received scholarships) went to Harrison College, the sons of the plantocracy went to Lodge and the sons of the emergent middle-class coloureds joined white pupils at Combermere. Once they left school, each had their respective clubs to join. Old boys from Harrison joined the Wanderers club if they were white or Spartan if they were black. Lodge old boys joined Pickwick, and black and white Combermere old boys joined Empire and Pickwick respectively (Stoddart 1995a). Similar situations existed in Guyana, where the Georgetown Cricket Club was dominated by the Portuguese elite, in Trinidad (James 1963), and in Jamaica where the highly prestigious Kingston Cricket Club had restrictive policies preserving the club as a bastion for whites (St Pierre 1995). However, cricket clubs run by, and for, *non*-whites operated similar exclusion policies. Jamaica's Melbourne club was dominated by the coloured professional classes and instituted a complex fee structure which effectively, if not officially, limited working-class membership.

The game's competitive structures mirrored these exclusionary membership practices. The Barbados Cricket Committee (BCC), established in the late nineteenth century, was made up almost entirely of whites. Stoddart (1995a: 67) describes the BCC as 'a self-appointed, self-constituted, self-selected and self-perpetuated group', whose role was to organize local competitions and host touring teams. Although the BCC was superseded by the Barbados Cricket Association in 1933, such was the continuing feeling of exclusion amongst lower- and working-class blacks that the Barbados Cricket League was established three years later to cater for the cricketing needs of this section of the population. Similarly, where the concentration of Chinese and Indian populations was sufficiently large, they too established leagues of their own (Stoddart 1995c). Caribbean cricket, like Caribbean society, was organized as a 'multilayered pigmentocracy' (James 1993: 234).

After the incorporation of black slaves into military cricket practice and the post-slavery establishment of cricket clubs for blacks, the next significant dynamic in this development of Caribbean cricket was the institutionalization of inter-island competition. The first such match (between Demerera and Barbados) was staged in 1865 but by 1896 St Kitts, Antigua, Trinidad, Jamaica, St Vincent and St Lucia had all joined the regional cricketing network (Beckles 1995b). As with intra-island competitions these games were organized and played almost exclusively by whites. Significantly, however, inter-regional fixtures came to be seen as forums in which Island elites could demonstrate their superiority over their counterparts in other territories. Initially, the major consequence of this was that white and non-white players *within* the various colonies became increasingly integrated. While remaining largely excluded from the formal structure of both intra- and inter-island competitions, 'friendly' games between black teams and the white elite were organized in an effort to improve the skills of the white representative players. Status-emphasizing practices similar to those used in England to distinguish amateurs and professionals were employed during this early phase of integration. For instance a degree of distance was maintained by the exclusion of black players from clubhouse refreshment breaks during and after the game. Blacks began to be employed on an individual basis with increasing frequency, with the role of the professional in English cricket as the template for their employment. As St Pierre (1995: 108) states, 'in Barbados … the caste-like stratification system, based on race/colour, allotted to black Barbadians – they were known as "professionals" – the role of bowlers and fetchers of balls delivered during practice sessions in which whites batted and blacks bowled'. By 1895, the six Barbadian clubs employed fourteen (black) ground staff who performed similar bowling and pitch preparation duties to their white professional counterparts in England (Stoddart 1995b). The practices were probably both conscious attempts to signify status differences, but also an unconscious part of the colonists' cultural baggage.

These regional matches plus the reciprocal tours with England that started in 1895 'signaled the beginning of the non-racial democratizing process in selection policy' (Beckles 1995b: 197). The inclusion of black players enabled territories such as Trinidad to compete with the most powerful cricketing teams such as Barbados. Moreover, English administrators such as Pelham Warner noted that unless black players were selected for the West Indian team the region would remain far behind the 'Mother Country' in playing terms and when the West Indies side came to England they would risk having embarrassing defeats inflicted upon them by the English counties. White attempts to hold on to their dominance within the sport (and, indeed, society more broadly) worked in opposition to these integrative forces. The Guyanese representative side remained dominated by the members of the Georgetown Cricket Club and was always captained by a white or Portuguese player from that club. During the 1890s, Barbados refused to play Trinidad in the Challenge Cup if the latter included black players (Beckles 1995b). While the skills of the Barbadian professional William Shepherd were particularly influential in gaining black representation against touring teams from 1902 onwards, calls for the inclusion of black professionals in the Barbados Cup competition were consistently rejected on social rather than 'sporting' grounds.

The growing desire for playing success meant that Pelham Warner's words were heeded when the 1900 West Indian tour party to England was selected. The party of fifteen included five black players. This tour – the first to England by a West Indian side – was not granted 'first class' status and most of the games were lost. Tellingly, however, of the five black players, three were bowlers and two were all-rounders. When the subsequent tour party to England was selected in 1906, the team consisted of seven black and seven white players. This time the MCC decreed that all games would be 'first-class', but again, the composition of the tour party provides evidence of the positional segregation of black and white players and the continuity of 'class' distinctions in the English game. Four of the seven whites were picked primarily as batsmen whilst four of the seven blacks were picked primarily as bowlers.

Despite the growing number of blacks playing at all levels of West Indian cricket, selection committees rarely included black or 'coloured' members. Even as late as 1985 four of the thirteen executive officers on the BCA management committee where white. Moreover, as Stoddart (1995a) notes, there were fierce debates over the selection of regional sides until well into the 1920s. James (1963) for instance, discusses the non-selection of the black Trinidadian Wilton St Hill for the 1923 tour to England. Significantly St Hill was primarily a batsman, and 'the social aspirations to which his batting gave eloquent voice were those of the popular masses' (Lazarus 1999: 167). In contrast the inclusion of black bowlers was less contentious although judgements about appropriate temperament meant that some fared better than others. In 1923 Herman Griffiths was arguably the finest fast bowler in the Caribbean but H.B.G. Austin (the white captain) chose instead to travel to England with George Francis because he considered Francis more docile than Griffith. As a result of the limited opportunities for non-white players in the Caribbean, talented black players began to look elsewhere for employment. Some played for teams in North America but most came to Britain. Due in part to the stricter residency regulations, but also to the greater status-exclusivity of county cricket in England in the 1920s, cricketers from the Caribbean found it easier to obtain contracts in the Lancashire League. Learie Constantine's employment by Nelson Cricket Club (Hill 1994) was perhaps the most notable example of this.

Thus, while black Caribbean cricketers gradually came to represent their home territories, the region as a whole, and even towns in the North of England, certain cricketing roles remained more open to non-white participants than did others. The employment of blacks as groundsmen and bowlers became common but batting and the captaincy remained 'beyond a boundary'. The inclusion of black players, it seems, was crucial to improving West Indian playing standards and 'test status' was subsequently granted in 1928. St Pierre's (1995) analysis of the relative playing performances in early test matches illustrates how significant blacks continued to be to the success of the side. Between 1928 and 1960 the West Indies played England in ten test series. During this time white West Indians made no double or single centuries and only 25 scores over 50. In contrast, non-white West Indians made seven double, 29 single and 56 half centuries. Similarly white West Indians took four or more wickets in an innings only twice whereas non-white West Indians achieved this on 44 occasions. St Pierre (1995: 110) concludes that, 'since whites were not normally picked as bowlers and they did not perform as batsmen, then they must have been picked for some other reason'.

Moreover, from 1928 to 1960, with one exception, every manager, captain and vice captain of a West Indian touring team to England was white.

In 1947–48 there was much political manoeuvring in order to install the black batsman George Headley as captain of the Jamaican team to play England. The major 'breakthrough' came in 1960 when the black Barbadian, Frank Worrell, was chosen to captain the West Indies side on a tour to Australia. Coming at a time when the case for a region-unifying West Indian government was being made most vociferously (see James 1963: 217–243), Worrell's appointment has been interpreted as 'a classic statement of the link between emergent nationalism, anti-colonial struggle and sporting culture' (Searle 1990: 35). By this time all the region's political leaders were black and exclusion from the cricket captaincy increasingly came to be seen as untenable. Pro-Worrell campaigners noted that he had regularly captained teams representing the Commonwealth and had enjoyed considerable success. As James (1963: 224) noted, 'in cricket these sentiments are at their most acute because everyone can see and judge'. Worrell, of course, was primarily a batter. Moreover, despite a relative humble background, he had acquired an English university degree and had become 'acceptable within establishment circles in the Caribbean' (Stoddart 1995c: 249).

As stated in this chapter's introduction, the development of West Indian cricket has been documented in great detail and much of what is chronicled here – the complex interplay of individual agency and structural incorporation – is relatively well-established. Analytically however it is important to recognize the interdependence of ideologies, some specific to cricket (the relationship between class and playing role segregation) and some with wider currency (black docility, black physicality) in structuring the cricketing opportunities of black Caribbeans. This re-description of the development of West Indian cricket is therefore necessary for, as we will see, these ideologies would continue to contour the expression of social relations through cricket in the post-colonial era. Specifically, what is less well-charted (or at least less explicit) is the way these historical interdependencies subsequently shaped national self-assertion in the Caribbean and cricket-related identities. Moreover, this discussion highlights the analytic importance of conceiving of interdependencies in the round, and being equally cognizant of their intended and unintended outcomes for, it should be noted, it was the divisions between *whites* that were highly significant in enabling one power resource (playing ability) to assume the significance that it did. In the next section we see how identities, playing practices, and habitus (particularly attitudes towards, and perceptions of, violence) converge.

Cricket in the post-colonial Caribbean

The captaincy of the West Indian team by a black player, and therefore the removal of all white players from the side, signaled a selection policy guided more than ever by meritocratic principles. It was to establish the preconditions for the assertion of Caribbean self-identity and a concerted challenge to both the authority of the British within the game and the related notion of racial supremacy. The form of this challenge was partly structured by the historical legacy of the way in which the game was introduced as part of the colonization of the Caribbean. It also represents continuity in the significance of the mediating role of violence in cricket's development.

In the period from 1980 to 1994 the West Indies team won an unprecedented 79 per cent of all tests played and sixteen out of 24 test series, drawing seven others and losing only one (Wilde 1994: 176). More particularly the West Indies continually and comprehensively beat the England cricket team, winning all five tests in England in 1984, in the Caribbean in 1985/86 and four out of five tests in England in 1988. The team was now entirely composed of black players but the method by which the team dominated world cricket reflected the developmental dynamics of West Indian cricket. There were, of course, some very talented West Indian batsmen at this time but, as Wilde's analysis of the period between 1974 and 1994 shows, the side's dominance was based on fast bowling. Of all the fast bowlers who achieved fifty test wickets (and therefore relative success at this level) over a third (nine out of 26) were West Indian. Aggression, violence and injury (to the batter) were inextricably linked to fast bowling. Patterson (1995: 145) talks of 'the beautiful, sweet violence of the act' of fast bowling where, so often, 'it is "us" versus "them". "Us" constitutes the black masses. "Them" is everything else – the privileged, the oppressor, the alien, dominant culture'. In this the West Indies also dominated. In all test matches, played throughout the world between 1974 and 1994, a total of 88 batsmen retired from their test innings through injury (some were accused of feigning injury due to intimidation). Of these almost half (40) retired whilst playing against the West Indies (Wilde 1994). Thus, as the power of whites in the West Indies waned, black West Indians developed a cricket playing style which was far removed from the white-determined traditions of the game.

The reliance on fast bowling was not a specifically West Indian tactical innovation. Precedents had been set by England in the infamous 'Bodyline' tour to Australia in 1932/33 (see Chapter 3). Indeed the West Indies had a history of trying to use variants of this fast bowling tactic but, reflecting the broader structure of social relations, had censored themselves due to actual or perceived criticisms of status violation. During the 1926 England tour to the West Indies, England bowled bouncers to the West Indian captain, H.B.G. Austin. When the West Indies' Learie Constantine retaliated in kind and bowled bouncers at the England captain, the Hon. F.S.G. Calthorpe, he was implored by his colleagues to stop. James (1963: 111–112) recalls:

> 'Stop it, Learie!' we told him. He replied: 'What's wrong with you? It is cricket.' I told him bluntly: 'Do not bump the ball at that man. He is the MCC captain, captain of an English county and an English Aristocrat. The bowling is obviously too fast for him, and if you hit him and knock him down they'll be a hell of a row and we don't want to see you in any mess. Stop it!'

Constantine also recalled the 1933 tour to England during which he resented 'the blindness of some or our critics who professed to see danger in those balls (bouncers) when we put them down and not when English players bowled them' (cited in Marqusee 1998: 167). Twenty-five years later Ray Gilchrist was ostracized from the West Indian team and sent home from the tour of Pakistan and India for what West Indian cricket administrators deemed to be the inappropriate use of bouncers.

The West Indies were far from alone in exploring the use of these techniques. During the 1951–52 test series against the West Indies, the Australians regularly deployed bouncers to undermine the batting of the '3 W's' (Clyde Walcott, Everton Weekes and Frank Worrell) (Rae 2001). Similarly, during the 1957–58 South African series against Australia, one 56-ball spell of bowling by Heine and Adcock of South Africa included a total of 53 bouncers (Williams 2001). Criticisms were raised periodically. Rae (2001: 151) describes *Wisden* taking 'its traditional dim view' of events in 1951–52. In 1964, *Wisden's* editor talked of bouncers as 'one of the curses of modern cricket' (1964: 92) and two years later the editor reiterated his feelings, arguing that treating cricket like 'warfare' had led to various controversies, including 'the use of the bumper to frighten and threaten the batsman with bodily harm' (Wisden 1966: 78–79).

Indeed the origins of the dramatic escalation in the use of short-pitched fast bowling from the mid-1970s did not lay with the West Indies but can more properly be located in England's tour to Australia and New Zealand in 1974–75. Prior to the mid 1970s short-pitched fast bowling was rarely used against the weaker batters. There was commonly thought to be a 'fast bowlers union', an informal, unspoken agreement that fast bowlers would not bowl bouncers at each other (note the class-connotations of the term 'union'). But in 1974–75 a number of English players suffered at the hands of a new Australian pairing of fast bowlers, Dennis Lillee and Jeff Thomson:

> Dennis Amiss and Bill Edrich had their hands broken; David Lloyd's box was, in his own words 'completely inverted'; [Brian] Luckhurst, Fred Titmus and Derek Underwood all took crunching blows; and Thomson got a ball to cannon into the covers via Keith Fletcher's skull. Lillee bowled a beamer at Bob Willis, while the bumper he bowled at Geoff Arnold was described by Jim Laker as the most vicious ball he had ever seen. Willis, Underwood and Arnold were all established tail-enders. (Rae 2001: 158)[1]

Some (though not all) of these injuries occurred when batters faced short-pitched fast bowling. England also bowled short and fast and, like the Australians, targeted the weaker batsmen. When England moved on to New Zealand, debutant and tail-end batsman Ewan Chatfield had to be resuscitated at the wicket. England's matches in Australia and New Zealand inspired the editor of Wisden to address the issue of short-pitched fast bowling in *four* separate pieces in the Editor's Notes section of the 1975 edition.

Thus neither the proliferation of short-pitched fast bowling nor the decline of conventions protecting certain players were West Indian innovations.

Rather the continued use of short-pitched fast bowling can more closely be linked to Australia, and the involvement in cricket of media baron Kerry Packer. As a consequence of his failure to secure the rights to televise Australian test cricket, Packer, recruited players for his own, rival, competition. Marketing glamourized the confrontational and dangerous aspects of 'Packer cricket', leading one commentator to describe him as 'the Godfather of fast bowlers' (Wilde 1994: 68–9). Injuries occurred regularly. England's Dennis Amiss stated that 23 batsmen were hit on the head during the first Packer season (Wilde 1994). Ray Robinson (1978), writing in *The Cricketer*, counted a *mere* sixteen during the Australian 1977–78 season as a whole. Fuelling this alarm, no doubt, was the active role Australian crowds took in encouraging this style of play, through chants such as 'Kill, kill, kill, kill' (Rae 2001).

Despite these antecedents, it was the West Indian team which would become 'the most vilified and maligned in sporting history' (Williams 2001: 117). In part this stigmatization stemmed from race-ideologies of black physicality and violence. Sport remains one of the few areas of social life in which relatively violent conflict is largely tolerated (Elias and Dunning 1986) and, as Carrington (2010: 96) notes, 'the fantasmatic figure of the uncivilized and uncivilizable black athlete' has a long history. The use of short-pitched fast bowling stemmed from the historical legacies of the development of cricket in the Caribbean, but the West Indian refinement of this tactical approach produced the 'most efficient form of attack yet devised' (Wilde 1994: 10). Perceptions of the danger posed by this style of bowling were heightened because cricketing success became inextricably bound to the assertion of a West Indian 'national' identity. As Carrington (2010: 5) notes:

> Sports have historically provided an opportunity for blacks throughout the African diaspora to gain recognition through *physical struggle* not just for their sporting achievements in the narrow and obvious sense but more significantly and fundamentally for their humanity in a context where the structures of the colonial state continue to shape the 'post/colonial' present. (Emphasis in original)

A key turning point in the West Indian tactical development was their defeat by India in Jamaica in 1976. Clive Lloyd declared the West Indian second innings leaving India to score what at the time seemed an impossible 403 to win the game, but India reached this target and calls for Lloyd's resignation soon followed. Determined to win the next game, Lloyd replaced a spin bowler with an additional fast bowler (making three in total). The trio repeatedly bowled bouncers, hitting the Indian batsmen several times. Indian captain Bishen Bedi declared their first innings closed with four batsmen still to come to the crease and had five players 'absent hurt' in the second innings, in what was 'the nearest anyone has come to surrendering a test match' (Wilde 1994: 55).

A significant motivation behind this development may have been the West Indian desire to shed the image of 'happy go lucky' players (Wilde 1994: 51), or the perception of being talented but 'less cautious and more flamboyant' cricketers (Williams 2001: 116).[2] Others, however, place more emphasis on the role of violent and aggressive resistance. Burton (1985), for instance, has described the West Indian style as a mix of 'flamboyant', 'contemptuous' batting and 'attacking', 'violent', fast bowling. According to Burton as the power of whites in the West Indies waned, black West Indians developed and negotiated a cricket playing style which was far removed from the white traditions of the game. But regardless of player motivations, this form of cricket proved very popular with spectators in the Caribbean. As St Pierre argues, 'Performance before an audience of West Indians equally emphatic about violent and aggressive cricket, conspired to produce a change in this "beautiful, difficult English game"' (St Pierre 1973: 15). For Searle (1990: 36) this was 'cricket of resistance and assertion, which mirrored an entire people coming into their own, rejecting colonial divisions imposed upon them and bringing a new confidence and will for cultural construction'.

The nomenclature used by critics of the West Indian use of fast bowling is also revealing. 'Brutal', 'vicious', 'chilling', 'thuggery', 'vengeance' and, commonly, 'violent' were terms which regularly appeared in the English mainstream and specialist cricket press. The West Indian slip catchers became known as 'Death Row', and whereas in 1963 Wes Hall had been described as the 'cheerful executioner' (cited in Wagg 2005: 188) from the 1970s their bowlers acquired nicknames such as 'Whispering Death' (Michael Holding). Malcolm Marshall was referred to as 'a cold blooded assassin' (cited in Williams 2001: 117). Wisden carried articles, pictures, or editorial notes commenting on short-pitched fast bowling in eight of the ten issues between 1975 and 1984 and thrice more in the next eight years. In 1979, for instance, the editor noted: 'In modern times, the act of deliberate intimidation to make the batsman fearful of getting some severe injury has become almost systematic with all countries, except India, exploiting this evil deed' (Wisden 1979: 79–80). In 1984, the Editor added 'the viciousness of much of today's fast bowling is changing the very nature of the game'. Eight years later Wisden's editor invoked the game's aristocratic roots in arguing that, 'there was never any reason for cricketers to behave like members of the House of Commons. Cricket should be a civilised game and a civilising one, and if that sounds high-falutin I make no apologies' (Wisden 1992: 49).

The weight of opinion led English, Australian and Indian cricket officials to seek to curb the use of short-pitched fast bowling (and thus West Indian success). In 1976 the ICC condemned the intimidation of batsmen, urged umpires to enforce the law more rigorously, and insisted that test match sides should attempt to bowl a minimum of 17.5 six ball overs per hour (curbing a development concomitant with the dominance of fast bowling, which led to both an intentional – to reduce the batting team's rate of scoring – and unintentional – ironically fast bowlers take longer than slow bowlers to complete their overs – reduction in the number of overs bowled). The following year the ICC accepted a recommendation that countries could mutually agree to restrict the number of bouncers to two per over and not more than three in any two consecutive overs (Williams 2001) but this, and a similar scheme introduced in 1979 (Wisden 1979), faltered when players unilaterally abandoned their agreements during play. A 'bouncer immunity' scheme for non-specialist batsmen was tried but again faltered due to problems of defining which batsmen should be included in the scheme and in defining how long the immunity lasted for tail-end batsmen who scored a significant number of runs (Wilde 1994). All such regulations remained voluntary until 1991 when the ICC introduced a three-year experimental scheme which limited bowlers to one short-pitched delivery per over (defined as any ball which would pass over the batsman's shoulder). In 1994 the laws were revised to permit two bouncers per over ('dangerous and unfair bowling' are regulated under Law 42.6).

These incidents illustrate that the West Indian dominance of world cricket post-1974, facilitated as it was through a reliance on fast bowling, signaled a final stage in the 'gradual supplanting of whites by blacks' (Yelvington 1990: 2). Given that the early 'excesses' of 1976 were not subsequently repeated, we can only assume that elements of West Indian self-censorship continued. However, in contrast to previous controversies of this nature, West Indian players objected to the implication that their success was 'based not on skill but on intimidation and brute force' (Holding and Cozier 1993, cited in Williams 2001: 119). The West Indian authorities actively and openly opposed the new rule changes perceived to have been imposed as a challenge to their cricketing success and style. Clyde Walcott, President of the West Indian Cricket Board called it 'a fundamental and unnecessary change in the way the game is played', while the West Indian cricket captain, Vivian Richards, spoke of racism and hypocrisy: 'I know damn well that there are people at the top of the cricketing establishment who feel that the West Indies have been doing too well for too long' (cited in Wilde 1994: 195). In 1991 the *Caribbean Times* asked whether there had been 'a white supremacist plot to undermine Westindies long-standing status as kings of cricket' (cited in Williams 2001: 125).

Conclusion

The debate over short-pitched fast bowling during the 1970s and 1980s undoubtedly had a 'racial' dimension. West Indian cricket, and black West Indian cricketers, had developed to such an extent that they exerted a significant influence over the cricket world. The ascent to unequivocal world leaders was closely related to the neo-colonial assertion of a West Indian 'national' identity. It simultaneously represented a challenge to the traditional balance of power. Notably, however, the nature of this challenge was rooted in the legacies of the colonial development of Caribbean cricket.

The importance of the West Indian case to the study of cricket and empire lies in the fascinating balance of incorporation and resistance, of co-operation (i.e. playing cricket) and conflict (adaptation of cricketing conventions) which it reveals. It shows quite acutely how relationships formed during one phase of the colonial process came to have significant unintended consequences generations later. In many ways it is the archetypal example of cricket as the imperial game and it provides an important segue into the final section of this book in which we look at the influence of cricket and its historical legacies on the identities of black diasporic and other post-colonial migrant communities in Britain. Writ large in this analysis is the interdependence of identity, cricketing practices and their regulation. Emotions and psychological life (as gauged through (in)tolerance of practices perceived by some to be violent) directly relate to large scale processes such as de-colonialization. A propensity to use violence, and the almost inevitable censure of such a successful tactic, were structured by the inequalities fundamental to imperialism.

In the next chapter, however, we consider a development of cricket which radically disrupts the notion of cricket as the (British) imperial game; namely cricket in the Celtic nations of the British Isles. This examination both raises questions about what does or does not count as 'successful' cultural diffusion, and forces us to be conscious of the lazy elision of Englishness and Britishness which is required to sustain this idea.

6

Cricket and the Celtic Nations[1]

The paradox of two widely-held ideas lies at the heart of this chapter. Cricket is universally accepted as the quintessential *English* game, a game which encapsulates and generates Englishness. But cricket, as exemplified in Chapters 3, 4 and 5, is also the game par excellence of the *British* Empire. This chapter seeks to address this apparent contradiction for while cricket is so closely associated with England, it is generally perceived to have had little popular appeal in Ireland, Scotland and Wales. Indeed, 'the temperament of the Welsh, Scots, Irish and French were (sic) often used to explain the limited impact of cricket there' (Bradley 1995: 37). Pycroft, it will be remembered referred to the limitations of the 'volatile spirits' of the Irish and the 'phlegmatic caution' of the Scots. The co-existence of these contradictory beliefs therefore seems to rest on one of two rationales. Either cricket was played throughout the British Isles and therefore its distinctively English character has been exaggerated, or cricket reflects and continues to be subject to the traditional elision of English and British identities, the perception that Great Britain is simply 'Greater England' (Haselar 1996: 30). An analysis of cricket in the Celtic nations therefore expands our understanding of the role of cricket in the process of colonization and in contemporary relations between British national identities.

Colonization and the Celtic nations

One way to approach relations between England and Ireland, Scotland and Wales is to conceive of a process of 'internal colonialism' (Hechter 1975). The conquest and colonization of the 'Celtic fringe', it has been argued, acted as a kind of trial run of English, later British, imperialism. There are a number of parallels between the internal and external phases of colonialism which provide empirical support for this view. The various Celtic peoples were stereotyped and stigmatized in ways which bolstered English self-images of superiority. At times a civilizing mission was evoked to legitimize English expansion. In Wales and Ireland in particular, English communities existed in parallel with 'native' communities and dominated the main cities, occupied the best land, etc. The language and culture of English communities and their laws and administrative systems became pre-eminent. As in North America and Australia, the attitudes English emigrants expressed toward the 'mother country' fluctuated between anglophilia and angry resentment at their 'unfair' treatment. Forms of colonial resistance were evident throughout, and in Ireland particularly violent.

While Kumar describes the British Isles as 'England's first Empire', he argues that there are limits to the parallels that can be drawn between this and the later imperial phase. He describes the English conquest of the Isles as 'slow, piecemeal, largely unplanned and often the result of local initiative and local invitation' (Kumar 2003a: 84). At times the English were more concerned with their continental neighbours than their Celtic cousins. At times their continental neighbours, particularly France, were involved in the 'internal' affairs of Britain by supporting Celtic resistance. Most significantly the degree of political, cultural and economic integration between the nations meant that 'British society became a blurred patchwork of ethnic groups' (Kumar 2003a: 85).

As with the British Empire more generally, it is important to recognize variations within the process of internal colonialization. For instance, while Ireland's borders were more-or-less defined by the sea, and Offa's Dyke gave Wales a physical basis for separation, the Scottish-English border was relatively permeable and only settled in the thirteenth century. Each of the Celtic nations was internally divided, and only Scotland was able to form a (relatively) unified nation prior to English settlement. Kumar uses the term 'conquest and colonization' (2003a: 71) to describe the Welsh and Irish experiences, but chooses 'Anglicization by stealth' (2003: 77) to portray the Scottish case. Latterly the Welsh would share Protestantism with England while Catholicism would dominate in Ireland and wield considerable influence within Scotland.

More specifically, under the 1284 Statute of Rhuddlan Wales acquired English laws, courts and a county-based administration. Resistance led by Owain Glyn Dwr was briefly followed by a Welsh parliament between 1400 and 1405 but the 1536 and 1543 Acts of Union 'completed the "anglicization" of Wales' (Kumar 2003a: 73). While significant cultural differences remained – particularly in terms of language and literature – via the ascension of the Tudor dynasty in 1485, the Welsh became embedded in the 'English' monarchy. The Welsh gentry, benefiting under these structural arrangements, were at the forefront of assimilation. They became closely integrated with both English settlers in Wales, and with the political and economic powers in England.

In Ireland internal struggles provided the opportunity for Henry II's 1171 invasion. Anglo-Norman knights subsequently came to own significant quantities of Irish land, adopted a range of Irish customs and manners and, in the process, became distanced from the interests of the English. Ultimately, however, this group were never fully integrated, and formed the core of what subsequently became known as the Anglo-Irish. The military and political domination of Ireland would only take a more complete form in the eighteenth and nineteenth centuries but throughout 'the English were in Ireland but Ireland was not English' (Kumar 2003a: 76).

Scotland, developed its own cultural and political autonomy after internal conflicts saw the English-speaking Lowlanders overcome the Gaelic-speaking Highlanders. Subsequently the Scottish and English monarchies merged under King James (VI of Scotland in 1581, I of England in 1603). In contrast to Wales and Ireland, Scotland was never conquered in the sense of military occupation, but Scotland only escaped this colonization experience by culturally capitulating to the English to a far greater degree than did the Welsh and Irish. For Kumar, 'The Scots were not conquered by the English; they "Englished" themselves' (2003a: 78). For the Scots and Welsh participation in Great Britain was more a partnership (albeit as weaker partners) than a takeover, and even for the Irish the process of colonization was no straightforward case of dominance and acquisition.

The development of cricket in Celtic nations

What impact did these processes of colonization and political and cultural integration have upon sport, and cricket in particular? Despite the high degree of integration, distinct national identities continue to exist and be expressed through sport. As Holt notes, 'within Great Britain and the island of Ireland national difference is the very stuff of sport' (1989: 237). Reflecting their different histories, the sporting cultures of each of the three Celtic nations varies considerably. In Wales, rugby union became the most significant sport in the definition and construction of national identity. Popular initially in the Southern valleys and latterly in the developing industrial areas, rugby union was played by and popular amongst the working classes in Wales and therefore contrasted with the middle-class image of the game in England (Williams 1985). For the Scottish, football would become the primary sporting expression of national identity. Beating the 'auld enemy' in the annual football fixture became something of an 'obsession' (Holt 1989: 257), entangled with the evocation of a history of relatively successful military resistance, but characterized also by the conjoining of Scotland's sectarian communities which otherwise deeply divided the nation and its football clubs in particular. Within late nineteenth-century Ireland we see the coalescence of political and cultural nationalism, with the rejection of British sports by Irish nationalists, the ostracism of those who practised such 'foreign' sports, and the championing of Gaelic games as an expression of Irishness (Mandle 1977).

Cricket is often conspicuous by its absence in discussions of sport and British national identities; once again testament to the uncritical acceptance of the ideological link between cricket and Englishness. Holt's (1989) discussion of Celtic nationalism in *Sport and the British* contains no discussion of cricket, merely a single reference to the first football international which was held at the West of Scotland Cricket Club in 1872. Jarvie's (1999) anthology,

Sport in the Making of Celtic Cultures contains just three brief references to cricket. Was cricket never played in these Celtic nations? If not, why didn't the English implant the game into their 'first Empire'? If cricket was once played, what accounts for its subsequent apparent lack of popularity? To answer these questions we first need to briefly examine the development of cricket in Wales, Scotland and Ireland. An understanding of cricket in Celtic nations add to our understanding of the place of cricket in the process of colonization and is necessary for an analysis of the social significance of cricket in contemporary Britain.

Wales

Johnes argues that 'the whole chronology and character of sport in Wales has closely followed its equivalent in England' (2005: 115). He cites the demise of traditional Welsh rural culture and the importation and incorporation of rugby from England as supporting evidence. At first glance cricket appears to represent something of a disruption to this schema although unfortunately the 'almost total absence of Welsh cricket literature' (Lewis 1980: 513) means that the history of the game in Wales is largely unrecorded. However, according to the *Welsh Academy Encyclopaedia of Wales* (Davies and Jenkins 2008) the first recorded match was played in Llanegwad in Pembrokeshire and the first club was formed in Swansea in 1785 (implied also by Lewis 1980). Johnes (2005) argues that the first recorded match was played in 1783 in Camarthenshire. Despite these early beginnings it is clear that the Welsh did not follow the English and embrace cricket as a totem of national character or a vehicle for its expression.

What little we do know about the establishment and subsequent development of cricket in Wales largely conforms to the conventional pattern of the cricket and colonization process discussed in Chapter 3. As in India and the Caribbean, Welsh cricket was championed by the landed classes. Cricket was used as a vehicle for the Welsh gentry's anglophile aspirations, as an adjunct to social, business and political contacts. By means of a county-based administrative structure the Welsh were able to mirror the way the game was organized in England. Monmouthshire, Breconshire and Pembrokeshire had fielded teams by 1830. The Rebecca Riots and the Chartist movement led to an increase in the number of English troops in Wales in the first half of the nineteenth century which, Johnes (2005) argues, further stimulated the game. During the 1840s the Grammar School Act enabled the spread of the English educational model within Wales and the game became diffused to a broader social demographic including the urban working classes. Indeed, so common was the game that in the romanticized social history *How Green was my Valley*, Kate Olwen Pritchard referred to three co-existing cricket clubs in close proximity (Evans *et al.* 1999). Thus cricket in Wales developed on a number of fronts, stimulated by the usual combination of social elites, military and education.

These developments were largely a consequence of integration, for parallel to developments in political and economic circles Welsh cricket sought to become part of the English cultural infrastructure. The South Wales Club was formed in 1859 and conducted an annual London tour including games against the MCC and Surrey. In 1864 a young W.G. Grace followed the example of his elder brothers and played for Neath because the club was thought to play at a higher standard than Grace's local Gloucestershire club. Cricket had such a significant presence in Wales at this time that the sport provided the organizational basis for the development of what would become the Welsh national sport. Swansea and Cardiff rugby clubs were both formed out of cricket clubs, in 1873 and 1876 respectively (Johnes 2005). While Neath Cricket Club would fold in 1888, in the same year Glamorgan CCC was founded. In 1921 Glamorgan became the first and only non-English representative in the County Championship.

Integration with the English game had both enabling and constraining effects for Welsh cricket. The existence of a County Championship side enabled Welsh cricketers to be continually exposed to relatively skilful levels of play and thus ensured that they remained competitive. Llanelli-born all-rounder Emyr Davies played for 'England' in the 1920s, as did public school educated batsman Maurice Turnbull in the 1930s. In 1972 probably the most notable Welsh cricketer, the Swansea born, Cambridge University educated Tony Lewis, captained England on his test match debut (Lewis later became MCC President). Integration also ensured that a significant level of funding flowed into Welsh cricket (all counties are heavily reliant on central funding generated by the England men's team). However, integration also led to the suppression of a separate national identity voiced through the sport. A national structure for Welsh cricket – in the shape of the Welsh Schools Cricket Association, the Welsh Cricket Association, and an amateur Welsh national side – did not arise until the late 1960s/early 1970s (Lewis 1980). The curiously anonymous history of Welsh cricket is thus probably a consequence of a failure to either passionately embrace the game (as evident in the Caribbean) or to reject it outright (as in America). Rather, for much of the game's history the Welsh have appeared to be content for their game to quietly become subsumed by its English big brother.

Scotland

Scottish cricket appears to have even earlier origins. As noted in the Introduction, there are claims that the game was played by Scots c. 500 AD. More concretely Penman (1992) claims that records of cricket played at Perth date back to 1750, but a match played at Schaw Park, Alloa in 1785 is generally identified as Scotland's first cricket match (for example Mair 1980). The ground was owned by the Earl of Cathcart and both teams are believed to have been made up of aristocrats. The Scottish lowland aristocracy seem to have been particularly significant in the early playing of the game (Penman 1992). For instance, during the 1780s the Duke of Hamilton was said to have limited his business affairs due to playing cricket every afternoon (Burnett 2000). Mair argues that the aristocracy's motivation for playing the game was 'rather as a means of gambling than as a source of exercise' (1980: 510). Thus there is reason to suggest that the Scottish aristocracy took to cricket because they perceived themselves to be similar to, rather than because they were trying to assimilate with, their English counterparts.

In the early 1800s the game was popularized through a number of channels. The first two of these are familiar: education and military. Cricket became popular in educational establishments modelled on the English public school system, with evidence of the game being played at the Old High School, Edinburgh in 1817. Cricket teams were established at both Edinburgh and Glasgow universities in the 1830s and former pupil's clubs were established in the third quarter of the nineteenth century (Penman 1992). The military also played a significant role with some of the earliest clubs such as Kelso and Perth formed in garrison towns. But interest in the game was also stimulated by the commercial ventures of English travelling cricketers. In 1849 William Clarke's All-England XI began the more-or-less annual visits of professional touring teams. Just as it could be argued of W.G. Grace's place in English culture, so he became Scotland's first sporting celebrity following his tour to the country in 1872 (Burnett 2000). As in America the game is thought to have been spread by English workers who migrated to exploit various industrial opportunities.

The scale of the adoption of cricket in Scotland is consistent with the idea that to a considerable degree the Scots 'Englished themselves' (Kumar 2003a). Burnett claims that 'it seems as though every village had a team, in mining as well as in country districts' (2000: 58). Such games had more in common with cricket played in the Lancashire and Yorkshire leagues than the stereotype of village green cricket in England's rural south, reflecting Colls' contention that the North East of England had more in common with Glasgow or Cardiff than the South of England at this time (cited in British Council 2000). Nonetheless, Burnett (2000) estimates that there were 200 cricket clubs in Scotland in 1873. Cricket was particularly popular in central Scotland where public-school educated males dominated the game. In the Borders matches drew local and passionate crowds which some thought posed a danger to players and umpires. In Glasgow a number of works-based teams were formed. In Argyllshire the game blossomed under the patronage of the gentry (Jackson 1999). Teams in the North and the East of Scotland were marked by their relatively outspoken defence of amateurism in cricket. What was remarkable about the Scottish game therefore was its sheer diversity. As in England there were elements of class division and exclusion. As in England the game 'crossed the boundaries of ... class and locality' (Williams 1999: 183).

Such was its popularity that until the mid 1870s cricket drew 'as large a crowd as any sport, excepting horse racing' (Burnett 2000: 61). Tranter's (1987) data indicate that in the early 1880s one in twelve 15 to 29 year-old males were members of cricket clubs with only football more popular than cricket. As in Wales, cricket provided the organizational structure from which other sports developed. Hawick rugby club and Kilmarnock football club were formed when groups of cricketers bought balls as a means to keep fit in the winter. As noted above, the first football international was held at the West of Scotland Cricket Ground, Partick in 1872.

The relative independence of Scottish cricket can be seen in a number of ways. The first 'Scottish XI' played in 1865. In 1871 a crowd of between 3,000 and 4,000 watched Scotland play against an All England XI. In 1882 a Scottish team defeated Australia by 45 runs in a single innings exhibition match (Mair 1980). Organizationally Scottish cricket demonstrated considerable progress around the turn of the century. The Western Union and the North of Scotland League were formed in 1893, the Border League in 1895 and the Scottish Counties in 1903. In 1909 the Scottish Cricket Union (SCU) was founded.

Relative independence was to have distinct enabling and constraining consequences. While the formation of the SCU formalized the independence of Scottish cricket from its English counterpart, separation probably also retarded the development of the game. The absence of a counterpart to Glamorgan meant that Scottish cricket remained semi-detached from the mainstream first class game. Fixtures with English counties seem rarer for Scottish than for Welsh clubs until 1980 when Scotland was admitted into the Benson and Hedges Cup, a one-day competition for English county sides. Although Scotland beat an English county for the first time in 1959, and had their maiden victory over the MCC in 1961, the MCC withdrew first-class status from its annual fixture with Scotland in 1969. Scottish cricket was to decline in popularity – the 10,000 who saw Bradman in Aberdeen in 1948 being the last large cricket crowd in Scotland – at the same time (not necessarily because) football and rugby established stronger popular bases. There have been, however, a number of notable Scottish born cricketers who have played for England. In particular, Gregor MacGregor played for both the England cricket team and the Scottish rugby union team during the 1890s, the Oxford educated Ian Peebles played test matches for England in the 1920s and 1930s and Mike Denness captained England in the 1970s. Mention should also be made of the South African born Tony Grieg and the Indian born Douglas Jardine who both captained England by virtue of their Scottish born parents (Bairner and Malcolm 2010). Yet as Mair (1980: 512) argues, 'the fact that no team from Scotland competed in the English County Championship gave to the cricket world an image of Scotland as a non-cricketing country even though club cricket flourished in Scotland for over a hundred years'.

Ireland

Given that political conflict between Ireland and England has been more pronounced than between England and the other Celtic nations, and given the centrality of Gaelic games in Irish nationalist resistance, one would expect cricket to have been more vigorously resisted here than elsewhere in the British Isles. Not only is this *not* the case, for, 'Irish cricket boasts a lengthy heritage that compares favourably with any national side outside of England' (Gemmell 2010: 17), in marked contrast to historians' neglect of the Welsh game, Irish cricket has attracted a detailed and diverse body of research.

As in Scotland and Wales, cricket in Ireland has a long history marked by periods in which the game showed remarkable popularity. Cromwell's commissioners did ban a game called 'Krickett' in 1656 but Siggins (2005) suggests that they probably mistook it for a version of hurling due to the similarity of the 'bats' each employed at this time. Whilst right to question whether the banned game was what we now understand to be cricket (see Chapter 1) it is equally likely that this was not hurling in the modern sense either, but a folk game which combined elements of what would become separate modern sport forms. A similar logic should be applied to Rowland Bowen's (1970) claim that cricket may have originated in Ireland. Rather, it is most likely that folk forms of cricket were played in Ireland as they were across England prior to the game's codification by the London-based English aristocracy (see also Gemmell 2010). Indeed, as we saw earlier, in 1727 an Anglo-Irishman – Matthew Brodrick – was a central party to the oldest surviving set of cricket laws.

It is more widely held that the first cricket match played in Ireland took place in 1792 at Pheonix Park, Dublin, adjacent to the home of the Viceroy, Lord Westmoreland. The teams consisted of members of the British army garrison playing against 'All Ireland' for 1,000 guineas. The garrison side was captained by Lt-Colonel Lennox, a founding member of the MCC, while the All Ireland side included gentlemen such as Arthur Wesley, the future Duke of Wellington, Edward Cooke, under-secretary at Dublin Castle, Major Hobart, Secretary at War and a member of both the Irish and English Houses of Commons, and five further members of the Irish parliament (Gemmell 2010: 19). As in England, therefore, Ireland's parliamentarians were prominent in the development of Irish cricket. Evidence for the staging of this match comes from a scorecard and description published in the *Freeman's Journal*. The journal, which Hone (1955: 1) describes as 'the organ of the Catholic and popular party', stated that 'the game of Cricket is in England what that of Hurling is in Ireland'. Similar to the American case, therefore, there were people keen to define cricket as an English game. As in America, this did not make cricket 'foreign', more the province of a distinct, and hyphenated, group within the nation.

Again the themes of military, gentry and education are prominent in the development of cricket in Ireland. The 1798 rebellion increased the number of English troops in Ireland leading, for instance, to a Coldstream Guard recording the first century in Irish cricket (Siggins 2005; Bergin and Scott 1980). The gentry took a central organizing role. The first cricket club is thought to have been founded by Lord Dunlo in Ballinasloe, County Galway, in 1825. The Dublin Club (later the Pheonix Club) was founded in 1830 and also had aristocratic origins. The Lord Lieutenant, the 7th Earl of Carlisle, established the Viceregal Cricket Club in 1856 and built a cricket field on the grounds of his lodge. The gentry 'saw themselves not as colonists, but as Irishmen who enjoyed English civil rights, and partook in civil life' (Gemmell 2010: 19) and thus adopted the game as a way of demonstrating their identity and status. The game facilitated the commingling of English, Anglo-Irish and Irish political leaders. The most presitigious educational institutions also embraced the game. Cricket was played at Trinity College from 1820 (Gemmell 2010), while the Jesuit college, Conglowes Wood in County Kildare, played from the 1820s, albeit according to local rule variations (Siggins 2005). Dublin University played its first match in 1827, and a cricket club was formed there in 1842 (Sugden and Bairner 1993).

The impact of cricket on early nineteenth-century Irish society was thus substantial. Cricket was 'all the rage' in Dublin in 1830 (Siggins 2005: 14) and in 1835 the Irish press announced proposals to build a cricket ground in Dublin equivalent to Lord's in London (Garnham 2003). The game spread north with the establishment of the Belfast Cricket Club in 1830 and Lisburn Cricket Club in 1836. Some spoke of the 'civilizing' potential of cricket for the Irish populace (Garnham 2003), others recommended cricket as a vehicle for the gentry to mollify potential political resistance (Davis 1994). Cricket was even popular in the latter-day strongholds of Gaelic games such as Kilkenny (Bergin and Scott 1980).

In an interesting parallel to cricket in America, the *Oxford Companion to Irish History* states that by 1860 the game had probably become the most popular sport in Ireland (cited in Gemmell 2010). Garnham (2003) argues that cricket's popularity peaked around 1870. At this time the game was played across all 32 counties of Ireland (Gemmell 2010). Cricket could not have been so popular had it not been played amongst all social classes and different religious communities (Davis 1994, Hunt 2007). The enthusiasm for cricket amongst leading figures in the Irish nationalist movement such as John Redmond and Charles Stewart Parnell can be taken as one example of the depth with which the game penetrated Irish society. Quirkily, Dublin-born Samuel Beckett is the only Nobel laureate to appear in Wisden. Bateman refers to James Joyce's blurring of colonial binaries through his Anglicization of Irishness and Celticization of Englishness and cites the presence and use of cricket in the writings of James Joyce as an example of 'the power of a colonising culture to penetrate the consciousness and sub-consciousness of the colonised' (2009: 88). The blurred patchwork of relations in 'England's first Empire' (Kumar 2003a) is particularly evident in the relationship the Irish have with cricket.

Irish cricket had similarities with its counterparts in both Wales and Scotland. In a parallel to the Welsh experience, Irish cricket integrated with English cricket. As early as 1839 the Pheonix club travelled to Liverpool for a fixture and in 1851 I Zingari, the peripatetic touring team of Old Harrovians, played its first fixture in Dublin. The MCC played its first game in Ireland in 1853, the same year that the first English professional touring XI visited the country. In 1855 a fixture between 'Ireland' and the Gentlemen of England was played which the Irish Cricket Union would subsequently identify as Ireland's first representative game (Siggins 2005). A notable participant for the Gentlemen of England was R.A. Fitzgerald who, though English born, later played cricket for Ireland. He also became the MCC's first paid secretary. An Ireland team beat the MCC at Lord's in 1858 and again in 1862. Davis (1994) states that by the 1860s and 1870s Irish cricket was on the verge of being on equal playing terms with the English. Crucially, however, the English do not appear to have defined the Irish as a 'foreign' team as they did both Aboriginal and 'white' Australian teams.

Ireland's cricketers also imitated the English game in much the same way as their counterparts in Scotland did. The Pheonix club employed its first professional in 1835 and by 1881 Ireland's census identified 161 individuals as making a living from 'billiards, cricket and other games' (cited in Garnham 2003: 34). An Ireland touring XI was established in 1853, though in contrast to its English counterpart it was entirely amateur. An Irish equivalent of I Zingari, Na Shuler, was formed in 1863 and continued to play until 1914. In 1865, just one year after John Wisden founded what would become the 'bible' of cricket, the *Handbook of Cricket in Ireland* was established and would subsequently be published on an annual basis for fifteen years. In 1879 an Irish team travelled to America at the invitation of the St George's Cricket Club in New York and so successful was this trip that additional tours were arranged (Bergin and Scott 1980). This curious juxtaposition of partnership and parallel structure resonates with Kumar's (2003a: 76) view that 'the English were in Ireland, but Ireland was not English'. But in cricket the Irish were not *un*-English either. Ireland's defeats of the MCC were not defined as international losses because Ireland was not defined as a separate nation.

The 'failure' of cricket in the Celtic nations

A comparison of the development of cricket in these three regions adds an interesting dimension to the cricket and colonization literature, and in particular perceptions in the success or failure of cultural diffusion. While there is little empirical evidence to suggest that cricket 'failed' more significantly in

Ireland and Scotland than in Wales, only the analysts of the game in the former two nations have sought to explain its relative decline. This perhaps says more about the subsequent relative independence of Ireland and Scotland in cricketing terms at least than the popularity of cricket in Wales. Moreover, each account of 'failure' is also somewhat unconvincing. Each falls short, as parallel accounts of American cricket do (see Chapter 4), because they confine themselves to issues internal to the respective nations and eschew an account based on a wider set of interdependencies.

With respect to Scottish cricket, Mair (1980) and Burnett (2000) both suggest that climate and environment may have played a part in the game's demise. Penman (1992) rightly identifies this as fallacious, noting that the differences between the East and West coasts of Scotland are more significant than between the North and South of Britain. Penman also rejects explanations based on the decline of aristocratic patronage, cost of the game and the links between the game's format and Scottish national psyche. He therefore concludes that, 'the comparative failure of cricket in Scotland was caused primarily by competition from other sports, mainly, but not exclusively, football' (1992: 313). As we have seen (Chapter 4), this kind of 'sports space' argument, where one sport 'replaces' another because two are deemed unable to co-exist, is generally problematic. Football is also more popular than cricket in England but the two have been able to co-exist.

In the case of Ireland both Garnham (2003) and Davis (1994) give some credibility to the argument that cricket was adversely affected by the weather. Both also compare cricket to the popularity of other sports in Ireland, though neither accept a 'sport space' argument as convincing. Garnham, for instance, rejects the idea that the Irish preferred golf to cricket noting that golf was initially a winter sport in Ireland (and therefore did not directly compete with cricket) and that golf's rise in the 1890s came some time after the decline of cricket began. Davis considers why rugby union – like cricket, historically organized on a non-partition basis in Ireland – should become a more important vehicle for nationalist competition and suggests that there may be a connection between the relative violence of Irish resistance to British rule and the popularity of the relatively violent sport of rugby. Conversely, he argues, the relative absence of violence in Australian and Indian independence movements explains the popularity of cricket in these nations. This argument is, however, undermined by rugby's popularity in Australia, and indeed its status as the national sport of one of the more anglophile post-colonial nations, New Zealand.

Finally both Davis and Garnham, like Penman in relation to Scotland, challenge the importance of a 'national psyche' or character in the rejection of the game. Davis (1994) notes that the enthusiasm for the game amongst Irish-Australians suggests that there was nothing inherently problematic for Irish people about playing cricket. Garnham's (2003) position is more sophisticated for it places greater emphasis on *perceptions* of national character. Garnham suggests, therefore, that it was the *idea* that cricket was fundamentally English, an idea widely propagated by the English, which led to Irish disillusionment with the game. Indeed, it is counter-intuitive that the Irish rejected cricket because it did not fit with their 'national psyche' because it seems more likely that 'psyches' would converge in a context of more frequent Anglo-Irish interaction.

More compelling, but ultimately still flawed, are arguments which locate cricket's demise to the broadening of class and religious differences in Ireland. Garnham notes that 'the most recurrent theme' (2003: 32) in accounts of the failure of cricket in Ireland is that it was a casualty of the Land War which saw the propertied classes previously active in sponsoring the game in rural communities withdraw from social interaction with agrarian workers. Garnham points out that a problem with this thesis is that such patronage of cricket was being withdrawn some time before the game's popularity peaked in Ireland. Garnham also critiques the assumption that the GAA played a significant role in cricket's demise on similar grounds, noting again that the popularity of cricket had begun to wane prior to the GAA's proclamation about 'foreign' sports. To this we can add the evidence from studies which have revealed that cricket was as popular in GAA strongholds as anywhere else in the thirty-two counties. For instance, Bracken (2004) has charted the popularity of cricket clubs in Tipperary, and O'Dwyer (2006) argues that the popularity of cricket in Kilkenny peaked in 1896, at which point there were fifty teams in the county. For Hunt (2005), the steady growth of cricket in Westmeath throughout the 1880s and 1890s challenges the traditional perception of Irish cricket as an elitist activity.

Rather, our understanding of the 'failure' of cricket in the Celtic nations can be advanced via three key considerations. First, and akin to the arguments relating to cricket and American national character, it may be that the relative equality in social status – what Kaufman and Patterson (2005) would describe as a homophilious relationship – meant that the Irish both resented and were able to reject conceptions of English moral superiority. The point here rests on a subtle distinction. An interesting characteristic of Irish sport more generally was that although the motivation for the establishment of the GAA was the rejection of English cultural forms, the organization stridently defended the underpinning ethos of English sport, amateurism. In other words, the Irish were close enough to the English to wholeheartedly accept the *principles,* but not the belief that the English held a monopoly over such 'virtuous' behaviour. In contrast to rugby union where the zero-tolerance of professionalism was clear cut, cricket operated a complex and in many ways less consistent accommodation and subordination of professionals (Dunning and Sheard 1976). This may explain why the Irish did not continue such a strong engagement with cricket, but also why cricket continued to flourish as a recreational game in rural areas where the issue of professionalism simply did not arise. Second, though this remains a matter of conjecture, one has to think that the unstandardized nature of cricket in England, and in particular debates over legitimate bowling, had an impact on the game in Celtic nations. As the American example shows, it would be wrong to simply assume that the game being played in these Celtic nations was uniformly that codified and advocated by the MCC. All existing accounts of the demise of cricket in Ireland and Scotland are based on this flawed premise. Third, these accounts also fail to reflect the fluidity of relations between different nationalities. Cricket's popularity waned in these nations because the permeability of English cricket structures, the 'blurred patchwork' of social relations (Kumar 2003a), enabled some aspects of the game in each of the Celtic nations to be subsumed. Be it in terms of Glamorgan CCC or individuals of Celtic origin such as R.A. Fitzgerald and Gregor MacGregor, the English incorporated aspects of British and Irish cricket. Indeed, amongst the ten paid MCC secretaries since Fitzgerald there is Irish born Rowen Rait Kerr, as well as an 'Aird', a 'Findlay' and a 'Griffiths'. Cricket may not have been the 'superglue' of Britain as it was of the Empire, but neither has it ever been the irrelevance that its absence from work on sport and British national identities suggests it to be. In the Empire cricket diffused most effectively where its Englishness was most explicit and its character building properties most celebrated. In Britain it became most well-established where it's nationalism was most anonymous.

Celtic cricket and colonization

What does the development of cricket in the Celtic nations tell us about cricket and processes of colonization? In each of these accounts we can identify certain commonalities with the broader pattern as well as locally specific variations. A common theme is that in each nation there is evidence to suggest that the game was played so early that it would not subsequently be 'diffused' in the conventional sense of that term. Particularly in Ireland and Scotland, we see cricket-like folk games which had similar antecedents to, but emerged independently of, the game codified by aristocrats in London. Second, while the social elite were prominent in the organization of cricket in each of the three nations, there are interesting and subtle differences to be observed. For example, both the Irish and Welsh gentry took to the game as a way of assimilating with the English and thus fostering closer and more cooperative relations, but the Scottish aristocracy appear to have *modelled* their behaviour on their English counterparts, rather than sought assimilation through the sport. In some respects the links between the English aristocracy and their Irish counterparts seem to have been stronger than with the aristocracy in Wales or in Scotland. A third common theme is the role of educational institutions in developing the game, though again this includes some notable local variation. In both Ireland and Scotland it was the elite schools which were prominent in the early organization of the game, whereas the Grammar Schools were more significant in Wales. Similarly the universities in Ireland and Scotland were notable early founders of cricket clubs, whereas in Wales they were not. Fourthly there is the role of the military. While cricket playing English troops are identified in each of the nations, their role is more significant in Scotland and Ireland reflecting the greater (or later) militarization of these particular 'colonies'. Finally only in relation to Ireland was a discourse of the civilizing mission employed, and thus the potential of cricket for reforming the behavioural norms to be more in line with English expectations voiced.

But perhaps the most striking finding from this comparison is that the cricket in each nation should take its own distinctive route. Whereas in Wales the process was essentially one of *integration* into the English mainstream, in Scotland we see the greater assertion of *independence*. In 1909 Scotland became the first Celtic nation to have a national cricket association, coincidentally (or not) the same year as the ICC was founded. The Irish had proposed their own national association in 1890 but the move only came to fruition in 1923 shortly after the establishment of the Irish Free State. The Welsh waited until 1969. The Irish case is the most complex of all, but primarily reveals an attempt at *replication*. A model of cricket developed that was, for a brief time, as close a replica of the English model as cricket anywhere else in the British Empire.

This level of replication extended to Ireland not simply being a recipient, but also an instigator of the cricket and colonization process. Ironically, given the nation's subsequent independence from Britain, Ireland would have a greater impact than any other Celtic nation on shaping the imperial game. Initially it was the entrepreneurship of the Pheonix cricket professional, Charles Lawrence, which was fundamental to this. Lawrence epitomizes the fluidity of movement and identity which cricket enabled within both Britain and the Empire. One of Lawrence's early cricketing achievements was to take all ten wickets for Scotland against an England XI in 1849. On leaving Dublin's Pheonix club he travelled to Australia with the 1861 English touring side. He stayed in Australia and played for New South Wales until returning as manager of the touring Aboriginal team in 1868. While Ashley Mallet has argued that Lawrence could be described as the Father of Australian cricket, Siggins (2005: 25) adds, 'and more than any other, he was probably the Father of Irish cricket too'.

The impact of Irish migrants was also more significant on the global development of cricket than any other non-English group. Siggins (2005: 20) claims that more than 120 Irishmen have played first class cricket around the world (see also Bairner 2009). Their qualitative impact is perhaps even more remarkable than their sheer number. Tom Horan and John Blackham, who played for Australia in the first ever test against England in 1877 and the historic Ashes match at the Oval in 1882, both hailed from Ireland (Gemmell 2010). Leland Hone, who kept wicket for England against Australia in 1879 was born in Dublin. As Kibberd observes, 'only a rudimentary thinker would deny that the Irish experience is at once postcolonial and post-Imperial' (1997: 97).

Conclusion: Cricket and contemporary identities in the Celtic nations

This chapter began by identifying the paradox in cricket's status as both the quintessential English game and the game, par excellence, of the British Empire. We can also now see that far from being an irrelevance to the broader diffusion of the game, cricket in the Celtic nations played a fundamental though far from predictable role in the wider process of British imperialism. Therefore the resolution of this issue rests in the traditional elision of Britishness and Englishness. For while cricket is, on the one hand, the sport most closely associated with Englishness, ironically it is also the game in which the separate British and Irish nations are most effectively forged into one (Bairner and Malcolm 2010). While it seems that there were moves to establish international fixtures between England and Scotland and Ireland (though tellingly not Wales) the failure to recognize the separate national status of the Celtic cricketers deprived the peoples of these countries of the opportunity to forge a separate national identity through such sporting contests. In some ways the Irish cricketers preceded their Australian counterparts in defeating England at Lord's by some thirty years, but that victory occurred in a particular social context in which it simply was not defined as an international fixture. We return to this issue in the book's Conclusion.

Cricket in the Celtic nations has experienced something of a renaissance in recent years and this provides a convenient segue to *Globalizing Cricket's* final chapters. In large part Celtic cricket has been stimulated by the ICC's explicit globalization agenda. One consequence of attempts to incorporate Associate and Affiliate members of the ICC within the playing programmes of full member states has been to provide greater publicity for the exploits of countries where the game has traditionally been assumed to have a marginal cultural significance. The 2007 ICC Cricket World Cup in the Caribbean was unique in that the event included representative teams from England (and therefore Wales), Ireland and Scotland. Ireland's defeat of England in the 2011 ICC World Cup provided the former with perhaps the nation's most significant cricketing victory to date.

The renaissance of Celtic cricket is also a rather more unintended consequence of the reformation of the administration of the 'English' game. On 1 January 1997 the ECB was established as the single 'national' governing body for all cricket in England and Wales (ECB 1997). The board, located at

Lord's, assumed the responsibilities that had previously been carried out by the Test and County Cricket Board (TCCB), the National Cricket Association and the Cricket Council (which themselves had acquired control from the MCC as the English/British national governing body for cricket in 1968). The launch document for the ECB made no reference to cricket in Wales or of relations between the ECB and its Scottish or Irish counterparts. The move to an overtly national organization – the first governing body of cricket to have 'England' in the title – became a source of tension. Those in Welsh cricket circles spoke of the reinstatement of the silent 'W' (Harris 2006), but in truth the silence of the 'W' had only become apparent through the vocalization of the 'E'.

The fluidity of cricket migrants between Ireland and England has also stimulated awareness of national identity issues. In 2007 Ed Joyce became the first cricketer to play for two nations in the same competition, helping Ireland qualify before achieving residential qualification to play for England in the World Cup in the Caribbean. The Irish public were reported to have 'jammed radio phone-ins to voice their disapproval' on Joyce's selection for England (*Scotsman* 30 March 2007), and it was reported that Joyce's father supported Ireland against an England team which included his son (*Sun* 29 March 2007). Joyce himself seemed more sanguine, though he recalled how strange it was to put on an England shirt because he had been used to 'the green and blue of Ireland' (*Independent on Sunday,* 11 March 2007). Since this time not only has Joyce returned to play for Ireland, but Dublin-born Eoin Morgan has been selected as captain of an England Twenty20 side playing Ireland in Dublin. The selection was met with a pragmatic response from Irish cricket administrators and in post-match interviews Morgan thanked the Dublin public for their warm welcome and support.

Cricket in the Celtic nations has also been stimulated by the growth of Celtic nationalism, but it is important not to over-emphasize this. While there is some validity in Johnes' argument that Glamorgan has come to be seen 'as much representatives of Wales as they were of a county that was actually abolished in 1974' (Johnes 2005: 115) due to a more general growth of an anti-Englishness in Welsh sport, it is contentious whether this nationalist rivalry has ever been requited, and therefore fully consummated. It is also the case that Scottish and Welsh (and perhaps Irish) hostility to the England cricket team is qualitatively different to that expressed towards the England football or rugby team (see also Potter 1999). For instance, while a campaign to establish Wales as an associate member of the ICC has been ongoing since 2002 and has attracted cross-party political support, the integration of Welsh cricket has also advanced with the first 'England' home test match staged in Cardiff in 2009. As Bairner and Malcolm (2010: 198) note, 'this raised interesting questions. Why would a national team play its home games in another country except in unusual circumstances such as civil unrest or as a result of being penalised for unacceptable behaviour by fans?'. Indeed in the early years of the twenty-first century the Welsh were particularly active within the ECB. From 2002 to 2007, Tredegar-born David Morgan was Chair of the ECB and in 2005 Cardiff-born Hugh Morris was appointed Deputy Chief Executive and later Managing Director of the England (men's) cricket team. The Glamorgan captain and England off-spinner Robert Croft has publicly talked about the potential identity conflict of being Welsh and playing cricket for England but reconciled the issue by perceiving 'England' as representative of a supra-national team, the equivalent of playing rugby union for the British Lions or for Europe in golf's Ryder Cup.[2]

That said, we see that contemporary developments have clearly altered the relationship between cricket and national identities in the Celtic nations. What this brief discussion illustrates is that the globalizing of cricket impacts upon the relationship between the English and other nationals, between the English and emigrants who have taken the opportunities open post-colonialism and subsequently settled in England, and ultimately on the way in which the English view themselves and others. These issues will be developed in the next three chapters.

7

Cricket and Diasporic Identities in Post-Imperial Britain

One of the most notable features of cricket in post-imperial Britain is the incorporation of diverse minority ethnic groups. When West Indian batsman Brian Lara achieved a world record test match score of 375 he did so against an England side which contained the British Afro-Guyanese player Chris Lewis, British Indo-Guyanese player Mark Ramprakash, and from which the British Jamaican fast bowler Devon Malcolm had recently been dropped. Consequently Lara,

> touched the collective brain and heart of a dispersed people and fuelled their unity and hope ... the spectacle of cricket had provoked a sudden new regional pride and confidence ... (but) the Caribbean was unequivocally a part of English cricket too. Like the English health and transport systems, it could not function effectively without the essential Caribbean contribution. Lara's achievement had also been integrally linked to the diaspora ... Now the Caribbean was on both sides. (Searle 1995: 32)[1]

This chapter seeks to examine the relationship between cricket and identity in diasporic communities living in Britain. Again we see the importance of cricket's apparently paradoxical position as both the game of (British) Empire yet simultaneously the sport which most closely resonates with notions of Englishness. In this instance cricket provides a particularly fruitful case study of the multifarious ways in which identities are created, contested and negotiated. The role of cricket within diasporic communities is also fundamental to an assessment of the role of cricket in shaping contemporary identities in Britain.

Conceptualizing diaspora

The concept of diaspora has had an increasing impact on studies of race, nation, migration and identity in recent years. Prior to 1990 diaspora was largely used with reference to the Jewish and African experience of geographical resettlement which was almost always 'forced' (Kalra *et al.* 2005: 8). In this context diaspora was a descriptive term which 'referred to displaced communities of people who have been dislocated from their native homeland through migration, immigration, or exile' (Braziel and Mannur 2003: 1).

As the application of diaspora has broadened to encompass a wider range of peoples, so its theoretical purchase has increased, moving from a simple descriptive tool to a concept used to capture a multi-faceted and fluid social process (Kalra *et al.* 2005). Concomitantly, diaspora has developed from a term centrally concerned with migration, movement and geography, to being an area of study characterized by a concern with identity construction and contestation. In these more recent and more theoretically sophisticated analyses, diaspora has come to refer to 'the doubled relationship or dual loyalty that migrants, exiles, and refugees have to places – their connections to the space they currently occupy and their continuing involvement with "back home"' (Lavie and Swedenburg 1996: 14).

There are a number of reasons why diaspora has increasingly come to be preferred to terms such as migrant and migration. Many of the people whom we now describe as diasporic are not in fact migrants, but the off-spring – the second, third generations, etc. – of those who formerly experienced migration. Second, the term migrant reproduces nation-centric sociology, where nation and society are unproblematically equated and analysis is confined to the former. Third, migrant is to be rejected because, when used as a euphemism for 'not from this place', it marginalizes, racializes and 'Others' particular people. '"Immigration" has become, *par excellence*, the name of race, a new name but one which is functionally equivalent to the old appellation' (Balibar and Wallerstein 1991: 222). Fourth, migration implies a one-off event – an act of dis-/re-location – and a one-way process in which older affiliations are severed to be replaced by new affiliations. In contemporary societies migrations are more commonly multiple and multi-directional.

A central contribution of the development of diasporic studies has thus been to disrupt the traditionally held view that the links between place, culture and identity are immutable. Where previously it was assumed that there exists some strong bond between the nation and national identity, diaspora studies have highlighted that these connections are far from straightforward. But not only can diasporas be conceived of as 'Janus-faced', looking both forwards to where a person was and backwards to where they had come from, increasingly focus has been placed on the essential hybridity of diasporic people (Braziel and Mannur 2003: 9). Building on Anderson's (1983) notion of the nation as an 'imagined community', Appadurai (2003: 31) suggests that we consider *imagined worlds*; that is to say, 'the multiple worlds which are constituted by the historically situated imaginations of persons and groups spread across the globe'. Diaspora reflects the impact of both the local and the global on peoples' conceptions of self; a 'mutliplicity of belongings and identities' (Kalra *et al.* 2005: 16). For example, as Paul Gilroy (2003) argued via the notion of 'The Black Atlantic', Black British diasporic identity is a product of the intermingling of Caribbean, North American and British cultural styles.

The hybrid identities which characterize diasporic communities do not necessarily entail a postmodernist fragmentation of identity, in which 'culture becomes a free-floating mosaic, its pieces constantly in flux' (Lavie and Swedenburg 1996: 3). Rather, they are always and everywhere rooted in power relations – in political, economic and cultural processes – and must be viewed as the products of 'a long history of confrontations between unequal cultures and forces' (Lavie and Swedenburg 1996: 9). For instance, the hybrid identities of the Black and South Asian diasporas in Britain are rooted in the experiences of the British Empire. These experiences provide a set of social relations which both enable and constrain the contemporary construction of diasporic identity. Cricket, as we will see, is integral to this.

Use of the concept of diaspora allows us to develop different frameworks for understanding identity formation. For Stuart Hall (1990), diaspora consciousness is produced through difference, and this difference is most clearly marked in contrast to homogenizing notions of the nation. A stereotyped national culture is defined (in this case Englishness) against which the diaspora's 'pervasive image of otherness' is constructed (Burdsey 2010a: 316). '[C]ulture becomes a euphemism for "race" as, despite the changing nomenclature, cultures are interpreted as being fixed and discrete' (Burdsey 2006: 15). Symptomatic of this process is the development of 'new racism' (Barker 1981) which leads minority ethnic groups to be excluded not solely on the basis of race, but on the intersection of race, culture and nationality. The 'emphasis on culture allows nations and race to fuse. Nationalism and racism become so closely identified that to speak of the nation is to speak automatically in racially exclusive terms' (Gilroy 1993, cited in Burdsey 2006). Diasporas, therefore, do not lead to the disappearance of national identities; indeed as we will see sometimes quite the opposite. They may entail either the reinforcement of a sense of national belonging or even generate a new or more unified sense of nationhood within the diaspora than has previously been evident in the 'homeland'. While diaspora consciousness has most commonly been identified in cultural configurations such as music, film and literature, and while the use of diaspora in the study of sport is less common (Burdsey (2006) and Carrington (2010) are notable exceptions), it is no less applicable.

While the concept of diaspora has been embraced and advanced by writers more influenced by cultural studies and/or postmodernist or poststructuralist ideas about the fluidity of social relations, the main themes of diaspora resonate with the key ideas of Elias's sociology. Like Elias's sociology, diaspora is inspired by multidisciplinarity. Like Elias's sociological theory, the concept of diaspora focuses on the importance of process and the relational construction of identity. Diaspora is premised on the assumption that geographies, nationalities and ethnicities are socially constructed. But Elias's historical sensitivity alerts us to the fact that while the use of the concept of diaspora is relatively new, and indeed has changed in meaning in recent times, the human processes which it describes are not (Brubaker 2005). As we saw in the previous chapter, colonization entails many of the same features encapsulated in diaspora, including multiple movements, dual loyalties, and hybrid identities. What perhaps separates these two analyses is relative power. That is to say, while diaspora may be preferred to 'race', it continues to bear the legacy of inequality and discrimination which largely inspires the sociological study of race. Logically, however, it does not have to do so.

This chapter employs the concept of diaspora to structure and interpret the cricketing experiences of the Black and South Asian diasporas in Britain. The examination of the multiple ways in which British minority ethnic groups engage with cricket suggests that the game plays a unique role in the construction of diaspora consciousness. Through these various cricketing experiences we can clearly see the dynamism, hybridity and contextuality of identity construction. In illustrating the multiple ways in which these multiple communities culturally engage with cricket we can begin to understand the game's social significance in contemporary Britain.

The Caribbean diaspora and cricket spectatorship

In 1950, inspired by Sonny Ramadhin and Alf Valentine, the West Indies side beat England at Lord's for the first time. The reaction of the English press to this defeat was characterized by 'magnanimity and unthreatened paternalism' and a certain amount of pleasure that the 'imperial children (had) come partially of age' (Wagg 2005: 183). Contemporary journalists commented upon, and generally welcomed, the 'pleasantly strange' scenes of victory celebration at Lord's (cited in Wagg 2005: 183). The West Indians were congratulated on the joyous and skilful way in which they played the game. As we saw in Chapter 3, by implication the English could be self-congratulatory about the success of the imperial civilizing mission.

But the victory was also 'celebrated by elated West Indians throughout the Caribbean and Britain' (Searle 1990: 35). From this point in time, West Indian supporters became remarkable for both their number and the style of their support, particularly at the Oval in London, but to a greater or lesser extent at all of England's test match grounds. Whilst cricket crowds in the Caribbean were portrayed as rather more threatening (major crowd disorder incidents occurred in Georgetown, Guyana in 1953–54, Port of Spain, Trinidad in 1960 and Kingston, Jamaica in 1968), West Indian spectators at matches in England continued to be seen as carnivalesque and fun-loving. Following the 1963 series in England, a *Daily Mail* journalist suggested that, 'West Indian crowds seemed to have achieved as much as Frank Worrell's players ... (turning test cricket) into something everybody could enjoy' (cited in Wagg 2005: 191). Supporters from the Caribbean diaspora were juxtaposed against what Paxman (1999) calls their 'curiously passionless' English counterparts.

Initial experiences of day-to-day living in Britain entailed a significant disjuncture for the self-image of Caribbean immigrants. On arrival in Britain the subtle skin shade distinctions which had operated in the Caribbean (see Chapter 5) were rendered meaningless, with the British population perceiving black-skinned immigrants as a monolithic mass. The experiences of British racism led immigrants from the Caribbean to put aside their 'Island chauvinism' (James 1993: 240), and increasingly develop a shared Caribbean identity. Whilst almost inevitably such new identities were not clearly defined, the English 'helped Afro-Caribbean people in Britain "*feel* West Indian" and "*feel* black"' (James 1993: 244. Emphasis in original). This changing sense of identity was fuelled by cricket attendance. Television coverage of England-West Indies tests provided one of the few graphic depictions of the presence of large numbers of Black people in Britain and further projected an image of unity within the Black diaspora. Thus the visits of the West Indian cricket team not only served as one of the few forums in which a Caribbean identity could be demonstrated and celebrated, they acted as a centripetal force to create a greater sense of unity in the Black diaspora.

While expressions of Caribbean diaspora identity were initially received in a largely convivial, albeit inquisitive, manner, West Indian supporters would subsequently become depicted not simply as different or 'other' to English cricket spectatorship norms, but as intrusive and threatening. The 1976 West Indian tour was a turning point, for by the end of the summer – during which, it will be remembered, the legitimacy of the team's playing tactics were widely scrutinized – English cricket administrators asked the West Indies captain Clive Lloyd to address the behaviour of the team's supporters. Spectators were urged to be quieter on the grounds that noise levels, like the bowling which inspired them, were considered to be 'intimidatory' (Wagg 2005: 195). Subsequently, throughout the 1970s and 80s, 'complaints about the "endless din", "mindless cacophony", "inescapable racket" of the West Indian fans ... became commonplace on "Test Match Special" and in the columns of *The Times* and *Telegraph*' (Marqusee 1998: 171).[2] In 1984 it was claimed that supporters had assaulted England's Jonathon Agnew as they ran on to the pitch in celebration. 'In 1950 and 1963, West Indian supporters celebrated; in 1976 they made intimidating noise and left debris; now, in 1984, they "attacked"' (Wagg 2005: 198).

The stigmatization of spectator behaviour was augmented by substantive regulation. From the 1980s restrictions were imposed on the use of musical instruments (especially drums, klaxons, whistles) as well as on the display of flags and banners. The amount of alcohol that could be brought into cricket grounds was restricted, and bars were closed at various points in the day. Whilst the decade had opened with West Indian fans proudly proclaiming the 5-0 victory over England as a 'Blackwash', the decade ended with many commenting on the 'notable absence' of Black spectators at English test grounds. For Searle the motivation was quite sinister; 'the British cricketing establishment and its watchdogs were attacking expressions of the enthusiasm, loyalty and wit of the Caribbean people' (1996: 49). Marqusee likewise suggests that the message for West Indian supporters in England was clear: 'unless they behave like "English" people, they are not welcome at English cricket grounds' (1998: 171). This process reached its zenith (or nadir) when in 1990 Norman Tebbit, a leading member of Margaret Thatcher's Conservative government, announced his 'cricket test' which effectively used the support for national cricket teams other than England as the basis on which members of minority ethnic groups in Britain could be castigated for 'failing' to assimilate into British society. As Kalra *et al.* (2005: 36) argue, the 'Tebbit test', 'can be understood as a reactionary response to diasporic consciousness on the part of an overtly coercive nation-state unable to comprehend the openness of diaspora and the practical consequences of transnational, post-imperial movement'.

Cricket had thus contributed to the creation of a Caribbean identity amongst the Black diaspora; it provided a forum in which these identity 'games' could be played out. But in juxtaposing supporter styles and politicizing diasporic identities, cricket subsequently became a mechanism for the construction of exclusionary barriers which ultimately reduced this collective sense of self. Indeed Crabbe and Wagg (2000: 82) note that, more recently, West Indian sports fans have been discouraged by 'the cultural insularity and contingent racial inclusions' that characterize English cricket and have consequently identified more closely with the soccer teams of the individual islands, most notably Jamaica and Trinidad and Tobago. The history of 'othering' and regulation have therefore effectively reduced the potential of cricket to be a forum for the expression of both West Indian and Caribbean diasporic identities.

The South Asian diaspora and cricket spectatorship

This backdrop of restrictive regulation of West Indian support and the marked decline in the number of Black British cricket spectators meant that there was an underlying irony to the marketing of the 1999 ICC Cricket World Cup in England. Billed as a 'Carnival of Cricket', images of young Black males dominated publicity materials. Steel bands and calypso music were used at the media launch to bolster this impression. According to Crabbe and Wagg, 'carnival (was) invoked as a "non-British" cultural signifier' (2000: 71) in an attempt to broaden the appeal of the tournament and hence tap into a (assumed) latent demand for cricket within Britain's minority ethnic communities.

The irony was compounded by the major development in spectatorship trends which emerged during the tournament, for it was in 1999 that public attention began to focus on the presence and the passion of cricket fans from the South Asian diaspora. Commentators were struck by the degree to which the games involving Pakistan, India, Bangladesh and Sri Lanka seemed to be dominated by supporters from the South Asian diaspora whose spectatorship style, like that of the West Indian spectators fifty years earlier, was performative, celebratory and conscious of national identities. It did however have distinctly South Asian characteristics. When Pakistan won the 1992 ICC Cricket World Cup, British Pakistanis 'brought Bradford city centre to a standstill' (Williams 2001: 178). The emergence of a group of British Indian cricket supporters at the 2003 ICC Cricket World Cup in South Africa was dubbed the Bharat Army (Burdsey 2010b). When India won the inaugural Twenty20 World Cup in 2007 impromptu celebrations led to street closures in Leicester. For these fans 'games represented an important cultural space in which to celebrate both a love of cricket and distinctive elements of their ethnic identities' (Crabbe and Wagg 2000: 77).

Why did cricket spectatorship become central to South Asian diaspora consciousness much later than it had for the Caribbean diaspora? Although there are dangers in falsely universalizing British Asian experiences, Valiotis' (2009) discussion of the British Pakistani community may have wider relevance. Valiotis argues that cricket only became popular among British Pakistanis during the 1970s as the earliest migrants had 'lacked a strong consciousness of the concepts of nationhood' (2009: 1795). Most first generation migrants identified more strongly with their home regions and conceived of cricket as a recreation rather than as a vehicle for nationalism. Increased governmental interest and funding for the game in Pakistan, as well as some notable competitive successes, combined with a sense that a permanent return to Pakistan had become increasingly unlikely. Cricket was appropriated as a nation-building tool by Pakistani politicians, but its adoption by members of the Pakistani and Muslim diasporas in Britain was more complex. Among these groups cricket 'is not just a statement of defiance, nor is it about cultural exclusivity, it is a narrative for integration into English society as well as an additional discourse in the debate about Pakistani national identity' (Valiotis 2009: 1796). It may also be the case that changes to English cricket spectatorship, described in detail in the next chapter, helped legitimize the more vociferous expression of (Pakistani) national identity at English cricket grounds.

That cricket should come to play such a role in identity construction for the South Asian diaspora is no accident. Werbner (1996) has argued that cricket occupies a peculiar space for young Pakistani males in particular. For diasporic communities a challenge of living in the West is how to preserve and reproduce identities in ways which are not solely linked to high culture and traditions (for example through religion) but which transcend and transgress traditional Muslim communities. Cricket is an activity which is 'not specifically Islamic' but which 'mesh(es) with Islamic traditions' (Werbner 1996: 95).

As a sport with a colonial history which predates the formation of the Pakistan state, cricket is seen by elders in this community as a legitimate alternative to Islamic high culture and thus a permissible activity for the diaspora's youth. It provides 'an expression of controlled masculine aggression and competitiveness ... a popular expression of modern Pakistani nationalism and friendly competition' (1996: 94–5). 'Through support of the national team ... young British Pakistanis express their love of both cricket and the home country, along with their sense of alienation and disaffection from the British society' (1996: 101). But in using cricket in this way the diaspora also utilizes a cultural form which engages the emotions of white English/ British communities. Clearly distinct from, and in some senses oppositional to, English cricket spectatorship styles, supporting the Pakistan cricket team provides an escape from the restrictive normative codes of English cricket (Crabbe and Wagg 2000). There have certainly been racist and Islamaphobic incidents involving England cricket supporters and those from the Asian diaspora (Crabbe and Wagg 2000; Marqusee 1998; Williams 2001), but if one compares them for example to a sport like football, we can see that Valiotis' citation of 'numerous disturbances and confrontations' (2009: 1804) exaggerates the problem. While fundamentally expressing the hybridity of diasporic experience, ultimately 'When it comes to cricket, it seems, blood is thicker than the English rain' (Werbner 1996: 104).

Diasporic identities and grassroots cricket

Spectatorship at international cricket matches may be the most public forum for the expression of diaspora consciousness, but participating in the grassroots level of the game has provided more continuous opportunities for the generation of social identities. While continued engagement with cricket is not prohibited by migration to countries where cricket is a culturally marginal sport (see, for instance, Joseph O'Neill's (2008) fictional portrayal of the role of cricket in diasporic communities in New York in *Netherland*), settlement in Britain means that continued participation can as easily be seen as evidence of similitude as an act of separation. However while the game itself is not perceived as 'other' in this context, contestation over the practices and rituals performed as part of the game has emerged. In such contexts the hybridity and complexity that diasporic consciousness entails, are particularly prominent. It is in this context also that the most graphic fusion of culture, nation and race is evident.

A number of research projects in the late 1990s focussed on the role of race relations in grassroots cricket in Britain (for overviews see Malcolm 2002b and Williams 2001). Notable among these were the work of Greenfield and Osborn (1996) examining cricket league regulations for migrant or 'overseas' players, Long *et al.*'s (1997) examination of racism in local league cricket in Yorkshire, and MacDonald and Ugra's (1998) investigation of equal opportunities and cricket cultures in Essex and East London. The latter two studies highlighted elements of institutional and cultural separation within cricket. Examples of racial inequality and minority ethnic exclusion included experiences of racial abuse, instances when Black and Asian cricketers perceived themselves to be discriminated against in club cricket (i.e. the problems encountered trying to arrange fixtures against 'established' clubs with predominantly white memberships), and an inability to gain access to certain leagues or competitions.

A perception that different ethnic groups played the game in culturally specific ways was identified as the basis of much of this exclusion. Players at predominantly white clubs aspired to a mythical and monolithic stereotype of English 'village green' cricket, the core of which had been 'invented' in the nineteenth century by Nyren, Pycroft, etc. (see Chapter 2). They critiqued the cricketing cultures of the diasporas which included partisan support and/or eschewed alcohol-based post-match socializing. The regulation of migrant and overseas players in semi-professional cricket leagues was similarly identified as motivated by 'attempts to preserve part of the fast disappearing rural idyll' (Greenfield and Osborn 1996: 288). Black and South Asian players were thus depicted as 'other', and their presence was seen to undermine this ideal of cricket and Englishness.

The central consequence of the racist and discriminatory experiences of members of the Black and South Asian diasporas is to 'naturalis(e) social formation in terms of a racial-cultural logic of belonging' (Solomos and Back 1996: 19). Racial inequality became rationalized as a product of voluntarily adopted cultural difference. 'Caribbean' cricket clubs were formed in many communities as were leagues which sought to cater for South Asians, the most notable of which was probably the Quaid-I-Azam league catering for British Pakistani cricket teams. Cricket therefore also reveals the 'complexity and contingent nature' of ethnicities in contemporary Britain (Crabbe and Wagg 2000: 86). A more detailed picture of the impact of this process of 'othering' on diaspora consciousness can be illustrated through three further studies of minority ethnic participation in grass roots cricket.

First, based on a study of the Caribbean Cricket Club (CCC) in the Chapeltown area of Leeds, Carrington (1998) suggests that cricket has acted as a focal point for the broader Black community in an otherwise hostile white environment. Members enjoyed the 'relaxed and secure' setting which the club provided (1998: 285) and the cricket pitch and clubhouse acted as physical markers of the club's, and therefore the community's, existence. Consequently, the actions and attitudes of club members came to be seen as indicative of the Chapeltown African-Caribbean community more generally. It was important to members, for instance, that their facilities were clean and in good order for, they felt, visitors would use this as a gauge of standards of cleanliness within the broader community.

The club also came to be seen as a symbolic marker of the Black diaspora *per se*, with opposing players viewing CCC as in some way connected or akin to the West Indian test team. Matches became racially charged as victories by white teams came to be seen as revenge for English defeats (Carrington's research took place in the immediate aftermath of West Indian test dominance). Conversely members of CCC viewed winning as 'a way of challenging the logic and efficacy of the racism they faced in their day-to-day lives' (1998: 291). Victories on the field of play thus became a form of cultural resistance. Through cricket the Black masculine identities which have largely been subordinated to white masculine identities through the experiences of colonialism and post-colonial discrimination (Mercer 1994) were bolstered and strengthened. Though such fillips for racial and masculine pride may only be temporary, cricket ultimately provided an arena in which self identity, local community identities and a Caribbean identity were literally and metaphorically 'played out'.

Second Stuart's (1996) analysis of the Oxford Caribbean and Casuals Cricket Club (OC&CCC) illuminates aspects of local community politics and thus suggests that diasporic identities can be more complex and more internally contested than might be inferred from Carrington's study. The club came into existence following the merger of the Casuals Cricket Club and the Cowley West Indian Club. In contrast to Carrington's emphasis on the link between CCC and community identity, Stuart argues that players' club affiliations were primarily based on convenience and family and friendship ties rather than a broader diasporic identity. Casuals had revolved around two Barbadian families which 'allowed their friends to play' whilst the Cowley West Indian Club had been run by 'one or two individuals' (Stuart 1996: 125–126). Thus the idea that these two clubs have represented 'African-Caribbean identity (was) ... far from the truth' (Stuart 1996: 127). Rather, the influence of a few Barbadian elders led to the dominance of a particular version of Barbadian identity. Moreover, the Oxford Caribbean and the Cowley West Indian club merger was 'far from smooth' (Stuart 1996: 127) as individuals exploited the club as a vehicle to bolster their positions as community leaders. A 'Black' identity was only promoted during attempts to obtain public funding. Thus, 'the image of a unified and homogeneous African-Caribbean community was but an illusion ... far from representing the whole African-Caribbean population in Oxford, the cricket club represented a few individuals' (Stuart 1996: 125).

This is not to say, however, that cricket did not play a significant part in diaspora identity construction, as the names chosen for these clubs suggest. Stuart, like Carrington, notes that outsiders viewed OC&CCC as a surrogate for the West Indies test side. He further argues that players often pandered to this stereotype, attempting to play in the West Indian 'tradition' of aggressive fast bowling, flamboyant scoring and countering spin bowling with attacking batting. For such men, 'cricket represented social status [and] social mobility'

(Stuart 1996: 125) and playing in this particular style, against largely white teams, represented a form of resistance to the everyday racism encountered in Oxford. Cricket therefore served to bolster a generalized 'Caribbean' or 'West Indian' identity as well as a sense of Black masculinity. But Stuart's work also highlights the internally fractured nature of affiliations within the Black British diaspora. At certain times and places local/island-based identities came to the fore. At other times, divisions arose between those who wished to express a community identity through cricket and those for whom such identities had less resonance. It is clear, however, that members of the Black British diaspora, 'construct and select specific images from the Caribbean to produce a new identity in keeping with their experience in Britain', and that '[diasporic] communities in Britain [are] positioned and repositioned in relation to the dominant presence' (Stuart 1996: 128). Identities, however, are also constructed in relation to the presence of, and power relations *between*, diasporic factions.

Third Williams' (2001) discussion of British Asian participation in grassroots cricket suggests an even greater level of fragmentation and hybridity of South Asian diaspora consciousness. Williams argues that Asian participation in grass roots cricket has primarily been as part of ethnically homogeneous teams. Some of these, such as those in Bolton, were first formed in the 1960s and their number increased rapidly in the 1980s (Williams 1994). Reflecting Valiotis' (2009) account of Muslim and Pakistani diaspora identities, a key finding of Williams' work is that it exposes the danger of attributing 'false universalism' to Asian communities. Cricket clubs tend to reflect not only national affiliations but a wide variety of distinctive group identities: 'kinship, clan identity, language, residential area, religion and ancestral villages or towns in Asia' (Williams 2001: 176). Where initially caste had been a significant factor in the creation of Hindu cricket teams it has waned in significance post-1990. Since this time the number of Muslim teams has grown considerably (while overall the number of cricket clubs in Britain declined), stimulated in part by the success of the Pakistan national team, but perhaps also by a growing Muslim identity in Britain which in turn stems from a recognition within the diaspora that residence in the United Kingdom is likely to be 'irreversible', and thus an identity linked to nation (Pakistan) is problematic (Werbner 1996). Only the clubs which play at the higher levels of competition, such as Deane and Derby in Bolton, attract players from across religious, ethnic and class groups within the South Asian community (Williams 1994).

The complexity of identities is best illustrated through a number of contradictions. While most of Williams' respondents argued that 'cricket promotes inter-racial contact and ethnic harmony' (1994: 62) the failure of Asian teams to gain entry to the highest leagues in the Bolton Association is seen by some as evidence of discrimination. While Williams interprets the absence of leagues solely consisting of 'Asian' teams as evidence of limited prejudice, the prominence of ethnically homogeneous teams could be taken to imply the opposite. In addition to this, however, it is notable that some of the leading 'South Asian' clubs (for example Bolton Indians) have incorporated local affiliations into their titles as a way of indicating multiple aspects of identity. Another club, formed by Muslims with ancestral roots in a particular Indian village, is called Red Rose CC, and thus emphasizes Lancashire identity.[3] For Williams, 'cricket playing among Asians expresses a determination to maintain Asian identities and culture in England' (2001: 178). Williams contrasts the impact of South Asian cricket on British society to the invisibility of other South Asian cultural forms in Britain as a reason for the degree of significance with which the game is held.

Diaspora and professional cricket in England

As this chapter's introduction illustrates, diasporic communities have also became integral to the elite game in England. Research focussing on members of diaspora communities who engage with cricket at this level shows the continuation of certain themes in relation to identity construction – namely the dynamic hybridity of diaspora consciousness – but also some context specific characteristics which stem from the rather unique experience of being selected to be a nation's representative.

At its broadest, we can see that diasporic involvement in English elite cricket has been contoured by certain cultural stereotypes. Early sociological analyses of English cricket illustrated how a disproportionately large percentage of Black British and British Asian cricketers tended to be 'stacked' into particular playing positions (Malcolm 1997). Following the participation patterns established in the Caribbean, Black British cricketers were significantly over-represented in the role of fast bowler, while following the participation patterns established in the Asian subcontinent, British Asian cricketers were significantly overrepresented as batsmen and spin bowlers. This pattern of positional occupancy was replicated amongst the diasporic cricketers selected to play for the England cricket team. Starting with Ranjitsinhji in 1896, England's cricket selectors have showed a propensity to select British Asian batsmen (England captain Nasser Hussain would be another notable case in point) and spin bowlers (such as Min Patel), while also largely selecting fast bowlers from the Black British community (for example Devon Malcolm, Chris Lewis, Norman Cowans). These positional patterns have become less distinct in recent years as the dominant trend has been for the proliferation of British Asian, and a decline in the number of Black British, cricketers. For instance, Steen (2004: 24) noted that whilst the 1994 edition of *The Cricketers' Who's Who* featured thirty-three England qualified players of 'Caribbean extraction', the 2004 edition featured just eighteen. Williams (2001) demonstrates the growing number of British Asian county cricketers in the 1990s and Burdsey (2010a) estimates that in 2009 there were approximately twenty British Muslims playing for English first-class counties. However, it remains the case that such participation patterns have both influenced, and can be taken as an indication of, the role of cricket in the expression of diasporic identities.

Players from the Black and South Asian diasporas have experienced different degrees of racism as they have negotiated access into English county cricket. Although a report by the England and Wales Cricket Board's Racism Study Group (ECB 1999) found that none of the county players to whom they spoke in their research cited experiences of racial prejudice or discrimination (though 82 per cent of non-white respondents 'believed' racism existed in the game), a number of cases of racist abuse of Black players (tellingly all fast bowlers) by spectators have entered the public domain. In 1985 David Lawrence recalled how a group of Yorkshire supporters threw bananas at him and called him 'nigger, black bastard, sambo, monkey, gorilla'. In an incident at Southampton, Middlesex and England fast bowler Norman Cowans was subjected to chants of 'black bastard, black bastard' (Searle 1990: 33). Most famously controversy dogged the career of Devon Malcolm. Chairman of the England cricket selectors, Ted Dexter, invoked racist stereotypes by accusing Malcolm of 'having no cricketing brain' (Searle 1996: 52). When Malcolm questioned whether England cricket manager Ray Illingworth's treatment of him would have been different had he (Malcolm) been white, the ECB threatened to punish Malcolm for 'bringing the game into disrepute'. The ECB remained intransigent even when another England player, Dermot Reeve, alleged that he had heard Illingworth racially abuse Malcolm (for a fuller discussion see Marqusee 1998: 300–302). To compound the prejudice Malcolm experienced within the game, at a Buckingham Palace function to which both the West Indies and England cricket teams were invited, the Duke of Edinburgh asked Malcolm, 'Why are you wearing an England blazer?' (Searle 1995: 33).

Such experiences show that the practice of 'othering' similarly exists in elite cricket in England. Searle (1996: 51) for instance has spoken about the 'in-out' attitude of the selectors towards particular Black England players, illustrated through the high proportion of Black British players whom the press have dubbed 'one-test wonders' (i.e. Neil Williams, Joey Benjamin). The publication of Robert Henderson's (1995) *Wisden Cricket Monthly* article, 'Is it in the Blood', most publicly drew attention to diasporic identity issues amongst elite players. Henderson launched a debate about whether the inclusion of players born or brought up outside Britain was beneficial to the England cricket team on the (unsubstantiated) basis that the effort, or 'desire to succeed', could not be as great as amongst 'native born and bred players' (1995: 9).

Perhaps as a consequence of entering the game later, examples of overt racism directed towards British Asian players are fewer. Burdsey (2010b) notes that the impact of the Asian diaspora is such that it is now possible to speak of the British Asian cricket star. The most prominent British Asian cricketer of recent times has been Monty Panesar. The first Sikh to play cricket for England, Panesar's public reception stands in marked contrast to the 1990s debate about players of overseas 'origin'. It might be argued that the focus on Panesar's 'visual otherness' – his wearing of a turban and growth of a full beard – betrays a lack of respect for difference and thus exposes an undercurrent of racism. However, an equally significant aspect of the public reception for Panesar is the broad feeling of affection for the player, and the absence of the expression of hostility. His shortlisting for the 2006 BBC Sports Personality of the Year award is indicative of the breadth of his public appeal but the stance taken by the English press over the racial abuse of Panesar during the early stages of England's 2006–07 tour to Australia is probably more revealing. When Cricket Australia's James Sutherland was reported to have called Panesar 'a stupid Indian', the *Sun* (18 November 2006), traditionally a newspaper relatively antipathetic to multiculturalism, retorted, 'For your information, A – Monty's not stupid, B – He isn't Indian.' Whilst ten to twenty years previously it was English supporters and administrators who were alleged to have racially abused minority ethnic cricketers, in the twenty-first century racism started to be depicted as something others inflicted upon British minority ethnic groups. Consequently Burdsey concludes that 'cricket appears to represent a more progressive sporting space than sports such as football' (2010b: 261–2).

Burdsey's research with British Asians playing county cricket in England illustrates the central role the sport plays in the construction of 'a sense of diasporic British Asianness' (2010b: 256) which is dynamic, fluid, fragmented, context specific and, at times, contradictory. He points, for instance, to the varied signifiers which players from the Asian diaspora use to express their identities (Indian, English, British Asian, British Muslim, etc.). He also demonstrates how identities are further complicated by the representational nature of elite sport, for many of the players to whom Burdsey spoke expressed a sense of allegiance to, and a desire to play for, England (or at least the national cricket team). The embrace of this aspect of identity did not, however, equate with the rejection or marginalization of another, such as religion or heritage, but was a consequence and manifestation of hybridity; 'a desire to construct a multilateral social identity that simultaneously emphasises their British citizenship and ethnicities' (Burdsey 2010b: 264). These issues came to public prominence in 2006 when Sajid Mahmood represented the nation of his birth, England, against that of his father's, Pakistan. During the game Mahmood was barracked by sections of the Pakistan support who chanted words like 'traitor' and 'reject'. Interviewees reflecting on the case of Mahmood expressed little sympathy with the spectators. British Asian professional cricketers understood and supported Mahmood's embrace of multiple identity positions and denied that his embrace of English cricket could or should be equated with a rejection of his Pakistani heritage (Burdsey 2010b).

Burdsey's (2010a) focus on British Muslims' experiences in English professional cricket adds to our understanding of the relationship between cricket and identity amongst the South Asian diaspora by illustrating the interdependence of religious and national identities. While the degree of religious adherence varies markedly between players, many of those interviewed defined Islam as an 'all-encompassing way of life' (2010a: 324). They further expressed a preoccupation with being 'good' Muslims and correlatively inferred that their identity as elite cricketers was essentially marginal to their religious identity. While some noted that they had experienced elements of prejudice while playing, especially from spectators and away from their 'home' county, these could not be described as frequent. Players further argued that their cricket participation did not particularly conflict with their attempts at religious observance. Issues related to the consumption of alcohol, provision of halal or vegetarian food, and public nudity required negotiation at times, but players' comments suggested a relatively high degree of accommodation, or at least an increasing sensitivity towards difference in English cricket. Burdsey concluded by noting that some British Muslim cricketers argued that it was important that they used their relatively privileged and prominent positions to challenge dominant perceptions of Muslims as extremists and/or terrorists.

Conclusion

Cricket permeates diaspora communities and (male) consciousness in numerous ways. For some cricket may primarily be experienced as infrequent spectatorship at international games; for others it may be a physically active and more regular leisure pursuit. For a smaller number cricket may become a source of employment. But whether it is in relation to spectatorship or participation, and whether this takes place at a grassroots or elite level, cricket plays and has played a key role in identity formation of a variety of British minority ethnic groups.

The identity formation we see in relation to cricket and diaspora is particularly complex. Diasporic identities are dynamic as, for example, illustrated by cricket's status as firstly a centrifugal force for the generation of a Caribbean identity, which became superseded by a return to, and strengthening of, Island-based identities promoted through football. Individuals may hold a multiplicity of identities at any one point in time. Diasporic identities may be 'janus-faced' (for example British Pakistani) or characterized by an even greater degree of hybridity (such as the caste specific teams of Hindus in Lancashire). Religious (for example Muslim) identities commingle with national identities (such as Pakistani) according to changing social conditions (i.e. the belief that 'returning home' is a more distant possibility). Perhaps most significantly diasporas can create identities which are determined by neither 'heritage' nor contemporary conditions but are a product of the interdependence of the two. Diasporas do not just continue national identities, they are not always 'just' hybrid, they can be something unique, new and context specific.

The role of cricket in the identities of diasporic communities living in contemporary Britain is one consequence of the role that the game played in the British Empire. Because cricket was diffused at this particular time, and via particular routes, it came to hold a particular significance for the Black and South Asian diasporas which constitute the major part of Britain's minority ethnic communities. Much less obvious but equally significant in this equation is the nineteenth century construction of cricket as the quintessential English game, for just as the 'demand' for participation in the game is mediated by the game's significance in colonial cultures, so the 'supply' of opportunities is mediated by cultural ideologies of what it means to be English and what Englishness means.

Previous analyses of the multicultural character of cricket in contemporary Britain have largely focussed on aspects of racism and racial inequality. While the ever-present backdrop to this and thus to diaspora identity is the resistance of the 'host' community through the mobilization and realignment of forms of English national identity (Kalra *et al.* 2005: 36), one common failing is the logical inconsistency with which diasporic and 'domestic' identities are treated. As we have seen here, diaspora consciousness is fluid, relationally constructed, and context specific. It would, therefore, be something of a contradiction to consider English national identity as static and monolithic. Indeed there is considerable evidence to suggest that notions of Englishness and their expression in relation to cricket have also changed considerably in recent years. It is to an investigation of this that we turn in the next chapter.

8

Cricket and Changing Conceptions of Englishness

If, as has been shown, both the 'metropolis' and the colony were deeply affected by the colonial process and if, as we saw in the previous chapter, cricket has played an important role in the generation of postcolonial diaspora consciousness, one would expect that English national identity has also been radically shaped by the experiences of postcolonialism. Yet, as Brubaker (2005: 10) notes, 'Sophisticated discussions are sensitive to the heterogeneity of diaspora; but they are not always sensitive to the heterogeneity of nation-states.' Consequently, this chapter examines both the role of cricket in changing conceptions of Englishness in contemporary times, and the multifaceted nature of those who identify with this nation.

Sport, of course, does not exist in a vacuum and the ways in which English people more generally express their identity appear to have undergone rapid and overt change in recent years. Indeed feelings of English national identity were perhaps stronger at the end of the twentieth century than they had ever previously been (Kumar 2003a). There have been increasing calls for St George's Day to be celebrated more widely and more formally to parallel the celebrations marking the patron saint days of the other home nations. The traditional elision of English and British national identities has to some degree waned. For instance, data from British Social Attitudes surveys indicate that whilst 31 per cent of the population described themselves as English in 1992, in 2003 this figure had risen to 40 per cent.

The strengthening of English national identity is generally attributed to several broader social processes. Commonly cited in this connection are the moves toward greater European integration, globalization and the concomitant growth in the significance of local and regional identities (King 2006; Kumar 2003b; Smith 2006). Such processes explain the more general rise of nationalism in Europe at the end of the twentieth century (Day and Thompson 2004; Spencer and Wollman 2005a). However, a number of UK-specific processes are also believed to be significant in strengthening a sense of Englishness. Debates about migrant labour from within an expanded EU, the increasing number of people seeking asylum in Britain, and the growth of diasporic communities more generally have dispelled the 'powerful myth of the island fortress' (Bassnett, cited in British Council 2000) and contributed to a process by which '"their" difference is used to enhance the sense of "us"' (Wallman 1979: 3). Scottish and Welsh devolution firstly raised the issue of whether English regional parliaments should be established, and secondly about whether Scottish and Welsh MPs should be excluded from voting on certain issues in the House of Commons (Nairn 2000; Kumar 2003a).

Though clearly more deeply rooted, this changing sense of national identity has been particularly evident in the sports context. A notable trend has been the increased use of the flag of St George and, in particular, the phenomena of car-mounted flags which began during the 2002 FIFA World Cup. A number of writers have commented upon the emergence of this 'celebratory patriotism' (for example Perryman 2002: 30). Polley (2003: 18) argues that these developments indicate that 'English national identity in sport has been shifted to be more inclusive'. While such changes may be largely cosmetic (Crabbe 2004; Garland 2004), and it is debateable whether this changing sense of nationalism easily translates to other spheres of political and social life (King 2006; Abell *et al.* 2007), what is clear is that many people in England either feel the need or simply enjoy expressing their sense of nationalism in ways which they have previously not done.

We saw in Chapter 2 that Englishness and cricket have been closely associated since the early nineteenth century. We have also seen how this ideological connection was fundamental to the diffusion of the game as part of the process of colonization. And using the concept of diaspora, we have explored the processual, contested and fragmented character of (national) identities. In this chapter I want to explore how recent developments show that cricket remains deeply interconnected with the way the English imagine themselves, but also that there are multiple ways in which the English connect with cricket. Through this we can also see that aspects of national identity are subject to continuity and change. Cricket's enduring relationship with Englishness has been facilitated by a metamorphosis in relation to new sets of interdependencies allied to the continued perception that the game provides a stable reference point in a rapidly changing world.

In structuring my observations of changing conceptions of cricket and Englishness, I draw upon two models of Englishness identified in the work of Edmunds and Turner (2001). *Malign Englishness* is described as closed (e.g. resentful of other nationalisms), insular (e.g. threatened by European identities and multiculturalism), earnest (e.g. seeing national identity as 'in the blood' and rejecting the idea that traditions are invented), masculine (e.g. aggressive) and reactive (e.g. defensive of traditional and nostalgic notions of Englishness). *Benign Englishness* is open (e.g. tolerant of other nationalisms), cosmopolitan (e.g. enjoying the co-existence of different cultures and welcoming of multiculturalism), ironic (e.g. aware of the contingent character of national identities), feminine (e.g. pacifist), and creative (e.g. actively seeking to build an identity of openness, liberalism and tolerance). In using these models it is important not to replicate the false dichotomy of ethnic (malign) and civic (benign) nationalisms (McCrone 1998), or the value judgement distinguishing between 'good' and 'bad' nationalisms (Spencer and Wollman 2005b). Moreover, as my previous cautionary note suggests (cf. Crabbe 2004; Garland 2004; King 2006), evidence of benign Englishness does not necessarily mean that personalities have fundamentally altered, merely perhaps a growing reflexivity over how others perceive the English and how the English would want others to view them. Indeed in the next chapter we examine the continuing 'Othering' process to which postcolonial nationalities are subject. However, this typology does provide a useful heuristic device for organizing the empirical evidence of the changing ways in which Englishness and cricket have inter-related in recent years.

This analysis builds upon Chapters 3 to 7 to examine how the experiences of colonialism and postcolonialism impacted upon English conceptions of self. In the first section of this chapter I chart the development of a cultural defensiveness constructed around a romanticized conception of cricket and Englishness. The concept of malign Englishness seems to closely fit the characteristics evident in this form of nationalism. However, this represents only one phase in a broader process. Thus I subsequently argue that: a) epitomized by the establishment of the Barmy Army in 1994/1995; b) popularized through the Ashes victory in 2005; and c) ultimately embodied in Andrew Flintoff, English cricket's most significant twenty-first century celebrity, contemporary cricket has come to express revised versions of English national identity which are closer to a model of benign Englishness than those which dominated English cricket discourses at the end of the twentieth century. Despite elements of change, the veneration of Flintoff illustrates the importance of nostalgia and history in defining Englishness, and the role of cricket in continuing to provide a stable source of distinction for those looking to express their Englishness within the set of social relations unique to the contemporary context.

Malign Englishness

As epitomized in the West Indian example, throughout the twentieth century the cricket playing nations of the former British Empire underwent a process of de-colonization and national self-assertion. Gradually the English lost political control of both the Commonwealth and the game. The Imperial Cricket Conference became the International Cricket Conference in 1965, and the International Cricket Council in 1989. The convention that the Chairman and Secretary of the MCC be appointed ex-officio Chairman and ex-officio Secretary of the ICC respectively was abolished. Although the first elected Chairman was former MCC Chairman Colin Cowdrey, subsequently the post has been held by only one other Briton, David Morgan. In 1993 England and Australia's right to veto ICC policy changes was withdrawn. With key administrative positions now subject to a vote of the member nations, historically held assumptions about the ownership and control of the game became overtly challenged.

The unilateral right of the English to define the way in which the game should be played also declined. The initial challenge can be traced back to the 'Bodyline' test series in 1932–33 (see Chapter 3) which was the first time anyone 'challenged the imperial tradition that Britain set the standards for civilized behaviour' (Stoddart 1979: 126). Latterly, as we have seen, defeats on the pitch at the hands of the West Indies were viewed as rejections of colonialism's hierarchical relations. Allegations of ball-tampering which accompanied Pakistan's emergence as a playing force in the early 1990s (Williams 2001) can also be seen as a sign of English resistance to their waning power over the game and an increasing sense of insecurity in a politically changing world. Maguire, for instance, charted the contested nature of Anglo-Australian relations in 1992 when Prime Minister Keating's attempts to re-position Australia as politically closer to Pacific Rim nations by questioning the country's links with the United Kingdom were closely followed by England's victory over Australia in the ICC Cricket World Cup. Maguire detected a 'revamped aggressive Englishness' (1993: 314) within a discourse 'dominated by a patronizing "English" tone toward the upstart Aussies who had been firmly put in their place' (1993: 303).

An equally significant challenge to British dominance has been economically driven. Again the initial challenge came from Australia in the form of the Packer cricket series of the 1970s. Even so, such were the relative economic power and infrastructural resources that the first three Cricket World Cups (1975, 1979, 1983) were held in England. There will, however, be a twenty-year gap between the country's staging of the 1999 and 2019 events. These more recent economic changes can be more adequately described as the Indianization of cricket (Gupta 2010; Steen 2010). Twin manifestations of this development include the shift in the economic balance of power towards India and the proliferation of one-day cricket relative to test matches. The emergence of the Indian Premier League's (IPL) Twenty20 competition is perhaps the clearest illustration of this trend (see Mehta *et al.* 2009). Epitomizing this changing landscape of cricket, the ICC relocated from Lord's to Dubai in 2005. Yet (other people's) attempts to commercialize cricket have long met with English objections that the 'spirit of the game' will be damaged or lost (Wright 1993). Suggestions of cheating (for example relating to ball tampering in the England-Pakistan game at the Oval in 2006) and examples of 'fair play' (Indian captain Mahendra Singh Dhoni's decision to 'invite' Ian Bell to resume his innings at Trent Bridge in 2011)[1] have been seized upon by the English media in equal measure. The insertion of a Preamble to the Laws of Cricket on the 'Spirit of the Game' in 2000 and the inauguration of the MCC's Spirit of Cricket Cowdrey Lecture in 2001 can be seen as symbolic swansongs of the right of the English to define the way in which the game 'should' be played.

These changes have impacted upon the expression of Englishness. As discussed in the previous chapter, debates generated by Tebbit and Henderson, the variety of spectatorship styles demonstrated by diasporic peoples and perceptions of racial inequality at the grass roots of the game are illustrative of 'an inward looking nationalism', characterized by 'a preoccupation with "the enemy within"' (Crabbe and Wagg 2000: 70). Though written with reference to race relations in Britain more broadly, Burdsey's (2006: 15) words are striking in their applicability to cricket:

> Perceptions of a threat to England and 'Englishness' have resulted in the emergence of a defensive 'Little Englander' mentality. This worldview is constructed around the celebration of quasi-mythical English history and utopian images of suburban/rural life, free from the alleged problems of inner city (and ipso facto minority ethnic) communities. It stresses a perceived common ancestry and homogeneity of English culture and, in the process, constructs a notion of 'Englishness' that is palpably monocultural.

Such was the exclusivity and reactive insularity of English cricket at the end of the millennium that some predicted the game's imminent demise. According to Paul Gilroy (2001: xv):

> Men's cricket is in what appears to be terminal decline as a national spectator sport. Its old imperial logics lost and its civilizing codes increasingly anachronistic and unmoving in a world sharply and permanently divided into the two great camps: a select group of winners and an ever-expanding legion of losers. Few state schools have the time or the facilities to maintain teams. Tall boys want to play basketball rather than bowl and the fundamental idea that a wholly satisfying contest can endure for five days and yet produce no result, increasingly defies comprehension. Meanwhile, the dead weight of a corrosive class culture prevents the decomposing game from re-inventing itself.

Gilroy has, of course, been proved quite wrong, largely because he fails to conceive of Englishness and English national identity with the same fluidity, hybridity and heterogeneity that characterizes his (and others) analysis of diaspora. In the latter years of the twentieth century cricket would not only be re-popularized through re-invention, but re-invented in such a way as to remain the quintessential English game. Cricket became structured around a revised set of core values which re-positioned English national character and formed the basis of a more 'positive' sense of national identity. It is to this, and the convergence of both cricketing and broader society-wide social processes, that we now turn.

The Barmy Army and the emergence of benign Englishness[2]

The first signs of a cultural seachange in the way cricket articulated with notions of Englishness emerged in conjunction with the arrival of the Barmy Army. 'England's Barmy Army' was the name given to a vocal and boisterous group of England cricket supporters by the *Sydney Morning Herald* during the 1994/95 Ashes series in Australia. The particularly high financial, temporal and emotional commitment required of supporters travelling to watch the Ashes seem to have been the catalyst for the formation of this group, already bonded by common nationality, the camaraderie of a backpacking, hedonistic lifestyle and, not least, a love of cricket. This loosely organized but clearly identifiable group attracted considerable media attention. The Barmy Army organized parties attended by the England players and were allocated specific enclosures at grounds which attracted corporate sponsorship. By the fourth test match in Adelaide the Barmy Army trademark had been registered and by the end of the fifth 3,000 Barmy Army t-shirts had been sold. The Barmy Army have since become a major feature of the English cricket landscape and, most significantly for present purposes, their emergence was both inspired by and has provided a vehicle for revised expressions of the relationship between cricket and Englishness.

Leaders of the Barmy Army *claim* that their membership is 'representative of the full social spectrum' (*Guardian*, 7 February 1998). They have openly espoused an anti-racist and anti-sexist agenda and proudly claim to cut across the traditional divides of class, 'race', age, gender, and regional loyalty. In reality, however, the Barmy Army largely consists of white males aged between twenty and forty. In terms of social class, Vic Marks has argued that most work in 'solicitors' or accountants' offices' (*Observer*, 24 January 1999) while B.C. Pires conversely reported that the Barmy Army members he met in the West Indies 'appeared to be predominantly working-class lads' (*Guardian*, 7 February 1998). More concretely we can say that the Barmy Army's 'leadership' is largely drawn from relatively affluent social backgrounds. The three co-founders or 'party co-ordinators' (a term which signifies the underlying motivations and anti-hierarchical ethos) are Paul Burnham, Gareth Evans and Dave Peacock. When the Barmy Army was formed, Gareth Evans was a chartered surveyor with the supermarket chain *Sainsbury* and ex-public schoolboy Dave Peacock was a manager with *National Power*. Paul Burnham also went to a public school. Previously an 'executive' with *British Airways*, Burnham now works full time for the Barmy Army (Parry and Malcolm 2004; de Lisle 2006).

The most sociologically interesting aspect of the Barmy Army is the contrast between the supportership style and motivations of its members and that which has traditionally characterized English cricket spectators and which has long been taken to be an embodiment of English national identity. Initially the Barmy Army motto was 'To love England, to love cricket, to love the players' (though it was later changed to, 'to make watching and playing cricket more fun and more popular'). As the original motto indicates, three concurrent preoccupations fuelled the formation of the Barmy Army: fun; influence and nationalism. Compared to the tradition of restrained approval and curbed emotion, the

Barmy Army is vocal, self-conscious, partisan and carnivalesque. Many wear fancy dress, carry inflatables and paint their faces. Critics, in particular, have continually identified the drinking culture of Barmy Army members. The Barmy Army sell song sheets – *Barmy Harmonies* – are accompanied by 'Billy the Trumpeter' [Cooper] and in Vic Flowers (aka 'Jimmy', due to his resemblance to the late Jimmy Saville) provide their own master of ceremonies. The Barmy Army is outward looking in that it expresses a proactive commitment to convert/recruit other spectators at, and to, the game and may well have been influential in contributing to the growing popularity of test cricket in England since the mid 1990s.[3]

The second preoccupation – influence – also re-defines English cricket spectatorship. The Barmy Army employ various strategies in this regard. Songs and chants are directed at individual players or the England team collectively. In contrast to the traditions and norms of cricket spectatorship irreverent, insulting and even crudely abusive chants are directed at England's opponents. These have included accusations of paedophilia, homophobic abuse and reference to Australia's history as a penal colony. In 2005 some questioned the appropriateness of the barracking of Jason Gillespie which rested on a traveller 'racial' stereotype. In a further inversion of tradition the Barmy Army vociferously applaud opposing bowlers *only* when they have bowled badly. The use of masochistic and ironic self-depreciation, or 'gallows humour', also illustrates the revised sense of the importance of winning as part of this style of support. England players' public endorsements of the Barmy Army serve as a particular point of pride, especially given the hostility the group initially encountered in the media. In 2005 England captain Michael Vaughan said that the support of the Barmy Army was like having an extra player (de Lisle 2006).

The third major pre-occupation of the Barmy Army is the nationalistic nature of members' support. On the one hand this is relatively self-evident in that their *raison d'etre* is to follow and support the England cricket team. This overt nationalism initially led many commentators to draw parallels between the behaviour of the Barmy Army and English football hooligans. Ian Woolridge, for instance, writing in the *Daily Mail* in December 1994 spoke of, 'the extreme embarrassment of some 30 or 40 English hooligans … the detritus of the English national social security system … those morons seek confrontation with any Australians that will take them on … this small banal bunch of louts…'. Yet such depictions falsely describe the group's demographics and belie the hybridity of the Barmy Army supporter style, for it is perhaps more accurate to draw parallels between themselves and the 'Tartan Army' and 'Roligans' who follow the Scottish and Danish national football teams respectively. Each emphasizes that being a fan abroad involves a responsibility to actively and positively experience foreign cultures, and to socialize with opposing fans. In 1996, for instance, the Barmy Army staged a fundraising match for the development of township cricket in South Africa. Songs and chants may include aggressive, coded and racialized verbal abuse, but instances of disorder at cricket matches more commonly perceived to have been 'racially' motivated (see previous chapter) have not been thought to have involved the Barmy Army. Indeed the Barmy Army show more similarities with Caribbean and South Asian supporter styles (evident both in the respective domestic games and amongst diasporic communities) than with either the relatively aggressive nationalism traditionally associated with English football supporters, or the restrained traditions of spectatorship associated with English cricket.

Thus the Barmy Army's explicit rejection of pre-existing and contrasting forms of English cricket spectator behaviour indicate the expression of a new variant of English national identity. Just as the Barmy Army can be juxtaposed against 'traditional' models of Englishness and cricket spectatorship, so their new and distinctive cultural identity can be seen in marked contrast to the forms of malign Englishness described above. The Barmy Army consisted of a group of English/British people who were not 'inward looking' or defensive about either cricket or 'their' nation, but were open (relishing their co-existence with similar fan groups), ironic (in their rejection of cricketing traditions and use of humour), creative (promoting liberal values and opposing the 'establishment' of English cricket) and cosmopolitan (formed partly through a willingness to experience different cultures).

The social context of the Barmy Army's emergence

As with the initial emergence of an ideological link between cricket and Englishness in the nineteenth century, these developments can only be understood in the context of a broader social structure in which particular social processes were particularly evident. Specifically society-wide processes, sports-wide processes and cricket-specific processes can be identified. Combined they enabled the Barmy Army to assume considerable prominence both in cricket and society more generally. Moreover, this integration enabled cricket to remain relevant to contemporary English identities.

First, the Barmy Army is a product of globalization. Enabled by the increasing opportunities for international travel and increasing media exposure of different cultural forms (and the subsequent appropriation of these cultural forms), the Barmy Army are illustrative of the interplay between global and local (national) identities whereby the latter are paradoxically strengthened as a consequence of the former (Bairner 2001).

Being something of a male preserve (and as we saw in Chapter 2, national identity is a gendered phenomenon), the Barmy Army also appears to be closely related to changing expressions of masculinity in contemporary Britain, and 'New Laddism' in particular. 'New lad', through an emphasis on sport, alcohol and sexual divisions, has been seen as a reaction to the

1980s 'New Man' phenomenon (Rutherford 1988), and a partial reversion to 'traditional' masculine, largely working class, values (Edwards 1997). The Barmy Army has been described as the most visible example of 'cricketing Laddism' and a prominent feature of 'New Cricket Culture' which is partly a 'by-product of the sociological New Lad phenomenon' (MacQuillin 1996: 39). Barmy Army guest appearances on the sports comedy quiz *They Think it's all Over* (a prominent manifestation of New Lad culture (Whelehan 2000)) both indicated and reproduced the connection between 'New Laddism' and the Barmy Army. New Laddism's use of irreverent humour to rationalize sexist and coded-racist remarks as 'excusable' (Carrington 1998), is reproduced in the Barmy Army's questioning of opposition players' sexualities while espousing an ethos of social inclusion.

Second, the development of the Barmy Army has been heavily influenced by processes affecting sports spectatorship more widely. The Barmy Army draw on the long-standing tradition amongst football supporter groups to define themselves in terms of being an Army (for example, the aforementioned 'Tartan Army'). Like traditional English working class football support, the Barmy Army congregates in the cheapest areas (like football 'ends'), and attempt to influence the outcome of matches. Such parallels are not accidental. Over sixty different replica football club shirts were evident amongst England fans who 'joined' the Barmy Army at the 1995 Adelaide test match (Parry and Malcolm 2004). Moreover the Barmy Army also share many of the features of the 'fundamental regeneration of football fandom' (Brown 1998: 65) which stemmed from the post-Hillsborough economic transformation of English football. The Barmy Army fulfil many of the same organizational functions as the football supporter groups which emerged around this time. Groups like the Football Supporters' Association (FSA) seek to increase fan influence over the game and promote 'liberal' agendas such as anti-racism. The FSA also establishes 'supporter embassies' during international football tournaments and thus provides similar kinds of traveller support as the Barmy Army does for overseas cricket tours. Like the Barmy Army, football supporter associations tended to promote themselves as representative of a broad social spectrum while being dominated by white, middle-class, males (Nash 2001). Like those who launched the football fanzine movement, the Barmy Army leadership have been accused of economic exploitation of their position.

Finally, the emergence of the Barmy Army needs to be understood in the context of cricket-specific processes and in particular the peculiar economic structure of the English game. Since 1945 attempts have continually been made to increase cricket's popularity and revenue. Significant developments include: the removal of the distinction between professionals and amateurs in 1962; the introduction of sponsored one-day cricket in 1963 (The Gillette Cup); the expansion of one day competitions (the John Player League followed in 1969 and the Benson and Hedges trophy in 1972); and sponsorship of test match cricket from 1977. In each case the resistance of established groups attempting to 'defend' the traditions of English cricket have been overcome (Sandiford 1985). The wearing of coloured clothing, the musical punctuation of matches, day-night floodlit games and the 2003 launch of Twenty20 cricket are all extensions of this trend. These innovations have enabled the cricketing authorities to further exploit broadcasting rights income. This process significantly developed in 1990 when the (then) financially ailing Sky TV (latterly BSkyB) purchased the rights to broadcast England's tour of the West Indies. For the first time English cricket became part of a commercialized TV package. In 1998 the ECB opened the tender for home test match cricket coverage and the traditional TV broadcaster of cricket, the BBC, could no longer compete financially. The 2005 Ashes series was the last international cricket to be aired live on a terrestrial channel in the UK.

Commercial broadcasters have sought to market the game beyond its traditional audience. An appeal to a new 'football-type' audience, familiar with 'New Laddism', has led the relaxed, understated style of John Arlott, Brian Johnston, Peter West and Tony Lewis to be replaced by more spectacular coverage. Radio coverage and Test Match Special in particular has been subject to similar changes (Watson 2010, 2011). Technology – on-screen scores, slow-motion replays, 'hawkeye', 'snicko', 'hot spot', blogs and Twitter, etc.[4] – creates a more dynamic package. Broadcasters also attempt to convey to the viewer the atmosphere in the stadium and consequently spectator groups like the Barmy Army assume increased significance as ready-made, animated scenery which can be incorporated into the coverage. Cricket administrators subsequently formulated a strategy of co-option aligning official England merchandise with Barmy Army branded products and using the Barmy Army as a base to popularize the game, particularly amongst a younger audience. Thus, driven by the desire for increased income, English cricket authorities, media groups and advertisers have sought to utilize the presence of the Barmy Army, which in turn has justified the Barmy Army's continued presence, helped legitimize their actions, and increased their profile.

The Barmy Army represents a qualitatively new form of English national identity and, as with the nineteenth century 're-invention' of cricket as the quintessential English game, this has occurred concurrently with a combination of society-wide social processes and cricket-specific developments. With regard to the latter, the peculiar economics of cricket which have seen the English game continually struggle for existence have generated the social conditions in which pronounced change can relatively easily occur. The degree to which a discourse of malign Englishness had increasingly become associated with all things to do with English cricket similarly provided a context which structured the specific variant of Englishness to emerge. Just as malign Englishness was based on an 'othering' of particular social groups, so benign Englishness has stemmed from an 'othering' of the traditions and establishment of cricket. But just as we saw in relation to cricket and diaspora, these processes are not simple binary reactions, but entail a commingling of identities and cultural forms.

2005 Ashes and the popularization of benign Englishness

If the formation of the Barmy Army marked the emergence of benign Englishness, the 2005 Ashes series represented the point in time at which the relationship between cricket and this sense of national identity could be said to have entered a broader public consciousness. Newspapers reported increased sales of between 5 and 10 per cent (*Observer*, 18 September 2005), the *BBC Sport* website had its busiest ever Saturday, 66 per cent of the public said that members of the cricket team were 'much better role models' than England's footballers, and 80 per cent of respondents to a *Radio 5 Live* poll said that they now preferred cricket to football. Manchester United manager Alex Ferguson said that it was the first time in the history of the football Premiership that the start of the season had been overshadowed by Test cricket (*Guardian,* 22 August 2005). For Mike Selvey, the 2005 Ashes victory 'captured the imagination of the public in a manner that hitherto could only be dreamed of' (*Guardian*, 23 December 2005). But the style of patriotism with which this victory was celebrated was also inherently linked to the displays of a changing sense of English national identity emergent in the formation of the Barmy Army. To what extent did these celebrations align with Turner and Edmunds' (2001) model of benign Englishness?

In championing a team which incorporated players from diverse backgrounds, English cricket fans and media commentators implicitly recognized the contingent nature of such sporting/national allegiances. The team contained the Australian-raised, Papua New Guinean wicketkeeper (with a Welsh forename) Geriant Jones. The South African-born Kevin Pietersen, who had qualified to play for England through residency, had become one of the most popular and prominent England players. Andrew Strauss, also South African-born and married to an Australian, qualified to play for England because he had an English mother. Through his educational experience (Radley College and Durham University), he developed many of the characteristics of traditional, upper-class conceptions of Englishness and thus earned the nickname 'Lord Brocket'. But the contingent nature of national identities has most explicitly been commented upon by Ed Joyce, a Dublin-born cricketer who played for Ireland before subsequently qualifying and choosing to play for England. Reflecting on his shift of national affiliation, in 2007 Joyce stated,

> there's no doubt … [once] you supported anyone other than England. That's changing now. I think it's just time, a new generation. And the England team now have an interesting mix of people. There was Geraint Jones, and there's Kevin Pietersen and Monty Panesar and Sajid Mahmood. If you look at England and Britain as a whole it is a brilliant mix. I look at the team and see a progressive country here. (*Independent*, 11 March 2007)

Such remarks stand in direct contrast to Henderson's critique of player motivation a decade earlier.

In addition to both the recognition of the fluidity of national identity, and the embrace of rather than resistance to different identities, the 2005 Ashes series provided evidence to suggest that elements of the cricket community were becoming more 'creative' in their outlook, actively seeking to build an identity of openness, liberalism and tolerance. It was notable in the wake of the 2005 Ashes series victory that, and in sharp contrast to the traditional notions of cricket, the apparent classlessness of the England cricket team was celebrated. BBC correspondent Benjamin Dirs described the victory parade in Trafalgar Square as 'one big coming out party ... this is a very modern England with very modern fans'. The team were depicted as 'normal blokes'; 'these are men that you might like to have a few beers with ... England's footballers are remote by comparison and increasingly difficult to identify with'.[5] The cricketers were seen as down to earth and non-aspirational in material terms. A reporter in the Scottish *Evening News*, argued that the idea that cricket was 'only for sissies or for toffs from private schools ... is fast going out the window. Cricket is becoming a "normal" game' (20 August 2005). Andrew Collier in the *Scotsman* (15 September 2005) similarly argued that these events had radically altered the image of cricket: 'A piece of traditional England died this week, the notion of cricket as a game for gentlemen.' Centrally, therefore, this discourse portrayed as defunct the social hierarchies which have traditionally underpinned both cricket and Englishness. It was noticeable, moreover, that it was Scottish journalists in particular who stressed the significance of the changing class base of the game. *Pace* Gilroy, popularization *has* stemmed from the weakening of rigid social class boundaries and the increasing sense of democratization within the English cricket.

One could also detect elements of the feminization (similarly identified as a component of benign Englishness) of cricket. Television audiences grew significantly during the summer of 2005, with female viewers being one of the most significant growth areas. On the first morning of the first test only a quarter of viewers were female, but by the final day of the fifth test, that figure had grown to 39 per cent. The actual number of female viewers therefore increased from approximately 500,000 to around 3.25m (*Guardian*, 3 November 2005). Similarly the England women's cricket team, who also defeated their Australian counterparts that summer, were manifestly more integrated with the men's game than perhaps at any time previously. This was enabled by the Women's Cricket Association's merger with the ECB in 1998 (see Malcolm and Velija 2008; Velija and Malcolm 2010). In 2005 the women were included in the Ashes victory parade and both teams were invited to Downing Street to meet Prime Minister Tony Blair.

The response in Scotland to the success of the England cricket team illustrated the sense in which this nationalistic celebration was relatively 'open', more encompassing of, than oppositional to, other nationalisms. In the aftermath of the 2005 Ashes victory, MSP Christine Grahame submitted a motion to the Scottish Parliament entitled 'It's Simply not Cricket', which 'lamented the overwhelming UK-wide coverage of a sport of only marginal interest in Scotland'. This prompted four retaliatory motions condemning her 'petty and narrow minded nationalism' which was 'an insult to the thousands who play cricket in Scotland' (*Scotsman*, 15 September 2005). The critical voices in the ensuing public debate were largely directed at the London-based media rather than the English cricket establishment or the English *per se*. Many, like columnist Martin Hannan who described himself as a 'Fierce patriot … cut me and I bleed Saltires', 'confessed' to cheering on England (*Scotland on Sunday*, 11 September 2005). Craig Wright, captain of the Scottish men's cricket team said that England's success had been 'celebrated by people all over Scotland' (*Scotsman*, 15 September 2005). Television viewing figures seemed to support this, for whilst Scotland constitutes just 8.5 per cent of the UK population, viewers in Scotland accounted for 18 per cent of the total Channel 4 audience (*Scotland on Sunday*, 18 September 2005. It could however be argued that for some Scottish viewers this was not a manifestation of support, but borne out of the desire to see England lose).

Thus, some Scots seemed happy to support the England cricket team in a way unthinkable in other sports. Whilst Gordon Brown (a Scot) attracted considerable criticism for declaring his support for England during the 2006 Football World Cup, Scottish support for the England cricket team seems less problematic. Tom English, writing in *Scotland on Sunday* (11 September 2005), could revel in the aftermath of the England football team's defeat to Northern Ireland in September 2005, yet declare himself 'happy for the England cricket team … because from a distance they seem an altogether agreeable lot. But we draw the line at [England football manager] Sven's men'. Similarly broadcaster and columnist Nicky Campbell noted his (class-based) antipathy toward the England rugby union team – referring to 'Sir Clive [Woodward]'s Smarmy Army' – and asked, 'What's different about Test Cricket?'. Campbell's answer was that, 'We don't play you and, if we are good, we play for you and occasionally captain you' (*Guardian*, 15 September 2005). Thus the relationship between the English and the Scottish appeared to be more open and mutually supportive in cricket than in relation to other sports and built more upon Britain's historical legacy of a blurred patchwork of ethnic identities (see Chapter 6) than the divisions which tend to strongly characterize other sporting contests within the United Kingdom.

Illustrating both their social significance, and their location at the conjunction of these changing conceptions of Englishness, the Barmy Army were provided with a unique presence during the official celebrations and, specifically their own stage in Trafalgar Square, alongside that of the players for the conclusion of the victory parade. During the celebrations Kevin Pietersen beckoned Bill Cooper and Vic Flowers to join the players but they were stopped by security guards. Zimbabwean-born England coach, Duncan Fletcher, intervened to enable them to join the team (de Lisle 2006). The changing sense of Englishness that the Barmy Army both embodied and fostered was fully and explicitly recognized in the celebrations that brought it to the consciousness of a broader public in 2005.

Flintoff as the embodiment of Englishness

In concluding this analysis of changing conceptions of national identity I want to focus on the pre-eminent English cricketing celebrity of the twenty-first century. The recent boom in the study of celebrity culture stems in part from the social 'functions' celebrities are thought to perform. For instance celebrities are said to help generate cultural identities, provide an integrating function holding society together through common identification, and legitimate the process of capitalist exchange and commodification (Turner 2004). Celebrities may act as 'brands' which give security through familiarity and thus provide stability during times of rapid social change, and may contribute to meritocratic ideologies which underpin contemporary societies (Marshall 1997). One of the key elements of the study of *sports* celebrities is that they inevitably speak to themes of national identity (Andrews and Jackson 2001; Turner 2004). Although the nature of celebrity culture has changed markedly during the twentieth century, many of the changes are a continuation, rather than a disruption, of longer term processes. For instance, we saw earlier how W.G. Grace became an important sporting celebrity in England and Scotland at the end of the Victorian era. Similarly it could be argued that the popularity of Nyren's account of the Hambledon players stemmed from their use in generating an English identity, providing stability at a time of rapid social change, etc. Most interestingly though, the portrayal of Flintoff draws directly on the narratives introduced by Nyren and Pycroft in the nineteenth century. Consequently Flintoff provides an excellent vehicle through which to examine continuity and change in the relationship between cricket and English national identity.

Born in Preston, Lancashire, on 6 December 1977, Andrew 'Freddie' Flintoff's role in England's 2005 Ashes win propelled him to celebrity status, 'a name which, once made by the news, now makes the news itself' (Rein *et al.* 1997: 14). Yet Flintoff's post-2005 performances were as inconsistent as his fitness. He captained England to a 5-0 losing Ashes series in 2006–07 and was later stripped of the England vice-captaincy after the notorious 'Fredalo' incident during the 2007 ICC Cricket World Cup.[6] The 2009 season started poorly for Flintoff when he missed a pre-series trip to the World War I trenches in Flanders, resurrecting questions about his ill-discipline and relationship with alcohol. But Flintoff's series changed when, on the eve of the second test at Lord's, he announced that he would retire from Test cricket at the end of the Ashes series due to a persistent knee injury. Flintoff went on to take five wickets bowling unchanged on the final morning of the Lord's test to put England ahead in the series. Flintoff batted well but bowled ineffectually in the rain affected drawn third test before controversially being left out of the fourth, disputing the team management's assessment of his fitness. England suffered a humiliating loss and with the series tied Flintoff was recalled for the final Oval test. Set an improbable 546 to win a partnership of 127 between Australian captain Ricky Ponting and Michael Hussey looked like it might save the game and consequently retain the Ashes for Australia until Flintoff ran out Ponting with a direct hit from mid off. Shortly after England won the game and regained the Ashes. Though Flintoff had scored just twenty-nine runs and taken just one wicket in the match, he was accredited with inspiring victory. The 2009 Ashes would thus become seminal in defining Flintoff the celebrity.

Flintoff's emergence as a celebrity in 2005 firmly located him within the genre of nationalism fundamental to and evident in the development of the Barmy Army. Prominent, for instance, was his drunken behaviour during the Trafalgar Square celebrations and Downing Street reception where he reputedly asked the Prime Minister if he had anything to drink and urinated in the garden. He combined the 'New Laddishness' of these drunken antics (including writing TWAT on a teammate's forehead with an indelible marker pen) with elements of 'New Man' (for example, his devotion to family life). The most iconic image of that test series – a picture of Flintoff consoling Brett Lee mid pitch while the rest of the England team celebrated a narrow victory over Australia – positioned Flintoff as a compassionate man. Although Flintoff has subsequently (and jokingly) claimed that what he actually said to Brett Lee was 'It's 1-1 yer Aussie Bastard', this ultimately serves to highlight his embrace of an ironic humour also championed by the Barmy Army. Flintoff's 'sledging' of the West Indian tailender Tino Best (in telling Best to 'mind the windows' Flintoff induced a rash shot which led to Best's dismissal, much to the amusement of Flintoff and his team mates) and his 'not bad for a fat lad' comment in response to press criticism about his weight when accepting an ODI 'man-of-the-match' award in 2000, provide evidence of the centrality of humour to Flintoff's character. Post-playing Flintoff has become a panellist on the sports-comedy quiz, *A League of their Own* which in many ways is an organic successor to *They Think it's all Over*. But perhaps most significant to Flintoff's celebrity image is the passion with which he played and the manifest pleasure that playing the game brought to him. Flintoff and the Barmy Army were a natural fit due to their shared sense of fun, influence and nationalism. Thus Flintoff emerged as a celebrity at the convergence of the same processes that shaped the emergence of the Barmy Army and narratives of benign Englishness.

But if Flintoff's celebrity status stems from his connection to changing senses of national identity, it is also fundamentally rooted in his resonance with *traditional* conceptions of Englishness. These became particularly evident during the 2009 series. Flintoff was described as 'the embodiment of England'

(*Observer*, 5 July 2009), as 'a symbol of English belligerence ... there is a peculiarly English recklessness about his refusal to acknowledge physical disintegration' (*Guardian*, 21 July 2009). He was described as 'the solid oak of England', a 'big strong patriot who scares foreigners', whose 'exaltation at claiming an Australian wicket expressed large chunks of national character' (*Sun*, 4 August 2009; *Guardian*, 10 July 2009; *Guardian*, 16 July 2009). For Simon Barnes, 'Flintoff's most important role ... [was] as the antidote to fear. That's why he's the talisman. He intimidates' (*The Times*, 10 July 2009). Flintoff was, in many ways, the twenty-first century version of the 'unflinching, uncompromising, independent' Richard Nyren described by his son in 1833 in *The Cricketers of my Time* (Nyren 1833/1948: 18)

During 2009 the press represented Flintoff as a man whose previous ill-discipline had been redeemed through hard work. He was, for instance, prepared to 'run through a brick wall for his side ... he never knows when to give up' (*Sunday Mirror*, 26 July 2009). He had worked 'heroically hard on his fitness' (*Guardian*, 7 July 2009). The England medical team issued a statement praising the 'great determination and selflessness [in] making a conscious decision to push through discomfort in order to help England reclaim the Ashes' (*The Times*, 8 August 2009). Crucially effort was seen as an adjunct of honesty. It was claimed that 'Freddie never operates at anything less than 100 per cent' (*Sun*, 15 July 2009) and that he was 'the least cynical athlete in sport' (*The Times*, 16 July 2009). Former team mates and opponents were fulsome in their praise of Flintoff. In this respect Flintoff was reminiscent of Hambledon's John Wells, 'a creature of a transparent and unflawed integrity – plain, simple, and candid; uncompromising yet courteous; civil and deferential, yet no cringer' (Nyren 1833/1948: 35).

Flintoff's honesty was evident in both the simplicity of his game, and the modesty with which he reacted to his achievements. Again echoing the description of Wells, journalists wrote of, 'A carefree innings from a carefree man ... naturally committed to simple fun' (*Observer*, 23 August 2009). As if familiar with Pycroft's recommendations that conceit and vainglory were the 'enemies' of the cricketer (1851/1948: 67), Flintoff, reflected that he had not 'achieved greatness' on a par with players like Garry Sobers, Ian Botham and Ricky Ponting (*Sun*, 25 August 2009). While journalists sometimes questioned the role of PR advisors in constructing Flintoff's public character, it was thought that 'he never really set out to achieve greatness, doesn't yearn for it in the same way as [team mate] Kevin Pietersen. Flintoff plays for enjoyment, the company of mates' (*The Times* 20 August 2009).

This combination of character traits produced the kind of fundamentally unremarkable persona which traditionalists, since Nyren, have wanted to attribute for the genesis of the game. There was 'no player who enjoys a closer rapport with the fans. They view him as one of their own' (*Sun*, 19 August 2009), 'a player every cricket fan from all sides of the social divide could associate with' (*Sun,* 16 July 2009). Flintoff himself stated that 'If I wasn't a player I would be sat in the thick of the Barmy Army with a pint, singing away with the best of them' (*The Times,* 25 August 2009). Important in the presentation of Flintoff as 'normal' was the continual reference to his Preston roots, his embrace of northern, working-class culture and his support of the more 'local' Manchester City rather than the 'global' United. Thus 'much of Flintoff's appeal can be linked to this everyman approach' (*The Times,* 7 August 2009); 'a hugely inspirational figure, a man of his time and the undoubted hero of the masses' (*Sun,* 24 August 2009). On retirement Flintoff,

> bowed out an ordinary man ... This was understated Fred. This was ordinary Fred, the good lad Fred, bloke next door Fred who wonders what all the fuss is about when really he's just doing something he enjoys and happens to be quite good at ... [he] never betrayed his beliefs on how the game should be played and how the crowd should be entertained. (*Daily Mirror*, 25 August 2009)

Thus just as the nineteenth-century 're-invention' of cricket entailed the obfuscation of the game's elitist, aristocratic roots and the attribution of the game's origins to 'ordinary' English agricultural workers, so Flintoff was used to reiterate the narrative that cricket was a game of the people, embodying the people. Flintoff was both *one* of but also consciously *playing for* 'us' English. Like Hambledon farmer Thomas Brett, who bowled 'very quickly', and was a 'strictly honourable man' (Nyren 1833/1948: 17), Flintoff the sports celebrity was an everyday working man. The portrayal of Flintoff continued the tradition of using cricket as a mirror of social cohesion (Williams 1999).

As Hambledon and its cricketers had two centuries beforehand, Flintoff was positioned as a stable reference point in a changing world. Reflecting on England's victory in the second test, Matthew Syed wrote, 'The Ashes have once again shown us why the oldest rivalry in cricket, an anachronistic contest between a former colonial power and upstart nation, retains its vitality, urgency and relevance' (*The Times,* 22 July 2009). Following the Lord's victory it was claimed that 'cricket had reclaimed its place at the heart of British life' (*Daily Mirror,* 21 July 2009), while a Flintoff-less England at Headingley, 'played like a bunch of kids whose minds have been scrambled by too much internet surfing, cable TV channel hopping and Twenty20 cricket' (*Sunday People,* 9 August 2009). Flintoff had helped save test cricket from the perceived threat posed by the shorter and more commercially successful forms of the game like 'the white knight riding to the rescue' (*Daily Mirror,* 21 August 2009). In helping to return the Ashes to their 'rightful' status he challenged the 'Indianization' of cricket and provided a reminder of the days when England administered world cricket almost unilaterally. Resistance to these contemporary trends could just as easily have been described as counter to the 'march of intellect' as protests against the introduction of round arm bowling had been in the 1830s.

And just as had been evident almost two centuries earlier, the presentation of Flintoff was based upon the strong evocation of nostalgia. The portrayal of Flintoff evoked romanticized and mythologized aspects of the game. Flintoff was thus, 'one of a dying breed ... [and] a victim of the modern cricket calendar' (*Sun*, 16 July 2009). For former Australian cricketer Shane Warne, 'Freddie is a team player through and through ... People will remember him for his runs and his wickets in 2005, but also for how he played. He is one of the good guys, an entertainer who knows about the spirit of the game' (*The Times*, 16 July 2009). Others argued that his commiseration of Brett Lee in 2005 'will be used down the ages when erroneous stories are told about how the modern game is a degenerate version of the past' (*The Times*, 20 August 2009). Ahead of the final Oval test, Vic Marks referred to Flintoff's 'many old-fashioned virtues: generosity, politeness, loyalty, bravery and conviviality' (*Observer*, 16 August 2009). Invoking the transcental qualities of cricket and religion, the press referred to 'Flintoff ... bonding with the Lord's congregation' (*Guardian* 21 July 2009), of him 'deliver[ing] the kind of sermon everyone around the country wanted to hear' when announcing his determination to overcome injuries (*Daily Mirror*, 21 July 2009). The most explicit and extensive discussion linking Flintoff with nostalgia was written by Richard Williams at the beginning of the final test. He argued that:

> the importance of Andrew Flintoff lies in the way he provides a link to founding myths of English cricket ... (he) is as close as today's centrally contracted celebrity cricketers get to the blacksmiths and farmhands among whom the game took shape. His massive build and the apparent lack of science in his play combine to create a sense of cricket as it once was: a simple bucolic game. (*Guardian*, 19 August 2009)

Thus the presentation of Flintoff revolved around a familiar combination of English national character traits. The themes of bravery, commitment, honesty, simplicity and modesty essentially mirror those developed 200 years earlier when cricket was re-invented as the national game (see Chapter 2). Indeed much of what was written about Flintoff had direct parallels to Pycroft's (1851/1948: 62) description of 'The General Character of Cricket' in *The Cricket Field*. While Flintoff clearly was not 'sober and temperate', he possessed 'patience, fortitude, and self-denial ... obedience ... [and] an unruffled temper'. Flintoff demonstrated the virtues of perseverance but he was also amiable and recognized that cricket was a social game which should never, as Pycroft had argued, be over-serious. While Flintoff was projected as representing contemporary forms of masculinity, he also embraced 'the manly spirit that faces danger without shrinking and bears disappointment with good nature' (Pycroft 1951/1948: 69). Flintoff epitomized the view that 'no game is played in better humour – never lost till won – the game's alive till the last ball' (Pycroft 1951/1948: 69). Flintoff's sporting celebrity was based on his quintessential Englishness.

Conclusion

This chapter has sought to illustrate something of the fluidity and fragmented character of English national identity. Identity, however, is not a free floating mosaic in which various aspects can be picked at random, but fundamentally rooted in historical interdependencies. The Flintoff celebrity phenomenon epitomizes how contemporary themes are structured within a framework of relatively constant ideas of who the English are. Moreover, we can see that national identities are not monolithic. Newer forms of national identity may rise in conscious opposition to more traditional forms. They continue to be contested as illustrated in 2009 press debates about English cricket spectator behaviour during the Ashes series, and in particular elements of drunkenness and the booing of Australian captain Ricky Ponting. Thus it is important to emphasize that the malign nationalism that characterized English cricket prior to the mid-1990s has not entirely disappeared (or indeed that there was no benign Englishness pre 1994/95), but rather that there has been a shift in the relative prominence of their respective representations. It should also be noted that we cannot infer that there is some kind of direct relationship between the press narratives highlighted and the emotions and actions of self-identifying English individuals. We will return to this point in the Conclusion but for now suffice to say, as in the American case, it is unrealistic to imagine that national character (the character of a whole nation's people) can change quite so quickly. Rather there are some rather obvious attractions to developing the kind of positive self-image of benign Englishness which explains both its promotion to and reception among an English newspaper readership. Consequently, we also need to see how cricket is used as a vehicle for the characterization of other nationalities. It is to this that we turn in the next chapter.

9

Cricket, the English and the Process of 'Othering'

From its very inception as the national game, English 'ownership' of cricket has been bolstered by the concomitant belief that others have failed to embrace, and indeed are incapable of understanding, the sport. Given their geographical closeness and status competition, Anglo-French rivalry has traditionally been 'in a class of its own' (Paxman 1999: 26) and thus predictably manifest in perceptions of the quintessential English game. Consequently we see the terms French cut and French drive used to describe miss-hit shots. French cricket is used to describe a simplified form of the game, played mainly by children and always in informal settings. While it is a point of pride for the English that the French do not play cricket, more importantly, the French are portrayed as being *unable* to play cricket. For instance cricket historians have keenly seized on evidence which suggests that an English cricket team was about to depart for a game in Paris in 1789, but had to return home when revolution broke out (Goulstone and Swanton 1989). G.M. Trevelyan, Regius Professor of Modern English at Cambridge University would subsequently write, 'if the French *noblesse* had been capable of playing cricket with their peasants, their *chateaux* would never have been burnt' (cited in Holt 1989: 268) A brief examination of two examples of the way the English seek to demonstrate their (assumed) distinction from the French through cricket illustrates some of the broader points which underpin this chapter.

In 1889 the satirical magazine *Punch* responded to developments in France which would culminate in Pierre de Coubertin's establishment of the Modern Olympic Games by publishing a piece about 'Le Cricquette' and 'How he will be played shortly'. The article portrayed a match between 'ALL OF FRANCE v AN ENGLAND 'OME-TEAM'. The French team is dismissed for no runs with many of the players either paralysed with fear or injured. Three Frenchmen challenge the umpire (who is implicitly assumed to be English) to a duel. England score 6,333 runs in response but the game concludes when the umpire, 'with chivalrous generosity', declares a draw. Consequently it is decided that cricket in France should be played with a soft ball (to compensate for a lack of courage), that the wickets should be enlarged (to compensate for a lack of skill) and that 'the umpire, a grave anomaly in a game cherished by a liberty-loving people, should be instantly suppressed' (cited in Rayvern Allen 1985: 61).

A century later, marking the 2005 death of Jacques Derrida, a Miles Kington (2005) column in the *Independent* humorously juxtaposed the game and the French philosopher's ideas through a series of letters from fictional English cricketers. The first addresses Derrida's critique of essentialism. 'George "Gubby" Trotter' recalls Derrida questioning whether players can be said to be the same people at the beginning of a match as they are at the end: '"they are five days older. They may have changed their opinions, may have undergone significant experiences in the field. I think they may be different people"'. To this, Trotter responds, '"Jacques, you never change. You are an idiot" ... and he laughed.' In the second 'Lord Wilderspoon' portrays Derrida using a cricket example to formulate his critique of logocentrism based on binary oppositions: '"You know everything is relative" he [Derrida] told me one day in the slips. "You bowl medium-fast, with the occasional slow ball. I bowl slow and slip in the occasional quick one. Yet your slow ball is faster than my quick one! What does that tell us?"' The third lampoon's the French philosophic tradition more generally. 'Sir Ronald Cashew' asks Derrida to explain his philosophy to him and how it relates to cricket: '"An Englishman would never understand it ... The only true cricket is French cricket ... A bat, a ball, a pair of trousers. It is cricket reduced to its irreducible elements. Understand French cricket, and you can understand anything."'

These accounts draw on stereotypes which the English believe distinguish themselves from the French and which can be traced back to the conception of an English national character (see Chapter 2). French desire for liberty is contrasted with the ability of the English to achieve it. French intolerance of physical hardship leads them to respond with excessive violence (duelling), while the English, who possess the bravery to tolerate the violent aspects of cricket are paradoxically peaceable. The mocking of Derrida's ideas continues an English tradition of championing the practical over the abstract, the particular over the theoretical (Colls 2002). By invoking the imagery of French cricket, French philosophic traditions are portrayed as obfuscation rather than insight. Derrida is subject to the typically English insult of being 'too clever by half' (Haseler 1996: 21), while the English just get on with things and so get them done.

If, as Easthope (1999) argues, English national culture treats only cricket and its own sense of humour as transcental, then jokes about cricket which reveal how the English contrast themselves with others must hold considerable social significance. But the use of comedy as a vehicle to delineate competing identities serves an additional function. As we saw in relation to 'New Laddism', the use of humour 'at once permits, legitimates and exonerates an insult' (Pickering and Lockyer 2009, cited in Burdsey 2011: 269). Using humour enables people to distance themselves from the negative connotations of their identity construction practices and thus, for example, retain a benign rather than malign sense of national character.

Consequently this chapter seeks to develop our understanding of English national identity through an examination of the role of cricket in the 'Othering' of non-English peoples. Due to the influence of the colonial experience on Britain in general and cricket in particular, the Othering of Black and Asian populations is more frequent than, for example, the Othering of Americans or Europeans. Like the humorous accounts described above, these depictions demonstrate that English and 'Other' national characters are constructed relationally. But in addition to this, the very frequency and commonplace nature of such accounts makes them particularly influential and revealing. In contrast, for instance, to overtly political acts, they may not be subject to the same degree of critical reflection and thus illustrate in greater detail subconscious attitudes and beliefs. In contrast to humorous accounts, however, there is rather less ambiguity over their meaning.

Following a critical discussion of Said's concept of orientalism, this chapter presents an account of the media speculation over the death of former England cricketer and Pakistan coach during the 2007 ICC World Cup in the Caribbean, dubbed 'Woolmergate'. This, it is suggested, illustrates the way in which cricket acts as a vehicle for the juxtaposition of beliefs about English and 'Other' societies and people. The chapter concludes by arguing that a coherent set of ideas about self and other, about 'us and 'them', are consistently applied to frame a broad range of global cricketing issues, from allegations of match-fixing to the rise (and potential demise) of the IPL.

Orientalism

Edward Said's *Orientalism* is 'the classical framework in understanding relationships between the "West" (and the "Rest") and Muslims in particular' (Saeed 2007: 447). 'Orientalism' initially referred simply to the study of the social and cultural life of the East but latter day anti-colonial movements led to a questioning of the consequences of this genre of work. Said (2003: 2) argued that many orientalists had 'accepted the basic distinction between the East and the West as the starting point for elaborate theories', and thus one of the most significant achievements of orientalism is to construct *an* Orient, a single homogenized place which is believed to constitute a cohesive whole. Consequently a 'Them' and 'Us' is 'constructed as naturalized, binary oppositions' (Poole 2002: 18) in which Western cultures and societies are depicted as inherently superior to their 'alien' Eastern counterparts.

Orientalism constructs notions of an absolute and systematic difference between the East and West based on cultural generalizations or stereotypes that depict the Orient as 'irrational, aberrant, backward, crude, despotic, inauthentic, passive, feminine and sexually corrupt' (Macfie, 2000: 4). Conversely, in using antonyms such as rational, humane, developed and modern to depict the West, orientalism reveals inward self-reflection. Thus modernist Western identity – capitalist, secular, scientific – is logically dependent upon comparison with, and the establishment of difference from, non-Western cultures more broadly (Hall 1992). In this way European political and economic domination was/is augmented by cultural domination. This process can also be described as *Unthinking Eurocentrism* (Shohat and Stam 1994).

Said's (1997: xii) claim that, 'malicious generalizations about Islam have become the last acceptable form of denigration of foreign culture in the West' seems more pertinent post-9/11 than ever. Since 9/11 newspaper coverage of Muslims has increased dramatically (Whittaker 2002). Qualitatively, Richardson (2004: 75) suggests that the reporting of Islam and Muslims has been characterized by 'negative references' such as 'cultural backwardness', 'incivility', 'extremism', 'fundamentalism', 'barbarity' and 'intolerance', and he concludes that the similarities with 'Orientalist paternalism … are quite striking'. While British media representations of Black people have long focussed on an essential difference based on notions of the exotic, primitive and violent (Carrington 2010; van Dijk 1991), Asian males have come to replace Black males as the new 'folk devils' of British society. For Carrington (2008: 116) the 'Asian Muslim – a deliberate and powerful conflation of race, ethnicity and religion – becomes the new Other, against which British liberal democracy must stand'. Given the relational way in which identities are formed, it is perhaps not entirely coincidental that a benign nationalism entered the public consciousness of the English in 2005, for that was also the year of the 7/7 London bombings and thus a time when the events of 9/11 assumed a heightened level of significance for many in Britain.

Orientalism is a much debated text. It has been argued that Said was selective in his evidence, falsely presented Western scholarship as monolithic, ignored the role of the 'native' in developing the discipline, and failed to account for the way Westerners (as we saw in the previous chapter) have been affected by their own colonial experiences (Poole 2002; Richardson 2004). Consequently, in simplifying, homogenizing and dismissing the West, 'anti-orientalism' risks being as reductionist as the orientalist discourse Said set out to de-construct. Further questions centre on Said's ontological position; if orientalism portrays a falsehood – for instance Said (2003: 1–2) describes the Orient as both 'almost a European invention', yet not 'merely imaginative' – what is the relationship between orientalist discourse and reality?

The enduring relevance of orientalism lies in the connection Said makes between historical specificity, knowledge and power (Poole 2002: 31); that is to say, people in particular contexts generate particular beliefs and their (in)ability to sustain those beliefs depend on the broader structure of power relations. In this respect orientalism shares a number of notable similarities with Elias's sociology of knowledge more generally, and theory of civilizing processes in particular (these will be discussed further in the Conclusion). For present purposes, however, we merely need to recognize that a critical application of Said's ideas enables us to see that Western representations of the East form a 'saturating hegemonic system' (Macfie 2000: 4), and that the broader principles of such a framework can be useful in helping us understand how (and why) the English 'Other' various social groups. Consequently, the next section illustrates how, despite apparent changes to English self-conceptions, orientalism has continued, and perhaps become even more intense, in structuring jingoistic and nationalistic caricatures in recent years. As will be seen, the stereotyping of post-colonial peoples and societies is a more general feature of how contemporary English people engage with cricket.

Woolmergate

In Jamaica on 17 March 2007 Pakistan was unexpectedly eliminated from the ICC Cricket World Cup after losing to Ireland. Bob Woolmer described the result as one of his worst experiences in cricket. He told reporters that he would 'sleep on his future' as Pakistan coach and went to his room on the twelfth floor of Kingston's Pegasus Hotel. He ordered lasagne from room service. During the night he sent an email to his wife Gill in Cape Town, South Africa, and told her that he was shocked and depressed by events.

The next morning Woolmer's dead body was found lying against the inside of his bathroom door. The majority of reports stated that the room was not disturbed and that there were no signs of forced entry. Whilst there was vomit, blood and faeces on the bathroom floor and walls, there were no external cuts or bruises on Woolmer's body. Woolmer was pronounced dead at a local hospital at 12.00pm on 18 March.

Woolmer had been suffering from stress, had Type II diabetes and sometimes slept with an oxygen mask. Given this background it was thought that he may have suffered a heart attack or stroke. Others speculated that he may have died from food poisoning. The initial post-mortem conducted by Dr Ere Sheshaiah was 'inconclusive' but on 22 March, following further toxicology and histology tests, Jamaican police commissioner Lucius Thomas announced that it was believed that Woolmer died from 'asphyxia as a result of manual strangulation'.

Mark Shields, an English-born, former London Metropolitan Police detective led the Jamaican investigation. The high profile multinational inquiry was closed on 12 June 2007 with the conclusion that Woolmer had not been murdered but had died from natural causes. In the intervening weeks, however, a range of theories about Woolmer's death were mooted by the Jamaican police, cricketers, cricket administrators and journalists. Woolmer's murder, it was speculated, had been committed: by a Pakistan player; by an angry Pakistan supporter; by Muslim radicals; by bookmakers who feared Woolmer might expose their match-fixing operations; following a bungled burglary attempt. The uncertainty over Woolmer's death enabled British journalists considerable scope to speculate. In so doing particular narratives emerged which both conformed to the perceptions of Englishness charted in the previous chapter, and revealed 'a reservoir of ideas, or core images' (Richardson 2004: 230) about Caribbean societies and 'the Orient'.

Woolmergate and cultural representations of the West

Posthumous tributes portrayed Woolmer as 'essentially' rational, humane and modern. Such positive and generous reflections are, of course, not unusual in obituaries, but the *particular* attributes to which writers drew attention reveal a broader set of underlying assumptions about the defining characteristics and thus inherent 'superiority' of the West, and the English in particular. The prominent narratives mirror those discussed in the previous chapter in relation to benign Englishness, and epitomized in the Flintoff celebrity.

Woolmer's rational character was elucidated by the former South African player Allan Donald who said that Woolmer 'never became flustered' and had a 'calm way' which was 'brilliant at diffusing potentially difficult situations' (*Sun*, 23 March 2007). Woolmer was accredited for 'the unusual period of calm' which the Pakistan team experienced under his stewardship (*Daily Mail*, 22 March 2007), and *Eastern Eye* (23 March 2007) spoke of Woolmer's 'calming influence on a team full of eccentrics'. The *Daily Mirror* (24 March 2007) stated that 'despite the vitriol' which followed Pakistan's defeat to Ireland, 'Woolmer handled the upset with typical dignity'.

A sense of humanity underpinned Woolmer's rationality. Not only had Woolmer 'done such a great service to international cricket' (*Daily Star*, 23 March 2007), his motivation had been largely altruistic. John Etheridge described Woolmer as 'a cricket man to his soul and (someone) who cared so much' (*Sun*, 22 March 2007). Others noted that despite the international demand for his coaching skills, he had accumulated relatively little wealth from his involvement in the game. Greater significance was attached to his experience of coaching in South Africa's townships than to his participation on a 'rebel tour' to South Africa in 1981 or his involvement with Kerry Packer cricket in the 1970s (*Observer*, 25 March 2007). For former England captain David Gower, 'nobody … better represented the high principles of sportsmanship that have been traditionally associated with cricket' (*The Sunday Times*, 25 March 2007). The *Daily Mail* (22 March 2007) suggested that whilst 'sometimes frustrated by the vagaries of coaching Pakistan, Woolmer had a love for the country and its people'. Allan Donald, David Gower and Colin Crompton (*Independent*, 19 March 2007), all explicitly linked Woolmer's tolerance and benevolence to his Englishness.

Woolmer was also depicted as a modern cosmopolitan. He was described as 'truly a citizen of the world' (*Daily Mail*, 22 March 2007) on account of the variety of appointments he had held in international cricket, including an ICC post with responsibility for developing the game in emerging nations. For Derek Pringle, Woolmer was 'an enthusiast ... (who) liked a challenge', but also 'a man of the world' (*Daily Telegraph,* 22 March 2007). Crompton mused that, 'It always seemed odd that he was prepared to coach in so many bizarre places but he was so deeply enamoured of the game' (*Independent,* 19 March 2007). At the heart of 'Woolmergate', therefore, was a 'victim' who was depicted as an embodiment of many of the positive characteristics the English attribute to themselves, and by extension to the West more generally. Where many orientalists implied that 'colonialism brought tranquility' to colonized lands (Said 1997: liv), so Woolmer was represented as an English cricket philanthropist, who used typically English traits to bring order to a hostile and chaotic environment.

Woolmergate and cultural representations of the Caribbean

The media's depiction of the Caribbean, and Jamaica in particular, focused on three inter-related themes. Centrally the English press portrayed Jamaica as a society heavily reliant on Britain; a society which, despite political independence, could only function with the former colonizer's continued support. This dependence, stemmed from the second and third themes: the violent character of Jamaican society and its relatively underdeveloped infrastructure.

Many of the early reports on Woolmer's death contextualized the suspected killing with reference to the commonplace nature of violence in Jamaican society. *The Times* (22 March 2007), for instance, spoke of 'endemic gun crime, Yardie gangs and drug culture', the *Independent* (1 April 2007) referred to Jamaica's 'soaring murder rate', and the *Daily Mail* (31 March 2007) substantiated such claims by identifying Jamaica as having the world's third highest murder rate per capita. Barbadian cricket journalist Tony Cozier provided a more emotive backdrop:

> Two days after his [Woolmer's] death, a gang shot dead the two-year-old daughter of a policeman and seriously injured her six-year-old sister and other young family members in a rough Kingston area known as Vietnam. 'Evil' was the headline over the report in *The Daily Observer* but, as heinous as it was, it was simply another statistic to add to the 1,000 or so killed every year. (*Independent on Sunday*, 25 March 2009)

Police comments, designed to counter suggestions that the murderer may have been Jamaican did little to counter this motif of violence. On 27 March the *Daily Mirror* quoted Mark Shields, leading the Jamaican investigation, as stating that, 'Most murders in Jamaica are internal affairs. Manual strangulation doesn't fit a local profile. Firearms or knives are the favoured weapons here.' Similarly the *Guardian* (30 March 2007) cited Shields' view that,

> It's so important that people realise that Jamaica is, by and large, a safe country for outsiders. Jamaicans kill Jamaicans for a whole array of reasons … but Jamaicans do not murder tourists. They might rob them as they do in Rome or London, but they don't go around killing visitors to the island.

The paper went on to underscore the Jamaica-violence narrative by noting that Shields initially transferred from London to investigate an alleged 'shoot-to-kill' policy in some sections of the Jamaican police (see also *The Times* 22 March 2007).

The violence portrayed as endemic in Jamaica was viewed as partly a cause, and partly a consequence, of the dysfunctional aspects of a 'backward' society. The *Daily Mail* (20 March 2007) argued that 'the chaotic preparation for the World Cup has meant much-needed medical equipment, including MRI scanners, had not yet arrived in Kingston hospitals in time for the start of the event'. Although *The Times* (31 March 2007) reported that Shields 'prided himself on bringing modern investigative technology and techniques to the Jamaican force', others referred to the 'maelstrom of policing that is Jamaica', and suggested that there was 'corruption at all levels which has resulted in public mistrust' (*Daily Mail*, 6 April 2007). As early as the beginning of April, the *Daily Telegraph* (2 April 2007) suggested that the inquiry was 'in danger of becoming mired in Jamaican bureaucracy, a system so plagued by inefficiencies that some cases dating back 10 years remain unresolved'. The coroners court – which *The Times* (31 March 2007) described as 'a tiny wooden, one-room venue', located 'amid the chaos of central Kingston', staffed by assistants who 'appeared to be doing nothing. Their desks were devoid of paperwork' – was reported to have a backlog of almost 4,000 cases.

The Times (31 March 2007) was equally critical of the Jamaican pathology service, citing 'antediluvian scenes' and 'a creaky and antiquated Jamaican infrastructure poorly equipped to deal with such a high-profile and complex case'. In similar vein the *Daily Mail* (31 March 2007) reported that, 'post mortems that should take two hours or more are rushed through in 30 minutes'. The paper further cited a UK pathologist with experience of working in Jamaica who recalled that examinations 'did not meet the basic requirements … hands were not bagged to prevent contamination; the bodies were piled up on each other on trolleys … body fluids mingle, bullets aren't "noticed"'. The *Observer* (15 April 2007) and *The Times* (31 March 2007) drew attention to the Jamaicans' rapid embalming of Woolmer's body which complicated re-examination. The *Daily Mail* inferred that such practices were a natural extension of Jamaican culture. Not only did the paper cite the Jamaicans for Justice (JFJ) pressure group's claims that 'bribes are routinely offered to change autopsy reports', but concluded that, 'It was in this chronically ill-equipped and flyblown hospital – whose patients must endure reggae music pumping out night and day, and the fug of ganja wafting around the wards – that Dr Sheshaiah conducted his widely questioned post-mortem.'

Partly as a consequence of the uncertainty in the initial autopsy findings, but partly because the diagnosis of manual asphyxiation seemed inconsistent with other evidence from the case,[1] the media reported a number of 'authorities' who questioned the coroner's report. The *Daily Mail* (30 March 2007) first reported the concerns of Dr Garfield Blake, past president of the Jamaican Association of Clinical Pathologists, whilst two days later (1 April 2007) *The Sunday Times* and *Sunday Express* (in nearly identical reports) noted that, 'Some of Britain's leading forensic pathologists have called for a second autopsy to examine Bob Woolmer's death after expressing doubts about the evidence suggesting he was strangled'. *The Sunday Times* (1 April 2007) claimed to have spoken to five leading British pathologists who agreed that if strangulation had been the cause of death, one would expect to have found marks on Woolmer's neck. *The Sunday Times* (8 April 2007) repeated these claims a week later, this time citing Derrick Pounder, Professor of Pathology at the University of Dundee, in whose experience, Jamaican pathologists were 'hackers, not cutters … I would be more comfortable if these findings were reviewed'.

In addition to the post-mortem, journalists highlighted the relatively unsophisticated nature of CCTV security equipment. The *Daily Mirror* (29 March 2007) reported that no cameras pointed directly at Woolmer's door, that recordings were made on VHS tapes rather than digitally, and that 'it is also thought the tapes were worn out from years of reuse'. *The Times* (30 March 2007) further reported Pakistani discontent at the progress of the investigation. Inspector General Malik, of Karachi's Anti-Corruption Establishment, was reported as saying, 'To my assessment, the investigation is not very sharp. How many days was it before they were looking at the CCTV footage? Almost a week. I don't know why. I am astonished that they do not know yet who visited every room.'

The combined portrayal of a violent and disordered society which was technologically and organizationally backward led to a narrative which both underscored Jamaica's deficiencies and its continued dependence on other countries, and the former colonial power in particular. On 1 April, the *Independent* reported that Scotland Yard, London would send three senior detectives to review the case. On 7 April the *Guardian* reported that a Scotland Yard 'forensic expert' had arrived in Jamaica, and on 15 April the *Observer* said that Scotland Yard detectives were flying home having made 'no apparent progress'. Nearly a week later the *Daily Telegraph* (21 April 2007) stated that it understood that London Metropolitan police detectives had reviewed the investigation and had made a number of recommendations. The United Kingdom had supplied analysis of toxicology samples (*Daily Express*, 16 April 2007) and 'closer scrutiny' (*The Times*, 16 April 2007) and 'digital enhancement' (*Independent*, 21 April 2007) of CCTV images. The United States supplied a pathologist to conduct the second post-mortem (*The Times*, 23 March 2007), FBI assistance (*Sunday Star*, 1 April 2007), and further toxicology tests (*Daily Telegraph*, 21 April 2007). According to the *Guardian* (7 April 2007), the arrival of an Interpol forensic expert, 'renewed conjecture that the postmortem examination was bungled'.

Woolmergate and cultural representations of the Orient

Despite the death occurring in Jamaica, a greater proportion of the British press coverage of Woolmergate focused on Pakistan. In part this might have been a consequence of Mark Shields' conviction that the *modus operandi* of Woolmer's murderer was not that of a Jamaican killer. More importantly for present purposes however, there were some interesting similarities and differences between the depiction of Jamaican and Pakistani societies in the Woolmergate coverage. Whilst Pakistan(is), like Jamaica(ns), was portrayed as both violent and backward, the overriding narrative of Pakistan(is) was not one of the continued dependence, but rather of inherent and unbridgeable difference.

The violent character of Pakistani society was initially depicted through descriptions of the behaviour of Pakistan supporters. Defeat to Ireland 'sparked riots in Pakistan' (*Daily Mirror*, 19 March 2007), 'sent angry fans wild … Pakistanis (are) fervent about their national side' (*Daily Mail,* 19 March 2007). According to the *Daily Telegraph* (22 March 2007), Pakistan's defeats had led 'mobs' to stone Woolmers' Pakistan apartment and burn effigies of Woolmer and the captain Inzamam-ul-Haq, 'to chants of "Death to Bob Woolmer, Death to Inzamam"'. The *Sun* (22 March 2007) told its readers that what occurred was quite normal; not only were players' effigies 'burned when the team loses … their houses are frequently attacked'.

It was widely speculated that the murderer might be 'a Pakistani supporter, angry at their abject performance', 'a mad fan' (*Daily Mirror,* 24 March 2007), or that Woolmer had been the 'victim of a supporter with a grudge' (*Guardian* 30 April 2007). Newspapers reported that the team feared for their lives in the 'lawlessness' of Pakistan (*The Times*, 28 March 2007), and thus would stay in London to delay their return to Pakistan (*Daily Star* 23 March 2007). *The Times* (29 March 2007) reported that in an attempt to protect the players, the Pakistan Cricket Board (PCB) had decided that the squad would not travel back together, and circulated misinformation which concealed players' return journeys. The paper further described how players on a flight arriving in Islamabad at 2.30am had been 'jostled angrily' and had their cars surrounded by crowds of fans; 'You wondered what it would have been like if Woolmer was alive. Because this was a country showing a sensitive approach.' Before the murder investigation, by contrast, 'the public were openly talking of attending the team's return with sticks'.

In the same way that it was mooted that Woolmer's death might have been linked to organized crime in Jamaica, the British press speculated over the involvement of gangs of 'Asian bookmakers'. There were claims that Pakistan players had told police that Woolmer had a 'blazing row' with an 'Indian bookie' (*Daily Mail*, 29 March 2007), whilst former Pakistan player, Sarfraz Nawaz, was quoted as saying that 'at least 5 bookies from Pakistan are in the West Indies and had been in touch with Pakistani players in attempts to fix matches' (*Sun*, 22 March 2007). These individuals were depicted as frontmen for more sinister networks, or '"vague, shady" Asian syndicates' (*Daily Telegraph*, 24 March 2007).

Violence, organized crime and corruption were therefore depicted as pervasive features of Pakistani society and Asia more generally. The *Sun* (22 March 2007) suggested that there were 'illegal betting markets in Pakistan and India', *The Times* (30 March 2007) reported that, 'In Karachi they may gamble on cricket, but the industry is controlled from Dubai and Bombay', and the *Guardian* (24 March 2007) claimed that much of the finance came 'from overseas, mostly in the middle east'. Crucially, however, such gambling was seen as a 'major earner for criminal elements in Asia' (*Daily Mail*, 22 March 2007) and consequently largely controlled by 'Triad gangs' (*Daily Express*, 23 March 2007). On the basis that 'it is not unknown for those involved [in these illegal betting markets] to meet an unfortunate end' (*Sun*, 22 March 2007), it was speculated that Woolmer may have been killed in a 'Mafia style "hit"' (*Sun*, 30 March 2007).

The media extended the description of organized violence by further extrapolating from the involvement of bookmakers to links with international terrorism. The bookmaker with whom Woolmer was said to have argued was reported to be 'linked to one of India's most notorious godfathers who is himself said to have links to Al Qaeda' (*Daily Mail*, 29 March 2007) The *Daily Mail* (22 March 2007) claimed that the 'godfather', Dawood Ibrahim, was 'on Interpol's wanted list for terrorism, organised crime and counterfeiting and is accused of funding Al Qaeda-linked groups'. He was 'rumoured to have links with Osama Bin Laden'. Using the headline 'Al-Qaeda link to Woolmer murder', the *Sun* (29 March 2007) also reported this case, though they identified the bookmaker to be Dawood Ibrahim's 'Pakistan-based' brother, Anees. Though not explicitly connecting him to Woolmer's death, the *Independent* (26 March 2007), *News of the World* (25 March 2007), *Observer* (25 March 2007), and *Sunday Telegraph* (25 March 2007) all published accounts of Ibrahim Dawood's cricketing-gambling-terrorist connections. The *Independent*, for example, stated that Ibrahim was 'linked with a 1993 terrorist bombing in Mumbai which killed 200 people', that he lived 'in Pakistan, under the patronage of that country's intelligence agencies', and that 'allegations of Ibrahim's involvement with cricket-fixing and other crimes have become so commonly accepted in the Subcontinent, that few now question it'. The violence pervading Pakistani society therefore ranged from fanatical supporters and illegal bookmakers to state-tolerated terrorism.

As with Jamaica, violence was seen to be both a cause and a consequence of the irrational organization of the Pakistan state and Pakistani society more generally. Former Pakistan cricketer turned politician, Imran Khan, pointed to nepotism within Pakistan, arguing that the 'only qualification' of the Chairman of the PCB 'is that the President likes him'. Broadsheet newspapers supported such claims by citing Richard Pybus, a Westerner who had coached the Pakistan men's national side prior to Woolmer: 'Pybus revealed how making plans proved futile as the present was always being overthrown' (*Daily Telegraph,* 23 March 2007). The *Guardian* (20 March 2007) referred to governmental influence over cricket by quoting Pybus: 'you're always sitting there waiting for someone to lob a hand grenade and waiting for it to go off'. As a consequence, the Pakistan side were labelled, 'one of the most dysfunctional groups in world sport' (*The Times,* 23 March 2007), plagued by 'constant infighting' (*Daily Mail,* 22 March 2007), and whose 'ability to ambush themselves is legendary' (*Daily Telegraph,* 23 March 2007). Such was 'the chaotic world of Pakistan cricket' (*Guardian,* 20 March 2007), that Woolmer's death was just 'the latest and saddest chapter … [Pakistan cricket] has always been a web of intrigue' (*Daily Express,* 22 March 2007).

Speculation over the possible poisoning of Woolmer further revealed journalists' implicit assumptions about the traditional and pre-modern character of Pakistan society. According to a number of newspapers (*Mail on Sunday,* 22 March 2007; *Daily Star,* 23 March 2007; *Daily Express,* 29 March 2007; *Daily Mail,* 30 March 2007), Woolmer was killed by a 'Deadly snake venom'. Other reports suggested that the poison might have been aconite. The poison narrative had the effect of reinforcing perceptions of Pakistan as a violent and lawless society for it was claimed that the substance had been used 'in several high-profile assassinations in Pakistan' (*Sun,* 20 March 2007). More than this though, aconite was identified as a natural and thus primitive substance, 'used in herbal medicine across Asia' (*Independent,* 21 March 2007) and 'derived from the wolfsbane plant' (*Independent on Sunday,* 22 March 2007). The name wolfsbane was attributed to the belief in the Middle Ages that touching the plant would turn a person into a werewolf (*The Times,* 20 March 2007). This was 'an ancient poison' (*The Independent,* 21 April 2007), which had been 'used for centuries as a means of assassination' (*Daily Express,* 20 March 2007).

Rather than leading to a notion of dependence (as in the case with Jamaica), this press narrative concluded with the assertion that there was an absolute and systematic difference between Britain and Pakistan, and perhaps the East and West more broadly. Woolmer, it was claimed, failed to come to terms with, 'the most impenetrable … international outfit in the whole of sport' (*Daily Mail,*

23 March 2007) due to the 'constant bickering within Pakistani cricket' (*The Times*, 22 March 2007). Other reports suggested that there was 'a bitter feud between murdered coach Bob Woolmer and senior Pakistan officials', that Woolmer had been close to resigning due to 'continuous sniping and harassment' from unnamed cricket administrators, and had 'faced constant verbal battles' with the team captain, which ended in the player's 'brooding silence' (*Daily Express*, 28 March 2007). Woolmer, said the *Daily Telegraph* (23 March 2007), could be excused: 'some challenges are insurmountable and Pakistan cricket, with its shifting agendas and personnel, proved beyond even him'.

Religion was identified to be at the heart of this difference. Woolmer was said to have been 'an outsider walking into a different world … not part of the deeply religious Muslim culture' (*Daily Express*, 22 March 2007). He was excluded from the team meetings held in Urdu (*Daily Express*, 28 March 2007). According to the *Daily Telegraph* (23 March 2007), 'the impression is that many of the players, are a law unto themselves with allegiance only to Islam'. Under a headline which claimed that, 'Woolmer "clashed with his team over prayer time"', it was argued that some of the team were 'more interested in praying not playing' (*Daily Telegraph*, 30 April 2007).

In the latter stages of the investigation, the press increasingly began to suggest that Woolmer may have been murdered by 'radical Muslims' (*Daily Mail*, 30 April 2007) or 'Islamic fanatics' (*Daily Star*, 30 April 2007). References to religion were regularly conjoined with adjectives which conveyed extremism. According to the *Daily Mail* (22 March 2007), the team had followed Inzamam and become 'strict adherents to Islam'. P.J. Mir, the team's former media manager, argued that Woolmer agreed with his view that 'some senior members of the squad, who were members of the strict Muslim movement Tablighi Jamaat, were more focused on religion than cricket' (*The Independent*, 1 May 2007). Indeed, on 30 April, three newspapers (*Daily Telegraph, Daily Mail*, and *Guardian*) repeated the claims of the *Daily Mirror* a month earlier (30 March 2007) that a fatwa had been issued against Woolmer because of his stance against religion in the team.[2]

This cultural representation of the Orient was most explicitly encapsulated by John Etheridge in an article written prior to the launch of the police investigation. Under the headline "Killed by the Mad, Mad World of Pakistan cricket" a link was drawn between the supposed violent and irrational nature of Pakistan and the dangers inherent in attempting to bridge the cultural differences. Etheridge wrote that,

> Whatever the rumours, conspiracy theories or sheer lies about his tragic demise, Woolmer would almost certainly still be alive if he had not taken the job of Pakistan coach. He found a culture of love and hate, ball-tampering and match-fixing, divisions and togetherness, falsehoods and withering truths, sackings and reprieves. (*Sun*, 22 March 2007)

Conclusion

In relaying these representations of the Caribbean and Pakistan my intention is not to enter into a debate about their truth or falsity, merely to demonstrate the existence of a 'saturating hegemonic system' (Macfie 2000: 4) which frames the way in which the English 'Other' postcolonial peoples. Yes, Jamaica does have a relatively high murder rate. Yes, Al Qaeda has strong roots in Pakistan. But just as cricket continues to perform a unique role in the maintenance of postcolonial relations, so it is also an important sphere in which attempts at ideological dominance continue to be played out. Such is the influence of this set of ideas that they are also present within the cultures which they caricature. For instance, the *Independent on Sunday* (25 March 2007) cited Kingston's *The Daily Observer* which wrote: 'While the world watched and waited, we appeared to be a little Third World country which could not even carry out an autopsy without overseas assistance. But then maybe that's exactly what we are.' Citation of the criticisms of Pakistanis such as Imran Khan and Sarfraz Nawaz lend an air of authenticity to the views expressed in the English press.

Whilst the British press may no longer be pre-occupied with an inward looking, defensive nationalism when reporting cricket-related events, the portrayal of 'Others' suggests little by way of the tolerance of difference or mutual co-existence intrinsic to the kind of benign nationalism evident in the post-2005 reporting of English cricket. Whilst changes to the representation of Englishness may be enduring or transient, a consequence of economic exigency or moral self-reflection, heartfelt or merely public relations exercises, the postcolonial portrayal of the former territories of the British Empire is clearly not cosmopolitan and creative. Through Woolmergate, both Jamaica/the Caribbean and Pakistan/'the East' were seen to be 'dysfunctional'; societies infused with violence, irrationality and organizational incompetence. The selection of these themes is a continuation of the ideas which, as noted earlier, stem from the advent of modernity in Western Europe (Hall 1992), and thus the advent of modern sport in England.

One criticism that could be levelled at the kind of qualitative content analysis presented here is that it does not indicate how dominant such themes are, merely their presence. However, the depth to which these orientalist themes penetrated 'Woolmergate' can be illustrated by reflecting on the six main theories of how Woolmer died. Underpinning five of the six theories is a portrayal of the East as necessarily different and inferior to the West. If Woolmer was murdered by bookmakers, it was because the (Pan-Asian) bookmakers are more deviant, corrupt, evil and violent than they are elsewhere in the world, and have terrorist links. If Woolmer was murdered by a cricket fan, it was because Pakistanis have an irrational attachment to their national cricket team and a propensity towards violence. If Woolmer was murdered by a Pakistan player, or indeed 'Muslim radicals', it stemmed from a devotion to Islam which illustrates the essential incompatibility of Eastern and Western cultures. Even if no other individual was involved, and Woolmer died from natural causes or committed suicide, he did so because of the untameable nature of Pakistani cricket/culture. The sixth theory, that Woolmer died during an attempted burglary, evokes different, but similarly negative stereotypes about Caribbean society.

These narratives of difference are so pervasive that they structure a whole range of diverse issues in contemporary cricket. For instance reactions to allegations that Hansie Cronje had been involved in match fixing in 2000 were initially met by incredulity, the argument that evidence may have been fabricated by Indian police, and the assertion that such actions were strictly against Cronje's religious commitments (Nauright 2005). For Sen (2001: 238) the South Africans, English and Australians' immediate denial that '"they" could have been involved in something so heinous' soon turned to the implication that the 'innate immorality of the subcontinent … had ensnared, seduced, and corrupted an erstwhile icon of white moral purity'. In contrast to this, the British media's response to allegations that Salman Butt, Mohammed Asif and Mohammed Amir had accepted money in order to facilitate spot-betting almost universally assumed guilt. Moreover, while Cronje's guilt was depicted as an individual's aberration, the case against the Pakistan players was taken as evidence of more systemic, society-wide, corruption and led to numerous calls for Pakistan to be banned from international cricket.

Similarly, these themes resurface in Gupta's (2010) analysis of the major threats to the Indianization of cricket and the continuation of the IPL. The three threats Gupta (2010: 56) identifies are: *administrative inefficiency* – the degree to which the Indian authorities are deemed capable of running international, commercial, entertainment events; *security* – fears over player safety; and *corruption* – whether the competition can be run with the sufficient degree of transparency. For each of these concerns there is, of course, supporting evidence. For instance, questions were raised about the organizational competence of the 2010 New Dehli Commonwealth Games Organizing Committee. The IPL has already been staged in South Africa due to security concerns and there was further debate about the viability of the tournament following a bombing at the Bangalore stadium prior to the 2010 IPL. Lalit Modi, Chairman of the IPL, was suspended by the BCCI in 2010, accused of being involved in match-fixing or, at least, of being ineffectual in monitoring or addressing corruption during the tournament in South Africa in which forty-odd players were involved in attempts to rig the results of matches. These are tangible threats, but their identification is also quite predictable in that it fits in to the broader structure of understanding and the overarching logic that can be seen in the 'Woolmergate' coverage. Through the prism of orientalism, as identified by Said, we can see how threats to the Indianization of cricket are not simply the commonsense identification of potential problems, but conform to a relatively coherent set of interconnected ideas that are based on a historical legacy of colonialism.

We can see therefore that not only does cricket play a central role in the identity construction of diaspora consciousness in Britain, and various and competing forms of English national identity, but also in the way the English understand 'Other' populations around the world. Before providing some theoretical reflections from this historical sociological study of *Globalizing Cricket,* the concluding chapter addresses the continuing social significance of the game in British society and seeks to explain why, despite such manifest changes, cricket remains the quintessential English game.

Conclusion

Cricket
as explained to a foreign visitor

There are two sides
one out in the field and one in.
Each player that's in the side that's
in goes out and when he's out he
comes in and the next player
goes in until he's out

When they are all out the side
that's out comes in and the side that's
been in goes out and tries to get those coming in out

Sometimes you get players still in and not out.

When both side have been
in and out including the not outs
That's the end of the game
Howzat![1]

The aims of this book have been to subject the 'paradoxical beast' of English cricket to sustained examination, to chart how the role and social significance of cricket have changed as the game has globalized, and to take our understanding of the 'cricket-Englishness' couplet beyond the somewhat pleonastic treatment it receives in both the sports studies literature and analyses of Englishness and English national identity. At the outset it was established that cricket was somewhat peculiar amongst contemporary global sports. Subsequently we saw how cricket emerged as a modern sports form, socially and geographically diffused within Britain and across parts of the Empire, and continues to structure the lives and identities of various groups within Britain today. Can we identify how the development and structure of British society relates to the way in which the game is played? Can we now say *why* this peculiar sport remains the quintessential English game?

An obvious and simple answer to this question is that cricket is the quintessential English game because people think it is; because they associate playing the sport with this specific ethnic group. Consequently, when cricket is described in this way people identify a close interrelationship between what are perceived to be English national characteristics and those characteristics attributed to the game and its players. Williams (1999: 1) for instance has noted that cricket has been 'celebrated as a metaphor for England' and inscribed with a peculiarly English moral worth. Indeed for cricket, and I would argue *only* for cricket, English national character traits such as independence, honesty, restraint, self-discipline and pragmatism are routinely and unproblematically defined as generated through, and embodied in those who play, the game. *Globalizing Cricket's* broad historical sweep shows that pretensions to these attributes were just as conspicuous in the initial claims for cricket as England's national game as they were in the key role attributed to the game in the latter years of the Empire. The Flintoff celebrity persona charted in Chapter 8 illustrates the contemporary manifestation of this enduring sense of the distinctive aspects of national life that both insiders and outsiders have described as characteristic of the English (Langford 2000). It is easily overlooked but the perception of cricket as a manly game is fundamental to sustaining the association between cricket and the equally gendered concept of Englishness. Perhaps most importantly of all, the emergence of a stable and consistently identified model of English national character occurred concomitantly with the social construction of cricket as the national game.

Cricket better fits the English 'national mood' of nostalgia (Ackroyd 2004: 442) than any other sport. While to some extent all contemporary English sports are infused with celebrations of a romanticized past (Maguire 1994), only cricket was 'defined' alongside the rise of reactive nostalgia which led in the early 1800s to the 'invention' of Englishness itself. Only in cricket is the construction of contemporary celebrity so significantly shaped by nostalgia. While the statistical nature of cricket enables temporal comparison (Williams 1999), the centrality of statistics is as much a manifestation as it is a consequence of the importance of nostalgia.

Cricket can also be seen to be inexorably inscribed into both English landscape and language. One of the reasons why cricket is widely used in marketing 'England' and promoting tourism is that it is so closely associated with ideas about the English national landscape (Bairner *et al.* 2007). The image of an English cricket ground is visually distinct (though not to say lacking in imitators) and the enduring images of both the game and the nation are deeply intertwined with its rural landscape and (Church of England) churches in particular. In the popular imagination the game can thus be conceived of as played and watched by people who are seen to 'truly' belong to the nation, inherently linked to its 'unique' and visually verifiable characteristics. Moreover, just as 'evocations of English landscape … [often project] a Southern Englishness in the name of the whole' (Matless 1998: 17), so cricket played in the Southern English counties dominates representations of the game (Williams 1999: 9). Cricket has been subject to a more extensive literaturization and thus is more closely connected to the English language than any other sport (Bateman 2009). Just as an emerging literary class helped define English national identity, so they also 're-invented' cricket as the national game in the early 1800s. As Simons (1996: 50) concludes, 'No other sport has produced such a plethora of popular representations or has had to carry such a cultural and political weight.'

Cricket and Englishness can therefore be seen to intersect in multiple ways. Just as it could be claimed that no other nationality is as obsessed as the English are with the weather (Paxman 1999; Fox 2005), so no other sport is as subject to changes in light, precipitation or humidity. Cricketers break for 'tea'. It is surely just a happy coincidence that St George's Day falls at the start of the cricket season in the Northern hemisphere, but it was nonetheless an influential stimulus to the development of cricket in such diverse places as Bermuda (Manning 1995), Corfu and New York.

Perhaps most significantly cricket and Englishness are both somewhat enigmatic. For Schwarz (1992: 46), Englishness is 'an indefinable matter of being, incapable of systematic explanation and beyond the powers of foreigners either to comprehend or to emulate'. Similarly Holt (1989: 1) has said of cricket that, 'To foreigners … [it] was a uniquely English and Imperial thing quite beyond ordinary understanding'. Maguire (1993: 297) has identified the commonality between cricket and Englishness in this respect, noting that 'just as Englishness is represented as an indefinable matter of being, and beyond the powers of foreigners to comprehend, so too with the subtleties of cricket'.

Yet as evocative and varied as these links are they amount to little more than re-description. As noted throughout *Globalizing Cricket*, 'national character' (and of course the same applies to sports forms) is a social construction. National character and national identity are 'more a matter of exclusion and opposition than some more or less unchanging cultural "essence"' (Reviron-Piégay 2009: 2). This is as true in the English case as it is in the American, and as true in the creation of self-identity as in the 'Othering' of French, Caribbean, or Pakistani people and societies. In linking cricket and English national character we merely see that the two have been defined according to similar social processes. The more searching question, therefore, is what are these processes and how do they impact on both the game and the national identity of these people. It is my contention that cricket and English national identity have been structured according to a set of interdependencies specific to: a) a shared historical development; b) successfully heading an Empire; and, perhaps somewhat paradoxically c) being a dominant but submerged nation within the British nation-state.

A central reason for the extensive cross-over between cricket and Englishness is that their histories are so deeply intertwined. The development of parliamentary democracy, the emergence of a consistent and coherent sense of English national character, and the rise and fall of Empire occur in conjunction with paradigmatic shifts in cricket. Moreover the national identity and the sport share a legacy of *pre*-modern formation. Citing a range of different 'origin' points, a number of authors have argued that English national identity predates the nineteenth-century rise of European nationalism and thus challenges the 'modernist' view of the development of nations and nationalism (see Chapter 2). Haselar (1996) argues that contemporary expressions of Englishness are underpinned by a pre-industrial trinity of land, class and race. Cricket (as noted in the Introduction) could also be described as *un*-modern in a whole range of ways. The existence of multiple game forms, the tolerance of inequality, the lack of playing role specialization and the *non*-embrace of spatial, temporal and environmental rationalization, are elements of the contemporary game which contrast with the defining characteristics of modern sports. The very organizational structure of cricket is based upon representative units (the West Indies, English counties, an 'England' national team that formally embraces but titularly excludes the Welsh, while covertly incorporating the Scots and Irish) that are incongruent with the identity groups which prevail in the modern world.

Cricket also correlates with a historical orientation which makes English national identity more or less distinct. In his comparison of English and French national identities, Kumar (2006a) argues that a distinguishing feature of the former is an assumption of a seamless historical continuity. This is contrasted against a French history punctuated by disjunctures. England has resisted invasion for almost 1,000 years whereas France has twice been occupied in the last 100 years. England's 'Glorious Revolution' of 1688 in which the authority of the monarchy was peacefully supplanted by parliamentary democracy is placed in contradistinction to the French Revolution in which the republican defeat of the monarchy was itself rapidly superseded by dictatorship. Cricket, above all sports, reinforces this English historical perspective. Cricket was formed before other (team) sports and it was claimed to be the national game at the point in time at which a sense of Englishness was consolidated into a relatively coherent form. Its own traditions, moreover, were 're-invented' 200 years ago to establish the now widely held perception that the game emerged organically out of old English folk culture, and thus emphasizes its historical continuity. In contrast, other major team sports such as rugby and football have much shorter histories, are more directly linked to modernist developments such as urbanization and industrialization, and emerged in a process of bifurcation stimulated by class conflicts between the established of Eton and the parvenus of Rugby 'public' School (Dunning and Sheard 1979/2005). Perhaps at a subconscious and symbolic level, the English veneration of forms of cricket which span a number of days and have component parts (innings) of considerable temporal variability, relate to this dominant (though not to say incontestable) interpretation of English history. The belief that a proposed cricket tour to Paris was cancelled on the eve of the 1789 revolution provides a perfect anecdote locating the game within the nations' respective histories of continuity and change.

Cricket also bears the imprint of the peculiarly British imperial experience. Further exploring the contrast between English and French national identity,

Kumar (2006a: 419) argues that while France was 'undoubtedly the second imperial power of the nineteenth century … Second was not enough'. There were also greater tensions between French colonists and colonized groups which stemmed from the former's attempt to impose a relatively standardized model of relations in their Empire. This again contrasts with the distinctly varied local relations within the British Empire (see Chapter 3). Thus, the relative success/failure of English and French imperialism led to opposite tendencies; 'unlike the French, the English have little tradition of reflection on nationalism and national identity' (Kumar 2006a: 423). It was against this backdrop that a 'curiously passionless devotion' (Paxman 1999: 204) became associated with English cricket spectatorship. Only relatively recently has the Barmy Army emerged, their style of support juxtaposed against the traditions of the game. Even now their presence continues to be a source of debate and tension.

The respective imperial legacies of France and England, and their subsequent impact on national identities, are also distinct. In contrast to the rather conflictual French imperial withdrawal, British de-colonization 'was remarkably peaceful' (Kumar 2006a: 421). The French showed a propensity towards assimilative social policies for immigrant groups from their Empire, while the British favoured pluralism and (until recently) an emphasis on multiculturalism. Cricket both mirrors and plays an active part in the peaceful dismantling of the British Empire and, as discussed in Chapter 7, the contemporary experiences of Britain's minority ethnic groups. Though neither the move from colonial to post-colonial relations, nor the shifting power balance in international cricket has occurred without their own tensions, both could be claimed to have been relatively consensual compared to similar processes in other societies or sports.

As this example illustrates, far from being incongruous, the notions of cricket as the quintessential English game and the game par excellence of the British Empire are directly connected. English nationalism is a form of imperial or missionary nationalism (Kumar 2006b). Imperial nations tend to develop a particular kind of nationalism, distinct from most forms of nineteenth-century nationalism, because Empires necessarily consist of multiple ethnicities. Consequently imperialists must define their distinctiveness and/or superiority in terms of their mission and their creation – the Empire – rather than in terms of the people who created it. Correlatively, 'the right attitude has to be modesty and perhaps even self-deprecation' (Kumar 2006b: 6). The way the English could rather paradoxically congratulate themselves on the cricketing achievements of Australians and West Indians is an apposite example of this attitude. Rather than English failure, such defeats demonstrated the success of a 'civilizing mission' and were cited as evidence of the strength of the Empire. The conventions which dictated that competing teams would wear near identical clothing and that spectators should treat the achievements of both sides with equal respect can be explained in similar terms. Imperial nationalism meant that it was the project, the game, which was cause for celebration, not the individuals who played it or the nations they represented. While the ethos that 'it matters not who won and lost, but how you played the game' applied across all British sports, only cricket, with its peculiar accommodation of contests with no definitive outcome, and the historical dominance of drawn games relative to victories/defeats, had a structure which served this very purpose. Thus a neat synergy arose: having an Empire constrained the celebration of English national identity; cricket was socially constructed in such a way that victories were relatively rare, and their overt celebration rarer still; cricket was the imperial game *par excellence*. Those in the colonies may not have always seen it in this light (see Chapter 3) but cricket consistently provided the English with opportunities for the manifestation of this particular kind of imperial nationalism. Only cricket allowed the English to 'substitute[d] pride in their empire for the assertion of their own national identity' (Reviron-Piégay 2009: 2).

The structural accommodation of inequalities which marks cricket out from most modern sports may also be attributed to imperial nationalism. Inequality was, of course, a fundamental principle of imperialism, but both cricket and British imperialism were shrouded in an ideological cloak of equity. Phrases like 'It's not cricket' projected an aura of equality on a game uniquely structured in ways which perpetuated and allowed for the existence of elements of unfairness. The cricket community's tolerance of South African apartheid was more pronounced and more enduring than that of any other sporting community. The insistence that sport and politics should not mix blunted attempts to upturn the status quo. Similarly the Empire was ruled by the apparently neutral notion of Law without inviting inquiry into whose laws, and in whose interests such laws were applied. As C.L.R. James (1963) was perhaps the first to elucidate, the desire to challenge the structures of political and economic discrimination of Empire was not matched by a desire to challenge sporting injustices. There remains a marked reluctance within post-colonial nations to question or challenge the organization of the international game into three discrete groups (full, associate and affiliate nations), even though access to the top tier has been granted just three times since 1954. The sustained nature of this inequality has meant that once attained, membership has never been revoked, either during extended periods when teams have failed to win a match (it took Bangladesh five years to win their first test and a further four years to win their second) or even simply to play a match (Zimbabwe did not play a single test between 2006 and 2011). FIFA by way of contrast provides all member states with equal voting rights regardless of competitive success.

The imperial influence on English nationalism also helps us to understand why cricket has remained a game in which international participation is relatively restricted. While, as noted in Chapter 2, national sports may either be fostered through sporting isolation or competition with a nation's rivals, cricket enabled Englishness to take a third path. Where sports like football, and to a lesser extent rugby, necessarily entailed competition with other nations, the somewhat stilted global diffusion of cricket both structured and was structured by the lack of nationalist self-reflection which has been identified as characteristic of English national identity. The balance meant that England was not so insular that cricket was an inward looking and entirely esoteric pastime, for such an arrangement would not have suited a people which has traditionally seen itself as inclusive and expansive (Kumar 2003a). Neither, however, was competition sufficiently international that more fundamental questions of identity and difference were inevitably posed. Rugby separated England from the Celtic Nations and thus provided a basis for the oppositional definition of these national identities. England competed against Europeans and South Americans at football. The structure of international competition in cricket suited the imperial character of English nationalism for while Ireland, Australia, South Africa, the West Indies, etc. were clearly not English, neither were they entirely alterior. Cricket was a family affair but the family was a flexible unit, as the biographies of R.A. Fitzgerald, Gregor MacGregor, Ranjitsinjhi, Basil D'Oliveria and Tony Greig demonstrate. Cricket augmented 'the absence of a tradition of reflection on the English state itself, and of its character in comparison with other states' (Kumar 2006b: 5).

Imperial nationalism can also be seen in the *active role* the English play in reproducing the enigmatic, ineffable character of cricket. The citation with which this chapter opens encapsulates this point. This anonymously authored verse, marketed by the MCC as 'classic', formally describes the relationship 'foreigners' have with the game. Yet more deeply perhaps it represents the fundamental *dis*-inclination of the English to share cricket indiscriminately. The ambiguity of the term wicket – the name for the twenty-two-yard playing area or pitch, the three stump and two bail structure at either end of that playing area, and a synonym for dismissed batters – is another example. It is remarkable that in a sport which has such extensive and complicated laws it is not thought necessary for key terms to be mutually exclusive. Rather cricket is subject to a largely unconscious but nonetheless systematic obfuscation and, through that obfuscation, an exclusionary boundary is constructed. The use of humour may absolve the English from the negative connotations associated with such boundary maintenance but English cricket discourse shares with English literature 'an odd see-saw between a frustrating reticence about the nation's actualities and an odd, chatty explicitness about that very reticence' (Wood 2004: 59). Cricket is a visually distinct manifestation of Englishness, but at the same time that everybody can see it, like a cryptic crossword, only some certain people have the 'code' required to make sense of it. Just as the English have 'always been reluctant to provide their own definition of Englishness' (Reviron-Piégay 2009: 1), so they have been reluctant to provide a clear explication of their national game. It is probably for this very (ironic) reason that cricket's laws are so extensive.

The construction of an imperial nationalism was however also a consequence of internal colonialism and thus also had ramifications for relationships between England and the Celtic nations. As Kumar (2006b: 8) points out, 'to have celebrated their own English identity, as the creators and directors of Great Britain, would have been impolitic in the extreme', and similarly the celebration of cricketing dominance had to be delicately managed. For centuries cricket has been played throughout the British Isles and at times it has been very popular in all three Celtic nations, but historically there has been a perception that although the Irish, Scots and Welsh (unlike, for example, the French) are equipped to understand the game, they choose not to play or attach any great significance to it. In their different ways each nation has collaborated with the English and freely donated its most valuable assets – its best players and administrators. English cricket quietly subsumed the Welsh and the more 'useful' aspects of Scottish and Irish cricket within their structures. For Ackroyd (2004: 237) 'Englishness is the principle of appropriation' and in cricket, more than any other sport, we see the appropriation of other nations' resources. Governance by a 'club' (the MCC) rather than a more conventional national governing body of sport – an association or a union – enabled such incorporation to pass either unnoticed or with minimal resistance. The quintessential English game assumed the mantle of the sport which united and defined the *British* Empire without debate or contestation. Thus cricket continued to be ascribed as the quintessential English game not through separation or distinction from its closest neighbours, but through the thoroughly and uniquely English trait of conflating England and Britain. As Kumar (2006b: 8–9) notes in relation to the British imperial commitment to free trade, 'It was a happy circumstance that allowed the English, as the core nation of British Society, to link themselves to a cause that both expressed their national interest and at the same time loudly proclaimed its non-national or anti-national character.' The very same could be said about cricket. Given the more general role of sport in dividing the British Isles and acting as a forum for the expression of national difference, perhaps the most English aspect of the quintessential English game has been the continuation of this elision for so long.

As a consequence of these three factors – historical development, imperialism, and relationship to the rest of Britain – cricket and English national identity incorporate similar elements of ethnic and civic nationalism. If Englishness is rooted in notions of primordialism expressed through a nostalgic reverence of a rural past, so myths regarding the emergence and development of cricket portray 'natural' or organic origins for the game within a single part of a single nation. Correlatively, cricket's relatively restricted global diffusion is explained in terms equally 'innate' to other people and places; namely 'limitations' in character (of, for example, Americans or the French) or climate (of, for example, Scotland, Ireland or Canada). With reference to civic nationalism, the constructs of firstly Britain and then Empire depended on citizenship being the primary criteria of membership. As we have seen, a peculiarly imperial nationalism emerged. Concomitantly, cricket is fundamentally linked to a notion of inclusion such that Australians, South Africans, sub-continental Asians and West Indians (if not the continental Europeans or Americans) can, and have frequently been, assimilated into the English game. The use of the term 'foreign *visitor*' in the chapter's opening quote is quite deliberate, for as exclusionary as cricket can be, the ultimate message is that if one were to stay long enough, one could come to understand the game and thus adopt the national identity. Perhaps the earliest example of this was Frederick Louis, Prince of Wales, who had cricket bats sent to his school in Hanover and later died from a cricket-inflicted injury. Amongst the most recent are Eoin Morgan, Kevin Pietersen and Monty Panesar. The embrace of white South African cricketers into the 'England' team in recent years – starting with Allan Lamb, Robin (and Chris) Smith, and most recently manifest through Pietersen, Jonathon Trott and Craig Kieswetter – is perhaps the most striking example. The process of 'Othering' that we saw in Chapter 9 again demonstrates the subtle distinctions in identities, constructing for the English not merely a dichotomous sense of 'us' and 'them', but an 'us', 'them' and an in-between category; people who in some ways are more like 'us' than 'them', but who remain, and will always remain, distinct from 'us'. Here cricket and English national identity exhibit a similar coalescence of ethnic and civic nationalisms.

Cricket has continued to be the quintessential English game because both cricket and English national identity have proved remarkably flexible. Like the English political system, flexible enough to retain the monarchy but strip it of all but symbolic power, radical organizational changes in cricket have been completed with remarkably little conflict. As governance has passed from the MCC to the TCCB to the ECB, the former has retained the role of 'guardian of the game' in a development which is akin to English cricket's own 'Glorious Revolution'. The decision to stage the first ever 'home' test match outside England (in Cardiff in 2009) is a further example. This flexibility can also be seen in the existence of multiple and mutually co-existing forms of cricket. New formats are a response to domestic economic challenges and the global development of interdependency ties but the retention of the traditional format belies the lingering influence of previously hegemonic groups. As Reviron-Piégay (2009: 4) notes 'one of the main paradoxes of Englishness [is that] it is both permanent and ever-changing, continuous and transient, fixed and flexible'. So too cricket.

Indeed, the relationship between Englishness and cricket has been strengthened rather than undermined by recent crises of English national identity. When 'questions of English national identity became a matter of public debate in the 1990s' (Kumar 2006b: 4) they were more tellingly observed in cricket than any other English sport. Cricket was used as the medium for exclusionary discourses such as those initiated by Norman Tebbit and Michael Henderson, and John Major's defensive rhetoric against the transference of powers from the United Kingdom to the European Union (Kumar 2003a). While elements of more celebratory nationalism emerged across a range of sports around the turn of the twenty-first century, the culture of spectatorship changed more radically and more markedly in cricket than in other sports. In contrast to the Football Association and Rugby Football Union which continue to view national affiliation as a redundant addition to their titles, cricket's governing body was reformed in 1997 to include, for the first time, the explicitly nationalistic mention of 'England'. *Jerusalem*, with its reference to 'England's green and pleasant land', started to be sung at the beginning of each day of home test matches, whereas the *British* national anthem ('God Save the Queen') is sung at football and rugby internationals. It is perhaps no coincidence that on-field performances have improved as well, with England winning their first international competition in 2010 – the Twenty20 World Cup – and becoming the world's leading test team in 2011. Once national identity did matter to the English so, it seemed, did winning at cricket.[2] Consequently, cricket would supply the sporting celebrity which most closely resonated with this emerging sense of Englishness. Footballer David Beckham may have greater global recognition but his celebrity persona is linked much more to cross-national trends in masculinity, and metrosexuality in particular (Cashmore and Parker 2003). The Flintoff celebrity, by contrast, incorporates characteristics traditionally defined as typically English. He is more rooted, more normal, less manufactured. He acts as a stable reference point in a changing world by evoking a strong sense of English nostalgia. His size, his strength, his battle with injuries, and even perhaps his relationship with alcohol, make him the very embodiment of Englishness. It is this combination of continuity and change, which makes cricket such a paradoxical beast, which leads to its acclaim as the quintessential English game, and explains its cultural significance today and for the last 200 years of British history.

Theoretical reflections

I stated in the Introduction that the underlying theoretical framework of this book was largely drawn from Norbert Elias's figurational sociology. While reference to Elias was more prominent in the earlier chapters, my intention was always that the debt to Elias's work and concepts should not dominate the narrative of the book. My goal was to make the global development of cricket, rather than the advocacy of a particular theory, the central theme. However, in concluding *Globalizing Cricket* it is important to reflect on the theory used to understand the mass of empirical data, and on the role of figurational sociology in providing an interpretative and analytic framework.

The structure of the book, the desire to produce a developmental analysis of a single sport over a number of centuries and human generations, fundamentally stems from a commitment to a specific kind of historical sociology. Cricket provides a particularly useful vehicle for demonstrating the validity of this approach. Its status as the quintessential English game, its social significance in certain parts of the world (and concomitantly its irrelevance in others), its influence in understanding the experiences of minority ethnic groups in contemporary Britain, and its role in structuring the way English people have conceived of themselves and other peoples over time, could not be undertaken without an acute sense of the importance of process. One does not need to be a historical sociologist to appreciate that an understanding of the game requires a sense of history for, as we have seen, historical sensitivity is a prominent feature of cricket discourses. But being a figurational sociologist does lead one to embark on research which foregrounds process over present; that focuses above all on changes over time. The comparison of media descriptions of Flintoff with Nyren's account of *The Cricketers of my Time* is a particularly pertinent example.

Equally important and similarly endemic throughout the text is the notion of interdependence. Interdependence and process should not be abstractly separated – both are characteristic of all social relations – but the contours of interdependence become most apparent when relations undergo the most radical change. The *changing* character of interdependent relationships between members of the English aristocracy provides the context for the emergence of a systematic and (semi-)standardized set of Laws for cricket. Interdependence between the English aristocracy and the masses, and between participants in the game from different social classes, explains the establishment of cricket as the national game (and all the myths that went along with this) in conjunction with the rather more esoteric development of tactical innovation (the introduction of round arm and over arm bowling). The development of interdependency ties as a consequence of Empire serves as the basis for an understanding of the global diffusion of the game, while the specificity of those ties (for example in America compared to the Caribbean, compared to the 'internal colonialism' of Britain), explains the adoption/adaptation/rejection of the game. They are also crucial to understanding further developments in the Laws and playing conventions such as Bodyline and the subsequent West Indian utilization of short pitched fast bowling. As shown in the concluding chapters, interdependence fundamentally shapes the way the English see themselves and others. National identity and national character are defined in opposition to specific groups of others, but to fully understand such relationships one must examine the dynamic interdependence, rather than simply the co-existence, of the respective parties.

There are, however, two fundamental premises of Elias's notion of interdependence that are particularly relevant here. First, Elias stressed the multipolarity of human relationships. We see the importance of this concept at various times in *Globalizing Cricket*. One can only explain the development of cricket in America with reference to the complex balance of interdependencies between different groups within this emerging nation, and between specific groups within America and Britain. This point is equally true for the development of cricket in the Caribbean. The very notion of diaspora discussed in Chapter 7 develops from an attempt to understand human relationships as relatively dynamic and fluid. Nowhere is this clearer than in the case of cricket in the Celtic nations. The emergence of the Barmy Army, marked by both the group's rejection of English cricketing traditions and their appropriation of football and alternative cricketing spectatorship styles, is another case in point.

Second, Elias argued that the unintended consequences of human action are equally if not more important than intended actions. *Globalizing Cricket* provides many examples of this theoretical emphasis. For instance there is no evidence to suggest that the codification of cricket was intended to aid the diffusion of the game within Britain or more widely. The 're-invention' of cricket in the early nineteenth century was not designed to enable the game to play a fundamental role in the construction of Empire, and the range of unintended consequences of cricket's diffusion as part of British imperialism are myriad. Certainly it was never envisaged, nor could it have been, that cricket should provide an antithetical focus for the development of American nationalism, that it should become an important vehicle for post-colonial national self-assertion, or a source of identity construction for latter twentieth century diasporas. No one could have foreseen that the one thing that would be able to unite twenty-first century India, a country 'with 22 official languages, differing customs and traditions, is probably cricket' (Nair 2011: 574). The development of an introspective and defensive national identity, what I have here called malign Englishness, undoubtedly acted as a spur for benign Englishness in ways that were clearly unintended. To return to an analogy used in the Introduction, human interdependence works like re-bounding ripples in a pond, intermingling in multiple, complex and unanticipated ways.

But as noted at the outset, figurational sociology (especially as applied to the study of sport) is largely associated with questions about the internal and external regulation of violence. This is a theme which is more-or-less present throughout *Globalizing Cricket*. Reference to violence is most explicit in Chapters 1 and 2 which draw on previous work in which I sought to demonstrate the relevance of Elias's theory of civilizing processes to the study of cricket (Malcolm 2002a. See also Malcolm 2004). While it was not the intention to undertake a further demonstration or defence of that thesis, re-examination of the early codification of the game and the emergence of additional empirical evidence reinforces the earlier conclusion that,

> one can identify a pattern so distinct that the clarification (and standardization) of a range of rules can most adequately be conceived as indicative of broader, more deep-rooted social change … [that] when we come to analyze why particular sports came to have the rules that we see today, we must recognize that the desire for standardization may take place in a context of status rivalry, and that … a significant aspect of that rivalry relates to violence and its control. (Malcolm 2005: 115)

But it is also the case that the broader content of this book *extends* our understanding of the relationship between cricket and civilizing processes. Violence and its regulation are persistent themes in the development of the game. In addition to the above, the establishment of cricket as England's national game took place amidst a debate about the emergence of relatively violent practices and the concomitant obfuscation of cricket's history of relatively violent and unruly conduct. The diffusion of the game within the British Empire is characterized by an explicit 'civilizing mission'. Postcolonial relations are mediated by notions of (un)acceptable levels of violence within the game (firstly in relation to Bodyline and latterly in the emergence of the West Indies as the pre-eminent team in world cricket). The response within Britain to the presence of different diasporic communities, and the continued characterization of 'other' peoples, is infused with the belief that differing degrees of violence characterize different cultures. While we see a distinct trend over the 300 years that codified cricket has existed towards lower levels of violence, we also see a concurrent shift from external to internal regulation such that expectations regarding social experiences of violence become less frequently prescribed and more ingrained as part of habitus. While cricket-related deaths in the eighteenth century were treated as regrettable but unavoidable parts of the game, an uneven pitch in Jamaica at the end of the twentieth century, was described as an unacceptable 'dice of death'.

Perhaps more compelling than all of this however is the persistence of the view that the English (and thus also the sport which epitomizes this national group) are distinguished by their peaceable nature. For centuries, the English have taken considerable pride in this (supposed) character trait, and cricket has been integral to sustaining that ideology. Cricket therefore meets the fundamental premise on which Elias defined civilizing processes. For Elias, 'civilization' is a concept which 'expresses the self-consciousness of the West. One could even say: the national consciousness. It sums up everything which Western society of the last two or three centuries believes itself superior to earlier societies or "more primitive" contemporary ones' (Elias 2000: 5). For the English, cricket is deeply implicated in this self-conception. This is why participation in the game is highly valued but not indiscriminately shared. When we talk about cricket as the quintessential English game, we refer to the way cricket is an expression of national consciousness; i.e. a sense of superiority. This sense of superiority consistently entails beliefs about the relative abilities of different groups to behave in emotionally and physically restrained ways.

The long term analysis of cricket therefore demonstrates that large scale social processes have impacted upon emotions and psychological life (van Krieken 1998), as expressed through social identities and the rules or norms which govern the way in which cricket is played. In terms of social identities, we can see that the parliamentarization of political conflict occurred concurrently with the British aristocracy's adoption of the game as a vehicle for status rivalry.

The 're-invention' of cricket as the national game occurred in a context of changing international and domestic relations; specifically, a shifting balance of power between the English/British state and continental European nations, and the reformation of the aristocracy in response to revolution in France and the rising power and wealth of an industrial middle class in Britain. Social identities as expressed through cricket were similarly influenced by the process of both 'internal' and 'external' Empire building. Playing the game became an expression of a new form of identity related to imperial insider/outsider status. It is no coincidence that the popularity of cricket began to wane in post-Civil War America, that the public extolling of the Empire-unifying properties of the game became most explicit as the 'colonial' era began to end, that cricket has been deeply implicated in post-1945 race relations in Britain, or that devolution, the political and economic unification of Europe, etc. has impacted upon the way in which the English express their national identity through cricket. These large scale social processes clearly and consistently impact on social identity in multiple ways.

But in addition to this we can see that broad changes to the social structure of society occur in conjunction with micro-level developments in emotional control. The codification of cricket, which converged with the wider pacification of English/British society, entailed a coherent pattern of violence regulation. The changing social status of cricket in English society during the nineteenth century entailed a new imagining of both a sense of English character and the symbiotic relationship of the game to that character. Beliefs about the consequences of playing the game on the development of a specific character and moral worth took on an added dimension under imperialism. The golden age of cricket (a period dominated by stylish amateur batsmen who expressed a particular masculine habitus) occurs at the high point of Empire (Maguire 1993). Not only did cricket cultivate the independent, forthright, self-disciplined persona of English national character, it countered the effeminate, weak and cowardly character traits perceived amongst the colonized populations. In the post-colonial period micro-level developments in personality can be seen through the revision of English national identity in which characteristics such as openness, tolerance and compassion become valued above those of a more insular and exclusive sense of Englishness.

Consequently figurational sociology provides us with a particular framework for understanding national character and national identity. I have stressed throughout that national character is a social construction. Nations consist of groups stratified by class, gender, region, etc., and the dynamics of such divisions are writ large on the development of cricket. Nations are also somewhat arbitrarily constructed, influenced by unanticipated migrations, geographical features, political alliances. The English perception of themselves as 'an Island race' is a pertinent example of the unreflective way people can respond to an imagined, not to say fallacious, unity (for Britain rather than

England is an island). The counter evidence to the notion that the English are a peaceable people – the violent origins of the early game, the subjugation of peoples through Empire building, the English 'invention' of Bodyline bowling, the frequency of injury in the game today – is another. But accepting such subjectivism does not mean that we must reject the concept of national character in its entirety. If, as we have seen here, micro-level changes in emotional control relate to broader social structural changes, then it stands to reason that people in different social structural arrangements – that is to say nations – behave in different ways.

Elias's sociology of knowledge helps us to understand that within any imagining of self-identity there will be a mixture of more or less sustainable beliefs. In his work on established-outsider relations (Elias and Scotson 1994), Elias described how 'fantasies' about social groups were related to power relations. He described how self-perceptions differ according to the social power of respective groups, with the relatively powerful able to generate and sustain ideas of their own 'group charisma' while concomitantly perpetuating 'group disgrace' beliefs about less powerful groups of people (which in turn were based on the behaviour of the 'minority of the worst' within that group). Elias further argued that what constitutes 'knowledge' is most likely to persist unrevised in situations in which that knowledge has use value for its holders. That value stems from the emotional comfort knowledge brings, either in the sense of that knowledge 'working' when practically applied in real life situations, or when holding that knowledge enhances well-being, such as feelings of security or superiority. But for Elias knowledge, as all social constructs, is a process. Knowledge that doesn't 'work' in either of the above senses is jettisoned over time, whilst knowledge which does becomes more concrete and becomes embedded as a system of beliefs.

Consequently, within the framework that Elias established, it is perfectly possible to argue that national character is relatively though not solely subjectively drawn, to suggest that within any national group there exists a variety of identities and behavioural norms which come to be seen (in unequal ways) as representative of that group, and that acts which contradict that group's charismatic representation (for example of violence perpetrated against subaltern populations during Empire) can be acknowledged to have occurred, but rejected as defining features of that population's behavioural norms. Similarly a group can maintain ideas about their own cosmopolitan openness are clearly contradicted by the negative conceptualizations they hold of other groups (see Chapters 8 and 9). Moreover an ideological notion of character can become more 'real', or at least more widespread, over time. As knowledge is a process, when dominant groups (particular social classes or nationalities) define themselves in opposition to the violence done by historical forebears or ethnic 'Others', this can act as a self-fulfilling prophecy and have a spiralling effect, refining behavioural control and emotional norms over time. Behaviour that is expected becomes habitually expressed. Within cricket this can most vividly be seen in England during the nineteenth century, as the game developed into the peaceable and national game it was prematurely claimed to be. It is only by tracing cricket's globalizing journey that such processes can be laid bare.

If *Globalizing Cricket* has made this peculiar sport more understandable then it will have served its purpose. If this book has more clearly delineated why cricket continues to play such a fundamental role in the way in which the English people imagine themselves and the way in which people self-identify, then so much the better. If as part of this exploration I have clarified or illuminated broader aspects of national character, national identity, nationalism or even aspects of figurational sociology, then it will have exceeded my expectations. But perhaps the most valuable function a book like this can serve is to demonstrate that sports, such prominent features of our social landscape, are not just commonsensical everyday phenomena which require little or no investigation or can be dismissed in a repetitive and perfunctory way. Rather sports are social constructions which can act as a prism via which we can seek to understand more about the social world in which we live. While cricket and Englishness is almost pleonastic, it remains the case that we cannot properly understand one until we have a fuller understanding of the other.

References

Abell, J., Candor, S., Lowe, R., Gibson, S. and Stevenson, C. (2007), 'Who Ate all the Pride? Patriotic Sentiment and English National Football Support', *Nations and Nationalism*, 13(1): 97–116.

Abrams, P. (1982), *Historical Sociology*, Wells, Somerset: Open Books.

Ackroyd, P. (2004), *Albion: The Origins of the English Imagination*, London: Vintage.

Adelman, M.L. (1990), *A Sporting Time: New York City and the Rise of Modern Athletics, 1820-79*, Urbana and Chicago: University of Illinois Press.

Allen, D. (2010), 'South African Cricket and British Imperialism, 1870–1910', in D. Malcolm, J. Gemmell and N. Mehta (eds), *The Changing Face of Cricket: From Imperial to Global Game*, London: Routledge, 34–51.

Altham, H.S and Swanton, E.W. (1948), *A History of Cricket*, London: George Allen and Unwin (4th Edition).

Anderson, B. (1983), *Imagined Communities: Reflections on the Origin and Spread of Nationalism*, London: Verso.

Andrews, D. and Jackson, S. (eds) (2001), *Sports Stars: The Cultural Politics of Sporting Celebrity*, London: Routledge.

Appadurai, A. (1995), 'Playing with Modernity: The Decolonization of Indian Cricket', in Carol A. Breckenridge (ed.), *Consuming Modernity: Public Culture in a South Asian World*, Minneapolis: University of Minnesota Press, 23–48.

Appadurai, A. (2003), 'Disjuncture and Difference in the Global Cultural Economy', in J.E. Braziel and A. Mannur (eds), *Theorizing Diaspora: A Reader*, Oxford: Blackwell, 25–48.

Arlott, J. (ed.) (1949), *The Middle Ages of Cricket*, London: Christopher Johnson.

Bairner, A. (2001), *Sport, Nationalism, and Globalization: European and North American Perspectives*, New York: SUNY Press.

Bairner, A. (2009), 'Irish Australians, Postcolonialism and the English Game', *Sport in Society*, 12(4/5): 482–496.

Bairner, A., Curry, G. and Malcolm, D. (2007), 'Ireland's Other National Sport? Irishness and the Cricket World Cup 2007', paper presented at North American Society for the Sociology of Sport Annual Meeting, Pittsburgh, Oct-Nov. 2007.

Bairner, A. and Malcolm, D. (2010), 'Cricket and National identities on "the Celtic fringe"', in C. Rumford and S. Wagg (eds), *Cricket and Globalization*, Newcastle upon Tyne: Cambridge Scholar Press, 189–209.

Bale, J. (1994), *Landscapes of Modern Sport*, Leicester: Leicester University Press.

Bale, J. (2002), 'Lassitude and Latitude: Observations on Sport and Environmental Determinism', *International Review for the Sociology of Sport*, 37(2): 147–58.

Bale, J. and Cronin, M. (2003), 'Introduction: Sport and Postcolonialism', in J. Bale and M. Cronin (eds), *Sport and Postcolonialism*, Oxford: Berg, 1–15.

Balibar, E. and Wallerstein, I. (1991), *Race, Nation, Class: Ambiguous Identities*, London: Verso.

Barker, M. (1981), *The New Racism*, London: Junction Books.

Bateman, A. (2003), '"More Mighty than the Bat, the Pen …" Culture, Hegemony and the Literaturisation of Cricket', *Sport in History*, 23(1): 27–44.

Bateman, A. (2009), *Cricket, Literature and Culture: Symbolising the Nation, Destabilising Empire*, Farnham, Hampshire: Ashgate.

Beckles, H. (1995a), 'The Origins and Development of West Indies Cricket Culture in the Nineteenth Century: Jamaica and Barbados', in H. Beckles and B. Stoddart (eds), *Liberation Cricket: West Indies Cricket Culture*, Manchester: Manchester University Press, 33–43.

Beckles, H. (1995b), 'The Making of the First "West Indian" Teams, 1886–1906', in H. Beckles and B. Stoddart (eds), *Liberation Cricket: West Indies Cricket Culture*, Manchester: Manchester University Press, 192–204.

Beckles, H. (1998a), *The Development of West Indies Cricket: Volume 1 The Age of Nationalism*, London: Pluto Press.

Beckles, H. (1998b), *The Development of West Indies Cricket: Volume 1 The Age of Globalization*, London: Pluto Press.

Beckles, H. and Stoddart, B. (eds) (1995), *Liberation Cricket: West Indies Cricket Culture*, Manchester: Manchester University Press.

Benning, D. (1983), 'The Emigrant Staffordshire Potters and their Influence on the Recreative Patterns of Trenton, New Jersey in the Nineteenth Century', paper presented at the 'Geographical Perspectives on Sport' conference, University of Birmingham, 7 July 1983.

Bergin, S. and Scott, D. (1980), 'Ireland', in E.W. Swanton (ed.) *Barclays World of Cricket: The Game from A to Z*, London: Collins, 508–9.

Birley, D. (1999), *A Social History of English Cricket*, London: Aurum Press.

Birley, D. (2000), *The Willow Wand: Some Cricket Myths Explored*, London: Aurum Press (2nd edition).

Bloyce, D. (1997), '"Just not Cricket": Baseball in England, 1874–1900', *International Journal for the History of Sport*, 14(2): 207–218.

Booth, D. (2005), *The Field: Truth and Fiction in Sport History*, London: Routledge.

Bowen, R. (1970), *Cricket: A History of its Growth and Development throughout the World*, London: Eyre and Spottiswoode.

Bracken, P. (2004), *A History of Cricket in Tipperary*, Kilkenny: Kilkenny People Printing Ltd.

Bradley, J. (1990), 'The MCC, Society and Empire: A Portrait of Cricket's Ruling Body, 1860–1914', *International Journal for the History of Sport*, 7(1): 1–22.

Bradley, J. (1995), 'Inventing Australians and Constructing Englishness: Cricket and the Creation of a National Consciousness, 1860–1914', *Sporting Traditions*, 11(2): 35–60.

Braziel, J.E. and Mannur, A. (2003), 'Nation, Migration, Globalization: Points of Contention in Diaspora Studies', in J.E. Braziel and A. Mannur (eds), *Theorizing Diaspora: A Reader*, Oxford: Blackwell, 1–22.

British Council (2000), 'Looking Into England: English Identities in the Context of UK Devolution', *British Studies Now*, Issue 13, London: The British Council.

Brodribb, G. (1953), *Next Man In: a Survey of Cricket Laws and Customs*, London: Sportsman's Book Club.

Brooke, R. and Matthews, P. (1988), *Cricket Firsts*, Enfield: Guinness Publishing.

Brookes, C. (1978), *English Cricket: The Game and its Players through the Ages*, London: Weidenfeld and Nicolson.

Brown, A. (1998), 'United we Stand: Some Problems with Fan Democracy', in A. Brown (ed.), *Fanatics! Power, Identity and Fandom in Football*, London: Routledge, 50–68.

Brubaker, R. (2005), 'The "Diaspora" Diaspora', *Ethnic and Racial Studies*, 28(1): 1–19.

Bryson, B. (ed.) (2010), *Icons of England*. London: Black Swan.

Burdsey, D. (2006), '"If I Ever Play Football, Dad, Can I Play for England or India?" British Asians, Sport and Diasporic National Identities', *Sociology*, 40(1): 11–28.

Burdsey, D. (2010a), 'British Muslim Experiences in English First-class Cricket', *International Review for the Sociology of Sport*, 45(3): 315–334.

Burdsey, D. (2010b), 'Midnight's Grandchildren at the MCC: British Asians, Identity and English First-class Cricket', in C. Rumford and S. Wagg (eds), *Cricket and Globalization*, Newcastle upon Tyne: Cambridge Scholar Press, 252–69.

Burdsey, D. (2011), 'That Joke isn't Funny Anymore: Racial Microaggressions, Color-Blind Ideology and the Mitigation of Racism in English Men's First-Class Cricket', *Sociology of Sport Journal*, 28: 261–283.

Burnett, J. (2000), 'Cricket', in G. Jarvie and J. Burnett (eds), *Sport, Scotland and the Scots*, East Lothian: Tuckwell Press, 54–68.

Burton, R. (1985), 'Cricket, Carnival and Street Culture in the Caribbean', *British Journal of Sports History*, 2(2): 179–97.

Cannadine, D. (1990), *Aspects of Aristocracy: Grandeur and Decline in Modern Britain*, New Haven: Yale University Press.

Carrington, B. (1998), '"Football's Coming Home" but whose Home? And do we want it?: Nation, Football and the Politics of Exclusion', in A. Brown (ed.), *Fanatics! Power, Identity and Fandom in Football*, London: Routledge, 101–123.

Carrington, B. (1998), 'Sport, Masculinity and Black Cultural Resistance', *Journal of Sport and Social Issues*, 22(3): 275–298.

Carrington, B. (2008), 'Where's the White in the Union Jack?' in M. Perryman (ed.), *Imagined Nation: England after Britain*, London: Lawrence and Wishart, 109–133.

Carrington, B. (2010), *Race, Sport and Politics: The Sporting Black Diaspora*, London: Sage.

Cashman, R. (1988), 'Cricket and Colonialism: Colonial Hegemony and Indigenous Subversion', in J. Mangan (ed.) *Pleasure, Profit, Proselytism: British Culture and Sport at Home and Abroad 1700–1914*, London: Frank Cass, 258–272.

Cashman, R. (1998), 'Australia', in B. Stoddart and K. Sandiford (eds), *The Imperial Game: Cricket, Culture and Society*, Manchester: Manchester University Press, 24–54.

Cashmore, E. and Parker, A. (2003), 'One David Beckham? Celebrity, Masculinity and the Soccerati', *Sociology of Sport Journal*, 20(3): 214–231.

Clarke, C.C. (1833/1948), 'Editors Introduction to *The Cricketers of my Time*', reproduced in J. Arlott (ed.), *From Hambledon to Lords: The Classics of Cricket*, London: Christopher Johnson (1948), 14–15.

Clifford, S. and King, A. (2006), *England in Particular: A Celebration of the Commonplace, the Local, the Vernacular and the Distinctive*, London: Hodder and Stoughton.

Cole, C. (2000), 'Body Studies in the Sociology of Sport', in J. Coakley and E. Dunning (eds), *Handbook of Sports Studies*, London: Sage, 439–461.

Colley, L. (1996), *Britons: Forging of a Nation, 1707–1837*, London: Pimlico.

Colls, R. (2002), *Identity of England*, Oxford: Oxford University Press.

Crabbe, T. (2004), '*englandfans* – A New Club for a New England? Social Inclusion, Authenticity and the Performance of Englishness at "Home" and "Away"', *Leisure Studies*, 23(1): 63–78.

Crabbe, T. and Wagg, S. (2000), '"A Carnival of Cricket?" The Cricket World Cup, "Race" and the Politics of Carnival', *Culture, Sport, Society*, 3(2): 70–88.

Davies, J and Jenkins, N. (2008), *The Welsh Academy Encyclopaedia of Wales*, Cardiff: University of Wales Press.

Davis, R. (1994), 'Irish Cricket and Nationalism', *Sporting Traditions*, 10(2): 77–96.

Day, G. and Thompson, A. (2004), *Theorizing Nationalism*, Basingstoke, UK: Palgrave MacMillan.

de Lisle, T. (2006), 'Inside the Barmy Army', *Daily Telegraph Magazine*, 25 November 2006.

Denison, W. (1846/1949), *Cricket: Sketches of the Players*, reproduced in J. Arlott (ed.), *The Middle Ages of Cricket*, London: Christopher Johnson (1949).

Dirlik, A. (2002), 'Rethinking Colonialism: Globalization, Postcolonialism and the Nation', *Interventions*, 4(3): 28–48.

Dunning, E. & Sheard, K. (1976), 'The Bifurcation of Rugby Union and Rugby League: a Case study of Organizational Conflict and Change', in *International Review of Sport Sociology*, 11(2): 31–68.

Dunning, E. and Sheard, K. (1979/2005) *Barbarians, Gentlemen and Players: A Sociological Study of the Development of Rugby Football*, Oxford: Martin Robertson/London: Routledge.

Easthope, A. (1999), *Englishness and National Culture*, London: Routledge.

ECB (1997), *Raising the Standard*, London: England and Wales Cricket Board.

ECB (1999), *Going Forward Together: a Report on Racial Equality in Cricket*, London: England and Wales Cricket Board, Racism Study Group.

Edmunds, J. and Turner, B. (2001), 'The Re-invention of National Identity', *Ethnicities*, 1(1): 83–108.

Edwards, T. (1997), *Men in the Mirror: Men's Fashions, Masculinity and Consumer Society*, London: Cassell.

Elias, N. (1978), *What is Sociology?* London: Hutchinson.

Elias, N. (1986a), 'An Essay on Sport and Violence', in N. Elias and E. Dunning, *Quest for Excitement: Sport and Leisure in the Civilizing Process*, Oxford: Blackwell, 150–174.

Elias, N. (1986b), 'The Genesis of Sport as a Sociological Problem', in N. Elias and E. Dunning, *Quest for Excitement: Sport and Leisure in the Civilizing Process*, Oxford: Blackwell, 126–149.

Elias, N. (1991), *The Society of Individuals*, Oxford: Blackwell.

Elias, N. (2000), *The Civilizing Process, Sociogenetic and Psychogenetic Investigations*, Oxford: Basil Blackwell.

Elias, N. and Dunning, E. (1986), 'Quest for Excitement in Leisure', in N. Elias, and E. Dunning, *Quest for Excitement: Sport and Leisure in the Civilizing Process*, Oxford: Blackwell, 63–90.

Elias, N., and Scotson, J. (1994), *The Established and the Outsiders: A Sociological Inquiry into Community Problems*, London: Sage (2nd edition).

Evans, J., Davies, B. and Bass, D. (1999), 'More than a Game: Physical Culture, Identity and Citizenship in Wales', in G. Jarvie (ed.), *Sport in the Making of Celtic Cultures*, Leicester: Leicester University Press, 131–148.

Ford, J. (1972), *Cricket: A Social History, 1700–1835*, Newton Abbot, Devon: David and Charles.

Fox, K. (2005), *Watching the English: The Hidden Rules of English Behaviour*, London: Hodder and Stoughton.

Frith, D. (2001), *Silence of the Heart: Cricket Suicides*, Edinburgh: Mainstream.

Garland, J. (2004), 'The Same Old Story? Englishness, the Tabloid Press and the 2002 Football World Cup', *Leisure Studies*, 23(1): 79–92.

Garnham, N. (2003), 'The Role of Cricket in Victorian and Edwardian Ireland', *Sporting Traditions*, 19(2): 27–48.

Gemmell, J. (2004), *The Politics of South African Cricket*, London: Routledge.

Gemmell, J. (2010), 'Naturally Played by Irishmen: A Social History of Irish Cricket', in D. Malcolm, J. Gemmell and N. Mehta (eds), *The Changing Face of Cricket: From Imperial to Global Game*, London: Routledge, 17–33.

Gemmell, J. (2011), '"The Springboks were not a Test Side": The Foundation of the Imperial Cricket Conference', *Sport in Society*, 14(5): 701–718.

Gilroy, P. (1993), *Small Acts: Thoughts on the Politics of Black Cultures*. London: Serpent's Tail.

Gilroy, P. (2001), 'Foreword' to B. Carrington and I. MacDonald (eds), *'Race', Sport and British Society,* London: Routledge, xi-xvii.

Gilroy, P. (2003), 'The Black Atlantic as a Counterculture of Modernity', in J.E. Braziel and A. Mannur (eds), *Theorizing Diaspora: A Reader*. Oxford, Blackwell, 49–80.

Giulianotti, R. (1999), *Football: A Sociology of the Global Game,* Cambridge: Polity Press.

Goudsblom, J. (1977), *Sociology in the Balance*, Oxford: Blackwell.

Goulstone, J. and Swanton, E.W. (1989), 'Carry on Cricket: The Duke of Dorset's 1789 Tour', *History Today*, 39(8): 18–23.

Green, B. (1988), *A History of Cricket,* London: Barry and Jenkins.

Greenfeld, L. (1992), *Nationalism: Five Roads to Modernity,* Cambridge, MA.: Harvard University Press.

Greenfield, S. and Osborn, G. (1996), 'Oh to be in England? Mythology and Identity in English Cricket', *Social Identities*, 2(2): 271–291.

Gruneau, R. and Whitson, D. (1993), *Hockey Night in Canada,* Toronto: Garamond.

Guttmann, A. (1978), *From Ritual to Record: The Nature of Modern Sport,* New York: Columbia University Press.

Guttmann, A. (1986), *Sports Spectators,* New York: Columbia University Press.

Guttmann, A. (1996), *Games and Empires: Modern Sports and Cultural Imperialism,* New York: Columbia University Press.

Hall, S. (1990), 'Cultural Identity and Diaspora', in J. Rutherford (ed.), *Identity: Community, Culture, Difference*, London: Lawrence and Wishart 222–237.

Hall, S. (1992), 'The West and the Rest: Discourse and Power', in S. Hall and B. Gieben (eds), *Formations of Modernity,* Cambridge: Polity Press, 275–320.

Hargreaves, J.A. (1994), *Sporting Females: Critical Issues in the History and Sociology of Women's Sport,* London: Routledge.

Harris, J. (2006), '(Re)presenting Wales: National Identity and Celebrity in the Postmodern Rugby World', *North American Journal of Welsh Studies*, 6(2): 1–13.

Harris, Lord (1907), *A History of Kent County Cricket,* London: Eyre and Spottiswoode.

Harris, M. (1998), 'Sport in the Newspapers before 1750: Representations of Cricket, Class and Commerce in the London Press', *Media History*, 4(1): 19–28.

Haselar, S. (1996), *The English Tribe: Identity, Nation and Europe*, London: Macmillan.

Hastings, A. (1997), *The Construction of Nationhood: Ethnicity, Religion and Nationalism*, Cambridge: Cambridge University Press.

Hay, R. (2003), 'The Last Night of the Poms: Australia as a Postcolonial Sporting Society?', in J. Bale and M. Cronin (eds), *Sport and Postcolonialism*, Oxford: Berg, 15–28.

Hechter, M. (1975), *Internal Colonialism*, London: Routledge and Kegan Paul.

Henderson, R. (1995), 'Is it in the Blood?', *Wisden Cricket Monthly*, 17(2): 9–10.

Hill, J. (1994) 'Cricket and the Imperial Connection: Overseas Players in Lancashire in the Inter-war Years', in J. Bale and J. Maguire (eds), *The Global Sport Arena: Athletic Talent Migration in an Interdependent World*, London: Cass, 49–62.

Hobsbawm, E. (1983), 'Introduction: Inventing Tradition', in E. Hobsbawm, and T. Ranger (eds), *The Invention of Tradition*, Cambridge: Cambridge University Press, 1–14.

Holding, M. and Cozier, T. (1993), *Whispering Death: The Life and Times of Michael Holding,* London: Deutsch.

Holt, R. (1989), *Sport and the British*, Oxford: Oxford University Press.

Holt, R. (1996), 'Cricket and Englishness: The Batsman as Hero', *International Journal for the History of Sport*, 13(1): 48–70.

Hone, W.P (1955), *Cricket in Ireland*, Tralee, County Kerry: The Kerryman Press.

Houlihan, B. (1994), *Sport and International Politics*, Hemel Hempstead, UK: Harvester Wheatsheaf.

Hughes, T. (1857), *Tom Brown's School Days*, London: Macmillan.

Hunt, T. (2005), 'The Early Years of Gaelic Football and the Role of Cricket in County Westmeath', in A. Bairner (ed.), *Sport and the Irish: Histories, Identities, Issues*, Dublin: UCD Press, 22–43.

Hunt, T. (2007), *Sport and Society in Victorian Ireland: the case of Westmeath*, Cork: Cork University Press.

Ickringill, S. (1995), 'American Sporting Isolationism: Cricket, Baseball and the Wright Brothers', in K. Versluys (ed.), *Insular Dreams: Obsession and Resistance*, Amsterdam: VU University Press, 141–155.

Jable, J.T. (1991), 'Social Class and the Sport of Cricket in Philadelphia, 1850–1880', *Journal of Sport History*, 18(2): 205–223.

Jackson, L. (1999), 'Sport and Scottish Gaeldom in Argyllshire 1790–1900', in G. Jarvie (ed.), *Sport in the Making of Celtic Cultures*, Leicester: Leicester University Press, 26–40.

James, C.L.R. (1963), *Beyond a Boundary,* New York: Pantheon.

James, W. (1993), 'Migration, Racism and Identity Formation: The Caribbean Experience in Britain', in W. James and C. Harris (eds), *Inside Babylon: the Caribbean Diaspora in Britain*, London: Verso, 231–287.

Jarvie, G. (ed.) (1999), *Sport in the Making of Celtic Cultures*, Leicester: Leicester University Press.

Johnes, M. (2005), *A History of Sport in Wales*, Cardiff: University of Wales Press.

Kalra, V., Kahlon, R.K. and Hutnyk, J. (2005), *Hybridity and Diaspora*, London: Sage.

Kaufman, J. and Patterson, O. (2005), 'Cross-National Cultural Diffusion: The Global Spread of Cricket', *American Sociological Review*, 70(1): 82–110

Kibberd, D. (1997), 'Modern Ireland: Postcolonial or European?', in S. Murray (ed.), *Not On Any Map. Essays on Postcoloniality and Cultural Nationalism*, Exeter: Exeter University Press, 81–100.

King, A. (2006), 'Nationalism and Sport', in G. Delanty and K. Kumar (eds), *The Sage Handbook of Nations and Nationalism*, London: Sage, 249–259.

Kington, M. (2005), 'Memories of a Thinker and a Cricketer', *Independent*, 10 January 2005.

Kirsch, G.B. (1989), *The Creation of American Team Sports: Baseball and Cricket 1838–72*, Urbana and Chicago: University of Illinois Press.

Kohn, H. (1940), 'The Genesis and Character of English Nationalism', *Journal of the History of Ideas*, 1, 69–94.

Kumar, K. (2003a), *The Making of English National Identity*, Cambridge: Cambridge University Press.

Kumar, K. (2003b), 'Britain, England and Europe', *European Journal of Social Theory,* 6(1): 5–23.

Kumar, K. (2003a), 'English and French National Identity: Comparison and Contrasts', *Nations and Nationalism*, 12(3) 413–432.

Kumar, K. (2003b), 'Empire and English Nationalism', *Nations and Nationalism*, 12(1): 1–13.

Lambert W. (1816), *Instructions and Rules for the Playing of the Noble Game of Cricket,* Lewes: J. Baxter Sussex Press.

Lambert, D. (1992), *The History of Leicestershire County Cricket Club*, London: Christopher Helm.

Lang, A. (1912), 'The History of Cricket', in P. Warner (ed.), *Imperial Cricket*, London: The London and Counties Press Association.

Langford, P. (2000), *Englishness Identified: Manners and Character, 1650–1850*, Oxford: Oxford University Press.

Lavie, S. and Swedenburg, T. (1996), 'Introduction: Displacement, Diaspora and Geographies of Identity', in S. Lavie and T. Swedenburg (eds), *Displacement, Diaspora and Geographies of Identity*, Durham and London: Duke University Press, 1–25.

Lazarus, N. (1999), *Nationalism and Cultural Practice in the Postcolonial World*, Cambridge: Cambridge University Press.

Levi-Strauss, C. (1967), *Tristes, Tropiques: an Anthropological Study of Primitive Societies in Brazil*, New York: Atheneum.

Lewis, R.M. (1987), 'Cricket and the Beginnings of Organized Baseball in New York City', *International Journal for the History of Sport*, 4(3): 315–332.

Lewis, T. (1980), 'Wales', in E.W. Swanton (ed.), *Barclays World of Cricket: The Game from A to Z*, London: Collins, 513–4.

Lillywhite, F. (1844), *Illustrated Handbook of Cricket*, London: Ackerman.

Lockley, T. (2003), '"The Manly Game": Cricket and Masculinity in Savannah, Georgia in 1859', *International Journal of the History of Sport*, 20(3): 77–98.

Long, J., Nesti, M., Carrington, B. and Gibson, N. (1997), *Crossing the Boundary: A Study of the Nature and Extent of Racism in Local League Cricket*, Leeds: Leeds Metropolitan University Working Papers in Leisure and Sport.

Loomba, A. (1998), *Colonialism/Postcolonialism*, London: Routledge.

MacDonald, I. and Ugra, S. (1998), *Anyone for Cricket? Equal Opportunities and Changing Cricket Cultures in Essex and East London*, London: Centre for Sport Development Research, Roehampton Institute and Centre for New Ethnicities Research, University of East London.

Macfie, A.L. (2004), *Orientalism: A Reader*, Edinburgh: Edinburgh University Press.

MacQuillin, I. (1996), 'Who's Afraid of the Barmy Army', in A. McLellan (ed.), *Nothing Sacred: The New Cricket Culture*, London: Two Heads Publishing, 37–54.

Maguire, J. (1993), 'Globalisation, Sport and National Identities: "The Empires Strike Back"?', *Society and Leisure*, 16(2): 293–322.

Maguire, J. (1994), 'Sport, Identity Politics, and Globalization: Diminishing Contrasts and Increasing Varieties', *Sociology of Sport Journal*, 11(4): 398–427.

Mair, N.G.R. (1980), 'Scotland' in E.W. Swanton (ed.), *Barclays World of Cricket: The Game from A to Z*, London: Collins, 510–13.

Major, J. (2007), *More than a Game: The Story of Cricket's Early Years*, London: HarperCollins Publishers.

Majumdar, B. (2008), *Cricket in Colonial India, 1780–1947*, London: Routledge.

Majumdar, B. and Brown. S. (2007) 'Why Baseball, Why Cricket? Differing Nationalisms, Differing Challenges', *International Journal of the History of Sport*, 24(2): 139–156.

Malcolm, D. (1997), 'Stacking in Cricket: A Figurational Sociological Re-appraisal of Centrality', *Sociology of Sport Journal*, 14(3): 265–284.

Malcolm, D. (2002a), 'Cricket and Civilizing Processes: A Response to Stokvis', *International Review for the Sociology of Sport*, 37(1): 37–57.

Malcolm, D. (2002b), '"Clean Bowled"? Cricket, Racism and Equal Opportunities', *Journal of Ethnic and Migration Studies*, 28(2): 307–325.

Malcolm, D. (2004), 'Cricket: Civilizing and De-civilizing Processes in the Imperial Game', in E. Dunning, D. Malcolm and I. Waddington (eds), *Sport*

Histories: Figurational Studies of the Development of Modern Sports, London: Routledge, 71–87.

Malcolm, D. (2005), 'The Emergence, Codification and Diffusion of Sport: Theoretical and Conceptual Issues', *International Review for the Sociology of Sport*, 40(1): 115–118.

Malcolm, D. (2006), 'The Diffusion of Cricket to America: A Figurational Sociological Examination', *Journal of Historical Sociology*, 19(2): 151–173.

Malcolm, D. and Velija, P. (2008), 'Female Cricketers and Male Preserves', in M. Atkinson and K. Young (eds), *Tribal Play: Sport Subcultures And Countercultures*, London: Elsevier, 217–34.

Mandle, W.F. (1977), 'The Irish Republican Brotherhood and the Beginnings of the Gaelic Athletic Association', *Irish Historical Studies*, XX(80): 418–38.

Mangan, J.A. (1984), 'Christ and the Imperial Games Fields: Evangelical Athletes of the Empire', *The British Journal of Sports History*, 1(2): 184–201.

Mangan, J.A. (1986), *The Games Ethic and Imperialism: Aspects of the Diffusion of an Ideal*, London: Frank Cass.

Manning, F. (1995) 'Celebrating Cricket: The Symbolic Construction of Caribbean Politics', in H. Beckles and B. Stoddart (eds), *Liberation Cricket: West Indies Cricket Culture*, Manchester: Manchester University Press, 269–289.

Markovits, A.S (1990), 'The Other American Exceptionalism: Why is there no Soccer in the United States?' *International Journal for the History of Sport*, 7(2): 230–264.

Markovits, A.S. and Hellerman, S.L. (2001), *Offside: Soccer and American Exceptionalism*, Princeton New Jersey: Princeton University Press.

Marqusee, M. (1998) *Anyone but England: Cricket, Race and Class*, London: Two Heads Publishing (2nd Edition).

Marshall, P.D. (1997), *Celebrity and Power: Fame in Contemporary Culture*, Minneapolis: University of Minnesota Press.

Mason, T. (1986), 'Some Englishmen and Scotsmen Abroad: the Spread of World Football', in A. Tomlinson and G. Whannel (eds), *Off the Ball: The Football World Cup*, London: Pluto Press, 67–82.

Matless, D. (1998), *Landscape and Englishness*, London: Reaktion.

MCC (2010), *The Laws of Cricket*, London: Gardners Books.

McCrone, D. (1998), *The Sociology of Nationalism: Tomorrow's Ancestors*, London: Routledge.

McCrone, K. (1988), *Sport and the Physical Emancipation of English Women*, London: Routledge.

McLean, T. (1987), *The Men in White Coats: Cricket Umpires Past and Present*, London: Stanley Paul.

Melville, T. (1992), '"De Gustibus Non Est Disputandum": Cricket at St Paul's School, and a Note on the Structural/Character Debate in American Cricket', *International Journal of the History of Sport*, 9(1): 105–110.

Melville, T. (1998) *The Tented Field: A History of Cricket in America*. Bowling Green: Bowling Green State University Popular Press.

Mennell, S. (2001), 'The American Civilizing Process', in T. Salumets, *Norbert Elias and Human Interdependencies*, Montreal: McGill-Queens University Press, 226–244.

Mercer, K. (1994), *Welcome to the Jungle: New Positions in Black Cultural Studies*, London: Routledge.

Mitford, M. (1879), *Our Village*, London: Sampson, Low Marston, Searle and Rivington.

Mitford, Rev. J. (1833/1948), 'Review of *The Young Cricketer's Tutor*', reproduced in J. Arlott (ed.), *From Hambledon to Lords: The Classics of Cricket*, London: Christopher Johnson (1948), 120–135.

Nagel, J. (2005), 'Masculinity and Nationalism – Gender and Sexuality in the Making of Nations', in P. Spencer and H. Wollman (eds), *Nations and Nationalism: A Reader,* Edinburgh: Edinburgh University Press, 110–131.

Nair, N. (2011), 'Cricket Obsession in India: Through the Lens of Identity Theory', *Sport in Society*, 14(5): 569–580.

Nairn, T. (2000), *After Britain,* London: Granta Books.

Nandy, A. (1989), *The Tao of Cricket: On Games of Destiny and the Destiny of Games*. New York: Viking.

Nash, R. (2001), 'English Football Fan Groups in the 1990s: Class, Representation and Fan Power, *Soccer and Society*, 2(1): 39–58.

Nauright, J. (2005), 'White Man's Burden Revisited: Race, Sport, and Reporting the Hansie Cronje Cricket Crisis in South Africa and Beyond', *Sport History Review*, 36: 61–75.

Newman, G. (1987), *The Rise of English Nationalism*, London: Weidenfeld and Nicolson.

Nyren, J. (1833a/1948) *Cricketers of my Time*, reproduced in J. Arlott (ed.), *From Hambledon to Lords: The Classics of Cricket*, London: Christopher Johnson (1948) 16–53.

Nyren, J. (1833b), *The Young Cricketer's Tutor*, London: Effingham Wilson.

O'Dwyer, M. (2006), *The History of Cricket in County Kilkenny – The Forgotten Game*, Kilkenny: O'Dwyer Books.

O'Neill, J. (2008), *Netherland*, London: Fourth Estate.

Parry, M. and Malcolm, D. (2004), 'England's Barmy Army: Commercialization, Masculinity and Nationalism', *International Review for the Sociology of Sport*, 39(1): 73–92.

Patterson O. (1995), 'The Ritual of Cricket', in H. Beckles and B. Stoddart (eds), *Liberation Cricket: West Indies Cricket Culture*, Manchester: Manchester University Press, 141–147.

Paxman, J. (1999), *The English: A Portrait of a People*, London: Penguin Books.

Penman, R. (1992), 'The Failure of Cricket in Scotland', *International Journal for the History of Sport*, 9(2): 302–315.

Perkin, H. (1989), 'Teaching the Nations How to Play: Sport and Society in the British Empire and Commonwealth,' *International Journal of the History of Sport*, 6(2): 145–155.

Perryman, M. (2000), 'Going Oriental', in M. Perryman (ed.), *Going Oriental*, Edinburgh: Mainstream, 17–38.

Pickering, M. and Lockyer, S. (2009), 'Introduction: The Ethics and Aesthetics of Humour and Comedy', in S. Lockyer and M. Pickering (eds), *Beyond a Joke*, London: Macmillan, 1–26.

Polley, M. (2003), 'Sport and National Identity in Contemporary England', in D. Porter and A. Smith (eds), *Sport and National Identity in the Post-War World*, London: Routledge, 10–30.

Poole, E. (2002), *Reporting Islam: Media Representations of British Muslims*, London: I.B. Tauris Publishers.

Potter, D.W. (1999), *The Encyclopaedia of Scottish Cricket*, Manchester: Empire Publications.

Pycroft, Rev. J. (1851/1948), *The Cricket Field,* reproduced in J. Arlott (ed.), *From Hambledon to Lords: The Classics of Cricket*, London: Christopher Johnson (1948), 56–117.

Rae, S. (2001), *It's not Cricket: A History of Skulduggery, Sharp Practice and Downright Cheating in the Noble Game*, London: Faber and Faber.

Rait Kerr, R.S. (1950), *The Laws of Cricket: Their History and Growth*, London: Longmans, Green and Co.

Rayvern Allen, D. (ed.) (1985), *The Punch Book of Cricket*, London: Grafton Books.

Read, W.W. (1898), *Annals of Cricket: With my own Experiences*, London: Sampson Low, Marston & Co.

Redmond, G. (1992), 'Viceregal Patronage: The Governors-General of Canda and Sport in the Dominion, 1867–1909', in J.A. Mangan (ed.), *The Cultural Bond: Sport, Empire, Society*, London: Frank Cass, 154–177.

Rein, I., Kotler, P. and Stroller, M. (1997), *High Visibility: The Making and Marketing of Professionals into Celebrities*, Lincolnwood: NTC Business Books.

Reviron-Piégay, F. (2009), 'Introduction: The Dilemma of Englishness', in F. Reviron-Piégay (ed.) *Englishness Revisited*, Newcastle upon Tyne: Cambridge Scholars Publishing, 1–27.

Richardson, J.E. (2004), *(Mis)representing Islam: The Racism and Rhetoric of British Broadsheet Newspapers*, Amsterdam: John Benjamins Publishing.

Riess, S.A. (1991), *City Games: The Evolution of American Urban Society and the Rise of Sports*, Urbana and Chicago: University of Illinois Press.

Robinson, R. (1978), 'Helmet History', *The Cricketer*, April 1978.

Roden, D.T. (1980), 'Baseball and the Quest for National Dignity in Meiji Japan', *American Historical Review*, 85(3): 511–534.

Rosenwater, I. (1970), 'A History of Wicket-Covering in England', *Wisden Cricketers' Almanack*.

Rumford, C. (2011), 'Twenty20, Global Disembedding, and the Rise of the "Portfolio Player"', *Sport in Society*, 14(10): 1358–1368.

Rutherford, J. (1988), 'Who's that Man?,' in R. Chapman and J. Rutherford (eds), *Male Order: Unwrapping Masculinity*, London: Lawrence & Wishart.

Ryan, G. (1998), 'New Zealand', in B. Stoddart and K. Sandiford (eds), *The Imperial Game: Cricket, Culture and Society*, Manchester: Manchester University Press, 93–115.

Ryan, G. (2004), *The Making of New Zealand Cricket 1832–1914*, London: Frank Cass.

Saeed, A. (2007), 'Media, Racism and Islamaphobia: The Representation of Islam and Muslims in the Media', *Sociology Compass*, 1: 443–462.

Said E. (1997), *Covering Islam: How the Media and the Experts Determine how we see the Rest of the World*, London: Vintage Books.

Said E. (2003), *Orientalism*, London: Penguin Books (3rd Edition).

Sandiford, K. (1985), 'The Professionalization of Modern Cricket', *British Journal of Sports History*, 2(1): 270–89.

Sandiford, K. (1994), *Cricket and the Victorians*, Aldershot: Scolar Press.

Sandiford, K. (1998a), 'Introduction', in B. Stoddart and K. Sandiford (eds), *The Imperial Game: Cricket, Culture and Society*, Manchester: Manchester University Press, 1–8.

Scott, J. (1989), *Caught in Court: A Selection of Cases with Cricketing Connections*, London: Andre Deutsch.

Schwarz, B. (1992), 'England in Europe: Reflections on National Identity and Cultural Theory', *Cultural Studies*, 6(2): 198–206.

Searle, C. (1990), 'Race before Wicket: Cricket, Empire and the White Rose', *Race and Class*, 31(3): 31–48.

Searle, C. (1995), 'Lara's Innnings: a Caribbean Moment', *Race and Class*, 36(4): 31–42.

Searle, C. (1996), 'Towards a Cricket of the Future', *Race and Class*, 37(4): 45–59.

Sen, S. (2001), 'Enduring Colonialism in Cricket: From Ranjitsinhji to the Cronje Affair', *Contemporary South Asia*, 10(2): 237–249.

Seymour, H. (1960), *Baseball: The Early Years,* New York: Oxford University Press.

Sheard, K. (1992), *Boxing in the Civilizing Process*, unpublished Ph.D. thesis, Anglia Polytechnic, Cambridge.

Sheard, K. and Dunning, E. (1973), 'The Rugby Club as a Type of Male Preserve: Some Sociological Notes', *International Review of Sport Sociology*, 8: 5–24.

Shohat, E. and Stam, R. (1994), *Unthinking Eurocentrism: Multiculturalism and the Media,* London: Routledge.

Siggins, G. (2005), *Green Days: Cricket in Ireland, 1792–2005*, Stroud: Nonsuch Publishing.

Simons, J. (1996), 'The "Englishness" of English Cricket', *Journal of Popular Culture*, 29(4): 41–51.

Simpson, J. and Weiner, E. (1989) *The Oxford English Dictionary Second Edition*, Oxford: Oxford University Press.

Smith, A. (2006), '"Set in the Silver Sea": English National Identity and European Integration'. *Nations and Nationalism,* 12(3): 433–452.

Solomos, J. and Back, L. (1996), *Racism in Society*, London: Macmillan.

Spencer, P. and Wollman, H. (2005a), 'Introduction', in P. Spencer and H. Wollman (eds), *Nations and Nationalism: A Reader*, Edinburgh: Edinburgh University Press, 1–19.

Spencer, P. and Wollman, H. (2005b), 'Good and Bad Nationalisms', in P. Spencer and H. Wollman (eds), *Nations and Nationalism: A Reader,* Edinburgh: Edinburgh University Press, 197–217.

Sports Council (1991), *Injuries in Sport and Exercise*, London: The Sports Council.

St Pierre, M. (1995), 'West Indian Cricket – Part I: A Socio-Historical Appraisal', in H. Beckles and B. Stoddart (eds), *Liberation Cricket: West Indies Cricket Culture*, Manchester: Manchester University Press, 107–124.

Steen, R. (2004), 'What Happened to the Black Cricketer?', *The Wisden Cricketer*, 1(11): 22–28.

Steen, R. (2010), 'Burning Down the House', in D. Malcolm, J. Gemmell and N. Mehta (eds), *The Changing Face of Cricket: From Imperial to Global Game*, London: Routledge, 240–250.

Stirk, D. (1987), *Golf: The History of an Obsession*, Oxford: Phaidon.

Stoddart, B. (1979), 'Cricket's Imperial Crisis: the 1932–33 MCC Tour of Australia', in R. Cashman and M. McKernan (eds), *Sport in History: the Making of Modern Sporting History,* Queensland: University of Queensland Press, 124–147.

Stoddart, B. (1995a), 'Cricket, Social Formation and Cultural Continuity in Barbados: A Preliminary Ethnohistory', in H. Beckles and B. Stoddart (eds), *Liberation Cricket: West Indies Cricket Culture*, Manchester: Manchester University Press, 61–85.

Stoddart, B. (1995b), 'Cricket and Colonialism in the English-speaking Caribbean to 1914: Towards a Cultural Analysis', in H. Beckles and B. Stoddart (eds), *Liberation Cricket: West Indies Cricket Culture*, Manchester: Manchester University Press, 9–32.

Stoddart, B. (1995c), 'Caribbean Cricket: The Role of Sport in Emerging Small-nation Politics', in H. Beckles and B. Stoddart (eds), *Liberation Cricket: West Indies Cricket Culture,* Manchester: Manchester University Press, 239–255.

Stoddart, B. (1998a), 'Other Cultures', in B. Stoddart and K. Sandiford (eds), *The Imperial Game: Cricket, Culture and Society,* Manchester: Manchester University Press, 135–149.

Stoddart, B. (1998b) 'At the End of the Day's Play: Reflections on Cricket, Culture and Meaning', in B. Stoddart and K. Sandiford (eds), *The Imperial Game: Cricket, Culture and Society*, Manchester: Manchester University Press, 150–165.

Stoddart, B. and Sandiford, K.A.P. (eds) (1998), *The Imperial Game: Cricket, Culture and Society*, Manchester: Manchester University Press.

Strutt, J. (1801), *The Sports and Pastimes of the Peoples of England*, London: Methuen.

Stuart, O. (1996), 'Back in the Pavillion: Cricket and the Image of African Caribbeans in Oxford', in T. Ranger, Y. Samad and O. Stuart (eds), *Culture, Identity and Politics*, Aldershot: Ashgate, 120–128.

Sugden, J. (1996), *Boxing and Society: an International Analysis*, Manchester: Manchester University Press.

Sugden, J. and Bairner, A. (1993), *Sport, Sectarianism and Society in a Divided Ireland*. Leicester: Leicester University Press.

Tranter, N. (1987), 'The Social and Occupational Structure of Organized Sport in Scotland during the Nineteenth Century', *International Journal of the History of Sport*, 4(3): 301–314.

Turner, G. (2004), *Understanding Celebrity*, London: Sage.

Tyrrell, I. (1979), 'The Emergence of Modern American Baseball c. 1850–1880', in R. Cashman and M. McKernan (eds), *Sport in History: the Making of Modern Sporting History*, Queensland: University of Queensland Press, 205–226.

Underdown, D. (2000), *Start of Play: Cricket and Culture in Eighteenth Century England*, London: Penguin.

Valiotis, C. (2009), 'Runs in the Outfield: The Pakistani Diaspora and Cricket in England', *International Journal of the History of Sport*, 26(12): 1791–1822.

Vamplew, W. (1980), 'Sport Crowd Disorder in Britain, 1870–1914: Causes and Controls', *Journal of Sport History*, 7: 5–20.

van Dijk, T. (1991), *Racism and the Press*, London: Routledge.

van Krieken, R. (1998), *Norbert Elias*, London: Routledge.

van Stolk, B. and Wouters, C. (1987), 'Power Changes and Self-Respect: A Comparison of Two Cases of Established-Outsider Relations', *Theory, Culture and Society*, 4(4): 477–88.

Velija, P. and Malcolm, D. (2010), '"Look, it's a Girl": Cricket and Gender Relations in the UK', in D. Malcolm, J. Gemmell, and N, Mehta (eds), *The Changing Face of Cricket: From Imperial to Global Game*, London: Routledge, 199–212.

Voigt, D.Q. (1966–83), *American Baseball*: 3 vols. University Park and London: the Pennsylvania State University Press.

Waddington, I. and Roderick, M. (1996), 'American Exceptionalism: Soccer and American Football', *The Sports Historian*, 16(1): 28–49.

Wagg, S. (2005), 'Calypso Kings, Dark Destroyers: England-West Indies Test Cricket and the English Press, 1950–1984', in S. Wagg (ed.), *Cricket and National Identity in a Postcolonial World*, Routledge: London, 181–203.

Waghorn, H. T. (1906), *The Dawn of Cricket*, London: Electric Press.

Warner, P. (1946), *Lord's 1787–1945*, London: Harrap.

Watson, C. (2010), 'Test Match Special and the Discursive Construction of Cricket: The Sporting Radio Broadcast as Narrative', *International Review for the Sociology of Sport*, 45(2): 225–239.

Watson, C. (2011), 'Test Match Special, Twenty20 and the Future of Cricket', *Sport and Society*, 14(10): 1383–1394.

Werbner, P. (1996), '"Our Blood is Green": Cricket, Identity and Social Empowerment among British Pakistanis', in J. MacClancy (ed.), *Sport, Identity and Ethnicity*, Oxford: Berg, 87–111.

Whelehan, I. (2000), *Overloaded: Popular Culture and the Future of Feminisms*, London: Women's Press.

Whittaker, B. (2002), 'Islam and the British press after September 11', http://www.al-bab.com/media/articles /bw020620.htm (accessed 14 October 2008).

Wilde, S. (1994), *Letting Rip: The Fast-Bowling Threat from Lillee to Waqar*, London: H.F. & G. Witherby.

Williams, G. (1985), 'How Amateur was my Valley: Professional Sport and National Identity in Wales 1890–1914', *British Journal of Sports History*, 2(3): 248–69.

Williams, J. (1994), 'South Asians and Cricket in Bolton', *The Sports Historian*, 14(1): 56–65.

Williams, J. (1999) *Cricket and England: A Cultural and Social History of the Inter-War Years*, London: Frank Cass.

Williams, J. (2001), *Cricket and Race*, Oxford: Berg.

Williams, M. (ed.) (1985), *Double Century: Cricket in the Times, Volume One 1785–1934*, London: Pavilion Books.

Wood, J. (2004), 'An Activity not an Attribute: Mobilising Englishness', in D. Rogers and J. McLeod (eds), *The Revision of Englishness*, Manchester: Manchester University Press.

Wright Mills, C. (1970), *The Sociological Imagination*, Harmondsworth, London: Penguin.

Wymer, N. (1949), *Sport in England: A History of Two Thousand Years of Games and Pastimes*, London: George Harrap and Co.

Wynne-Thomas, P. (1997), *The History of Cricket: From Weald to World*, London: The Stationery Office.

Yates, J. (1982), 'Rule Change and Style as Gestalt Phenomena to be Understood: the Case of Cricket', *Momentum*, 7(2): 2–9.

Yelvington, K. (1990), 'Ethnicity "Not Out": The Indian Cricket Tour of the West Indies and the 1976 Elections in Trinidad and Tobago', *Arena Review*, 14(1): 1–12.

Notes

Introduction: Globalizing Cricket

1 http://icc-cricket.yahoo.net/the-icc/icc_members/overview.php (accessed 17 January 2012).
2 Indeed, the one-day game itself is not a unified entity, with games having taken place on the basis of between 40 and 65 over innings. In recent years, largely driven by member nations' desire for international success in the ICC Cricket World Cup, the format of the game has standardized around 50 overs per side.

Chapter 1 The Emergence of Cricket

1 However, on 25 December 1997 a one-day match between India and Sri Lanka had been abandoned for similar reasons.
2 The idea of making the 'ring' was taken from boxing where it became common practice to make an inner ring for the fighters and their seconds, and an outer ring for the referee and fight backers. Other spectators stood outside this outer ring and hence it also performed the function of a barrier which stopped spectators – perhaps with a betting interest – from interfering with the 'playing area' (Sheard 1992).
3 The Star and Garter Club in London also played a key role in the foundation of horse racing's Jockey Club (Birley 1999: 31).
4 The imprecision of the word wicket is a further anomaly of cricket which stands it apart from other modern sport forms. Wicket is used to describe both the set of wooden sticks which stand at either end of the pitch and which the batter seeks to defend, and the 22 yard strip of grass (or pitch) which lies between those two obstacles.
5 It should be noted that the early laws of cricket often referred specifically to batsmen despite the apparent regular female participation in the sport. For reasons of accuracy such language will be repeated here although, whenever possible (i.e. when not citing from the laws) gender-neutral language (such as batter) will be employed. It is an interesting aside that the term for a batsman is specifically gendered while that of bowler or fielder is not. Subsequently, batting would become the more venerated activity, and epitome of Englishness, and thus the most 'manly' role.
6 By 1774 the laws no longer explicitly prohibited substitutes from entering the field of play and Rait Kerr argues that it is probable that they were allowed with the consent of the opposition's captain (1950: 70).

Chapter 2 The 'National Game': Cricket in Nineteenth-Century England

1 Interestingly it seems much more natural to speak of cricket as the national game rather than the national sport, something which perhaps stems from the tradition in English cricket of downplaying the importance of winning.
2 Elias (1986b) states that sport entered the English language from the French word 'desporter'. Desporter referred to an emotion describing a kind of excitement but

subsequent usage of its derivative – sport – led to a stronger association with a notion of fair play during the nineteenth century.

3   This correspondence is reproduced by Denison in his 'Sketches of the Players' (1845), which itself is reproduced in Arlott (1949). Subsequent references relate to this publication.

4   A beamer is a ball which is directed at the head but without pitching on the ground.

5   In 1933 Patsy Hendren wore a protective cap made from sponge rubber when playing against the West Indies. The Australian test player, Graeme Yallop, was the first to wear what could be described as a modern helmet when he played in the West Indies in 1976.

6   A similar incident occurred during the 2011 England vs India test match at Trent Bridge. England batter Ian Bell hit the final ball before the tea interval towards the boundary. The fielder fumbled the ball and Bell, thinking that a boundary had been scored and thus the ball was 'dead', started walking towards the pavilion. The fielder had, however, saved the ball from hitting the boundary and returned it to the wicketkeeper. Bell was given out by the umpires and while this was overturned during the interval (the Indian team withdrew their appeal) the Indian team were loudly booed by the crowd until Bell's reinstatement became apparent. The different response to these two incidents reveals something about the relative orderliness of crowds in contemporary cricket.

Chapter 3   The Imperial Game: Cricket and Colonization

1   http://www.cricketeurope4.net/CRICKETEUROPE/ (accessed 14 February 2012).
2   http://www.cricketcorfu.com/home.html (accessed 14 February 2012).
3   http://www.cypruscricket.com/about.asp (accessed 14 February 2012).
4   The Trobriand Islands are now called the Kiriwina Islands and are part of Papua New Guinea.
5   A bouncer is literally a ball which bounces up from the pitch, towards the batter's chest or head. It is also called a bumper or a 'short-pitched' ball. This style of bowling was only made possible by the development of over arm bowling.

Chapter 4   Cricket in America

1   'Broken time payments' refers to a form of financial award justified as *compensation* for the loss of earnings players incurred as a consequence of playing the game. Broken time payments were not defined as payment for playing and therefore enabled those who received them to remain 'amateur'.

Chapter 5   Cricket in the Caribbean

1   A beamer is a ball which is bowled directly (i.e. does not bounce) at the batters head. 'Tail-ender' refers to the final cricketers in a team's batting order and thus, normally the least proficient.
2   The contrast between the overly cautious Australians (discussed at the end of Chapter 3) and the rather reckless West Indian approach highlights the subjective nature of these caricatures. The only logical consistency, it would seem, is the English critique of styles of play which are not deemed to be like 'their' own.

Chapter 6 Cricket and the Celtic Nations

1 This chapter builds on prior collaborative work with Alan Bairner. I am grateful to him for allowing me to draw on ideas we discussed in previous conference papers (Bairner *et al.* 2007) and publications (Bairner and Malcolm 2010). Any errors in the current analysis are of course my own.
2 'Sports Talk: you quizzed Robert Croft', BBC Online Sports Talk, April 12, 2001. http://news.bbc.co.uk/sport1/low/sports_talk/1274017.stm (accessed September 19, 2007).

Chapter 7 Cricket and Diasporic Identities in Post-Imperial Britain

1 Lara's world record stood for 10 years until Australia's Matthew Hayden scored 380 against Zimbabwe at Perth in 2003-04. Shortly afterwards Lara regained the world record scoring 400, again against England, and again at the Antigua Recreation Ground.
2 Test Match Special is the BBC's radio coverage of international cricket. For an analysis of its importance in constructing understandings of cricket, see Watson 2010.
3 It should be noted however that use of these names may also be a strategic way of countering prejudice and enabling the club to arrange fixtures against predominantly white teams.

Chapter 8 Cricket and Changing Conceptions of Englishness

1 The word 'invite' is placed in inverted commas in recognition of the unusual process that led to Bell resuming his innings. The England captain and coach were said to have visited the Indian dressing room during the tea interval to ask the Indian captain to revoke his appeal. The Laws of Cricket however indicate that it is only the umpires who may make this request and, especially in light of the reaction of the predominantly England-supporting crowd, it may well have been that Dhoni felt pressured to comply with this request.
2 I am grateful to Matt Parry for allowing me to draw on some previous collaborative research in constructing this section.
3 The Barmy Army do, however, refrain from taking part in the Mexican Wave, as they believe it to be disrespectful to the players.
4 Hawkeye is a device for predicting the trajectory of the ball used primarily to assess the accuracy of LBW decisions. Snicko and hotspot detect sound and heat and thus are mainly used to assess whether the ball has hit the bat.
5 http://news.bbc.co.uk/sport1/hi/cricket/ashes_2005/4242220.stm (accessed 19 September 2007).
6 Flintoff was reported to have been drinking heavily one night and subsequently took a Pedalo boat and went out to sea.

Chapter 9 Cricket, the English and the Process of 'Othering'

1 Police suggested that Woolmer's size and strength made strangulation very unlikely. They also argued that in the absence of signs of forced entry, it was likely that Woolmer would have known anybody let into the room.

2   As a fatwa can only be pronounced by someone officially qualified to interpret
Islamic jurisprudence, they are relatively rare and the use here was more likely the
commonly used press shorthand for death threat (Richardson 2004: 93).

Conclusion

1   http://www.shopatlords.com/?page=shop&pid=3071&cid=149
2   Though winning still did not matter too much to followers of English cricket with
84% of readers of *The Wisden Cricketer* (January 2012) saying that England's
success in 2011 had not affected their interest in the game.

Index